EIGHT SURVIVED

Also by Douglas A. Campbell

The Sea's Bitter Harvest

EIGHT SURVIVED

THE HARROWING STORY OF THE USS *FLIER* AND THE ONLY DOWNED WORLD WAR II SUBMARINERS TO SURVIVE AND EVADE CAPTURE

DOUGLAS A. CAMPBELL

LYONS PRESS
Guilford, Connecticut
An imprint of Globe Pequot Press

Lyons Press is an imprint of Globe Pequot Press.

Text design by Maggie Peterson

Maps by Maryann Dube, © Morris Book Publishing, LLC

Library of Congress Cataloging-in-Publication Data
Campbell, Douglas A.
  Eight survived : the harrowing story of the USS Flier and the only downed World War II submariners to survive and evade capture / Douglas A. Campbell.
    p. cm.
  Includes bibliographical references and index.
  ISBN 978-1-59921-934-9
  1. Flier (Submarine) 2. World War, 1939-1945—Naval operations—Submarine. 3. World War, 1939-1945—Naval operations, American. 4. World War, 1939-1945—Search and rescue operations. 5. Submariners—United States—Biography. 6. Disaster victims—Sulu Sea—Biography. 7. Submarine mines—Sulu Sea—History—20th century. 8. Shipwrecks—Sulu Sea—History—20th century. 9. Survival after airplane accidents, shipwrecks, etc.—Sulu Sea—History—20th century. 10. Sulu Sea—History, Naval—20th century. I. Title.
  D783.5.F56C36 2010
   940.54'51--dc22

                                   2010026655

Printed in the United States of America

10 9 8 7 6 5 4 3 2 1

CONTENTS

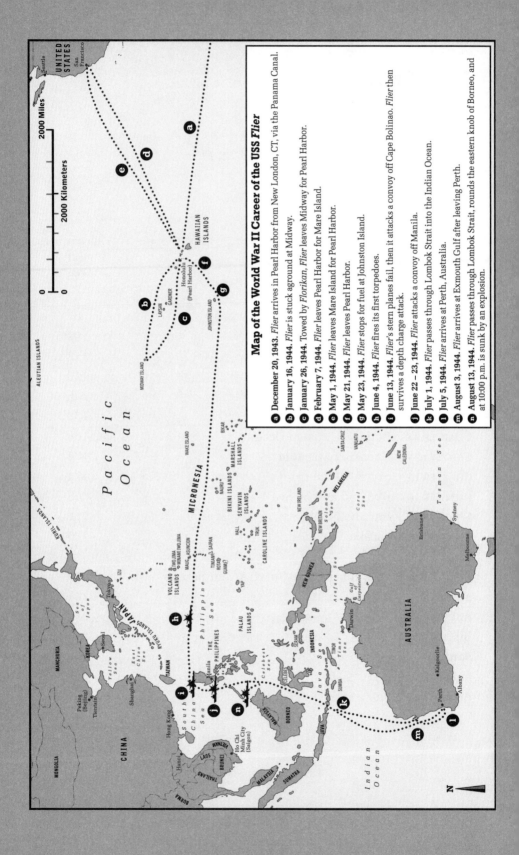

Map of the World War II Career of the USS Flier

a **December 20, 1943.** *Flier* arrives in Pearl Harbor from New London, CT, via the Panama Canal.

b **January 16, 1944.** *Flier* is stuck aground at Midway.

c **January 26, 1944.** Towed by *Florikan*, *Flier* leaves Midway for Pearl Harbor.

d **February 7, 1944.** *Flier* leaves Pearl Harbor for Mare Island.

e **May 1, 1944.** *Flier* leaves Mare Island for Pearl Harbor.

f **May 21, 1944.** *Flier* leaves Pearl Harbor.

g **May 23, 1944.** *Flier* stops for fuel at Johnston Island.

h **June 4, 1944.** *Flier* fires its first torpedoes.

i **June 13, 1944.** *Flier's* stern planes fail, then it attacks a convoy off Cape Bolinao. *Flier* then survives a depth charge attack.

j **June 22 – 23, 1944.** *Flier* attacks a convoy off Manila.

k **July 1, 1944.** *Flier* passes through Lombok Strait into the Indian Ocean.

l **July 5, 1944.** *Flier* arrives at Perth, Australia.

m **August 3, 1944.** *Flier* arrives at Exmouth Gulf after leaving Perth.

n **August 13, 1944.** *Flier* passes through Lombok Strait, rounds the eastern knob of Borneo, and at 10:00 p.m. is sunk by an explosion.

CHAPTER 1

TREACHEROUS PASSAGE

The sea was in a furious mood. Piled on its surface were great, gray waves, living monsters who could humble even the greatest warships. Yet, the USS *Flier* was but a submarine, at about 300 feet, one of the smaller vessels in the navy. Even when submerged, it pitched and rolled like a slender twig. But inside *Flier* were no ordinary sailors. They were submariners: men—most of them quite young—selected from the ranks for their virtues of fearlessness and its companion trait, optimism. Their mood was bright. Despite the beastly roar and hiss of the sea above them, none believed that on this day his death was at hand.

The Reaper might come later, when their boat reached the actual battle lines in this, the third year of World War II. And probably not then, either, they thought. The momentum of the conflict had turned in their favor. There was a sense, pervasive on board, that destiny was with the Allies. Everyone expected to be around for the final victory. These were young men—many of them green—led by a handful of sailors creased by the experience of having survived at sea. Death was for someone else, the enemy, even on January 16, 1944, even on the Pacific Ocean, the greatest naval battleground in history, a place where tens of thousands of Americans had already died.

But the men aboard the *Flier* could not ignore the thrashing as she bucked and twisted. For the one young cowboy in the crew, it had to make him think rodeo bull. He and his mates joked uneasily about the sobriety of the welders who had built the submarine back in Groton, Connecticut.

They had left Long Island Sound in the brand-new boat on November 23, 1943, after several successful sea trials there. The smell of fresh paint still competed with the ever-present stink of diesel fuel as they steamed south and then passed through the Panama Canal. The crew enjoyed the stop in Hawaii, basking in the warmth of the island winter days before resuming their westward journey toward the naval hot spots of the Pacific.

Now in these angry seas they approached the atoll known as Midway, one of the navy's refueling depots. Once beyond Midway, their first wartime patrol aboard *Flier* would begin, and their record—distinguished or dreadful—would be tallied in tons of enemy shipping sunk. With young hearts and a sense of invincibility, they knew that the slamming of their submarine by the sea was only a tune-up for the coming combat. And they had no fear.

Because it was daytime, *Flier* was running deep, avoiding the worst that the ocean was offering, drawing electricity from its huge banks of storage batteries to run its motors. The night before, when the storm was no less fierce, they had surfaced to run the diesel engines that charged the batteries. Then, the whole fury of a winter storm, with winds topping forty knots, was sweeping the sea, plowing up huge, heaving waves in endless ranks across the submarine's path. Now, even beneath the surface, the seventy-eight sailors aboard *Flier* felt the surge from the storm-driven seas that had raced thousands of miles unimpeded by land. But they knew that soon, they would get a break. The shelter of Midway was only hours away. Midway, where the Allies had won their first decisive battle of the war. Midway, a symbol of Allied destiny.

Just after noon, Commander John Crowley heard his radar operator in the conning tower report contact with land. The blip on the radar screen showed a small speck about fifteen miles away. Through his periscope, the skipper saw that while the seas were still running high, the storm above had eased—winds were force four, about fifteen miles per hour—and occasional rain squalls came from the mostly overcast sky. Once in a while, a hole in the clouds let sunlight through, enough so that *Flier*'s navigator could get a sun sight with his sextant.

Crowley, relying on the radar report of land, gave the order to steer due west, and by 1:15 p.m. he saw through his periscope the low group of islands that are the Midway atoll, about nine miles away. At two o'clock, *Flier* was two miles south of the entrance to Midway's channel and was sitting on the surface, with Crowley on the bridge, feeling the breeze on his left cheek. A detail of sailors was stationed on the rear deck, prepared to help in the anchoring of the submarine when it reached the dock. Fifteen minutes later, *Flier*'s semaphore light flashed a signal to a tower on one of Midway's islands and got a reply: "Stand by for pilot."

With the seas running high, it would be essential for a harbor pilot to steer *Flier* through the inlet. Even in calm weather, the naval base would dispatch a pilot, so hazardous were the coral reefs that surrounded the little port. Crowley, who had been at sea most of the thirteen years since he had graduated from the Naval Academy, was no novice sailor. He had served as a junior officer on two submarines and then had commanded the submarine *S-28* before taking charge of *Flier*. He had read the charts and the descriptions of Midway's channel, but he had never entered this port. Nautical charts are helpful, and a practiced eye can learn a lot from them. They show obstructions, depths, the placement of buoys that can be used to help navigate. But close to land, the seas are tricky. There are crosscurrents and the local effects of wind to be considered, and nothing helps navigate such waters more than local knowledge. So Crowley was relieved when the message came out from the tower on Sand Island, the larger of Midway's two big islands, that the pilot was on his way.

As *Flier* lay off the channel, waiting, crewmen who had no job for the moment headed for the crew quarters, where the bunks were stacked six high above the metal-plate floor, and they lay down because standing in the rolling submarine was too tiring.

There were more messages, more directions for Crowley.

"Moor port side to *Gunnel* south side submarine base dock."

"Pilot is under way now."

"Moor alongside *Herring* at south side NOB dock."

Standing behind a steel bulwark, looking north toward the channel, Crowley could see a small motor launch coming out from the islands, braving the big rolling seas that were lifting his own boat like a toy, and he noticed that a heavy ground swell was running in the channel, setting the launch steadily to the east, or his right. He told his crew to steam in a little closer to give the pilot's launch a shorter run. At about the same time, the skipper gave the order to switch to battery power and to stop the diesel engines, closing their air-intake valves to avoid flooding by the surf, whose crests at times towered above *Flier's* low-slung deck. This was a cautious move, a smart decision to avoid potential damage to the submarine's engines, nothing more.

Earlier that day, Crowley had radioed Midway. *Flier* was supposed to reach the atoll at 6:30, not long after sunrise, but heavy head seas had caused a delay.

When he got Crowley's message, the commanding officer at Midway—Captain Joseph A. Connolly—ordered that a watch be kept of the channel. He wanted the pilot dispatched once *Flier* was spotted. Strong southwest winds blew across Midway all morning, bringing with them blinding rain squalls and buffeting gusts of wind. Connolly knew that the pilot would have difficulty boarding *Flier* if these conditions persisted. He was more concerned with winds from another direction, though. Northwest winds would set up a surge in the entrance channel, which ran north and south, and could create a troublesome southerly current. In southwest winds and seas like these, which Connolly certainly considered rough, he had already seen submarines make the passage from the outside buoys—named "One" and "Two"—motoring due north through Brooks Channel to Gooney and Spit islands, which are embraced by Sand Island to the west and Eastern Island, to reach the shelter of the lagoon, where the seas were normally kept calm by the coral reefs that surround Midway.

Another squall passed over Sand Island about 1:30 p.m. while Connolly was inspecting the Midway Rest and Recuperation Center.

He had not yet heard of any sightings of the approaching guest, *Flier*, but when he returned to his office at two o'clock, he learned that *Flier* was waiting outside the channel entrance and that the pilot was on his way out to greet the sub. A radio squawked in the office, and Connolly heard his operations officer and the island's signal tower discussing *Flier*'s progress. First it was 200 yards from the channel entrance; then, curiously, it was 500 yards. *Flier* was drifting away. There was no logical explanation other than the surging sea.

Crowley stood at the bridge, his feet and knees compensating for the sideways roll of the submarine, his left cheek whipped by increasing winds. The hatch in the bridge floor that led down to the conning tower was open, and the skipper was in constant dialogue with his crew. Two officers shared the bridge with Crowley, and to the rear, the men of the anchoring detail waited for instructions, enjoying the bracing smell of the salt air, a refreshing change from the aroma of perspiration that, after a rough four-day transit from Pearl Harbor, had begun to vie with the paint and diesel smells in the buttoned-up boat.

Up in the channel, the little motor launch turned and hurried back toward the safety of the lagoon. Then Crowley saw a yard tug poke its bow out between Gooney and Spit islands, and in minutes the tug was tossing in the same surf as *Flier*. Someone on board was attempting to shout instructions through a megaphone, but the wind was screaming through the bridge and its superstructure, and the voices from the tug were swept away. The tug, about one-third the length of the submarine, made no effort to come up beside *Flier*, as the motor launch could have. The seas were too rough for such large vessels to raft together. There was no way for the pilot to get aboard *Flier*. The tug's semaphore flashed a signal to Crowley that confirmed this reality: "Follow me."

The tug turned toward the open sea, swung completely to the right, and headed north between the channel markers. Crowley gave the orders to follow, and like a dutiful guest, *Flier* fell in behind the tug, about a half-mile from the buoys, which the submarine passed in less than ten minutes. The tugboat and the pilot were about one thousand yards ahead, and Crowley called out course adjustments, attempting to steer his boat along the same path the tug was following. In order to keep a safe distance from the escort, he gave an order for two-thirds speed, or about ten knots. The skipper was unaware of the local custom during rough weather. Captains familiar with this channel knew that in order to maintain steering in these conditions, it was necessary to steam at fifteen knots. Any slower and the surf would actually pass the ship's rudder, eliminating its control over the vessel's direction. In his ignorance of the local waters, Crowley's main concern was that *Flier* not overtake the yard tug in front of him. With surf twenty feet or higher coming from the left, lifting the submarine and then dropping it in the following trough, he could not afford to get too close to another vessel.

And just now, there was another hazard. A severe squall had blown up, and rain was pelting the channel all around the submarine. Blinding as a blizzard, the rain came just when navigation was most difficult, as *Flier* reached the heavy ground swells in the channel. The first of the swells caught *Flier* as it passed through the entrance buoys, and the boat went involuntarily into a leaning, diving turn to the left. Crowley called down into the conning-tower hatch: "Course 355 true!"

The rudder responded, and the submarine began turning to the right. But now the next swell lifted the submarine's stern and, at the boat's slow speed, the wave overpowered the rudder. *Flier* leaned to the left and dove to the right, well past the new compass course Crowley had ordered.

The skipper called out for "left rudder," then "left full rudder!," and slowly, the boat seemed to respond, swinging rapidly to the left once more, well past the course needed to head up the channel's center.

In all the twisting mayhem brought on by the ground swells, and in the blindness of the passing squall, no one on the bridge seemed to notice how far to the right the submarine had traveled. It mattered little. For all the steering and attention to compass readings, the men aboard *Flier* had lost control of their boat. The sea, not a sailor, was at the helm, and now drove *Flier* clear of the channel, off into the reef-strewn surf line to the east.

The men in their bunks in the rear of the submarine, just ahead of the forward engine room, learned of all this at about the same time

Commander Crowley recognized his fate. They found themselves sprawled on the floor plates, thrown unceremoniously off their bunks in a heap of arms and legs. Scrambling to their feet on the tilting deck, they ran forward, past the mess hall and the galley, where pots, pans, dishes, coffee, and garbage were scattered across their path like debris from a tornado. *It must have been a collision!* they yelled to each other as they hurried by the cramped little radio room, heading for the control room and hoping for an explanation for the gruesome grinding sound and the sudden stop.

Up on the bridge, Crowley had the unwelcome answer. *Flier* had run aground. The boat was in the midst of its second wild swing to the left when the unmistakable, jarring sensation of its keel striking the hard ocean floor vibrated up through the steel and telegraphed into Crowley's legs. Just as quickly, the next surge lifted the submarine high off the bottom, only to drop it again on solid ground, bringing the boat to a dead stop.

Stopped, but not motionless. Each following swell lifted *Flier* slightly, giving the skipper hope.

"All ahead full!" he ordered, hoping to bully the submarine forward and off the coral reef that his vessel now straddled.

Flier's two propellers, each with a diameter several feet taller than a man, dug their huge blades into the green surf. But despite the desperate straining of the motors, the boat would not budge.

"Port stop! Left full rudder!" Crowley called down into the open hatch at his feet. He hoped that by using the power of the surf in combination with the starboard, or right side, motors, he could turn the boat and slip from the reef. His orders echoed down the tunnels of the submarine, relayed by men bracing themselves against the unnatural heaving of the submarine.

Now an urgent message came back to Crowley from the control room, two levels below the bridge. The voice of one of two sailors in the maneuvering room—a cubbyhole tucked back between the rear engine room and the after torpedo room, where the electric motors were operated—had shouted through the control-room intercom.

"Fire!"

In the control room, sailors quickly checked the dozens of brass and glass gauges and dials, looking for trouble. Nothing seemed out of order. The telephone system between cabins was working and the motors were running.

Whatever the problems in the maneuvering room, Crowley had more-immediate concerns. Someone else would take charge of the reported fire. The skipper had to wrest his boat from its perilous trap. Caught halfway across a reef, the submarine could get slammed broadside by a rogue wave. Even the surf that was now manhandling the boat could, in a wrong moment, roll *Flier* over. Then the skipper and his seventy-seven crewmen would be trapped, doomed to drown within sight of shore.

Hoping to make the submarine more buoyant, Crowley ordered that water be drained from tanks in the sub's belly that were flooded to keep the boat floating at a desired level. And he kept trying to steer the seesawing *Flier* out to sea. The starboard, or right, motors were racing forward while full power to the port, or left, motors was turning that propeller in reverse, the combined effect urging the sub, as long as a football field, to swing to the left. Each new swell lifted the sub, giving it a chance to move, and with each following trough *Flier* shuddered with the impact of the reef, a few feet farther to the east. The skipper knew that to save the submarine, he must either skip free of the coral that was grinding into the hull or turn the boat completely around to face into the mountainous seas. If that turn could be made, even if *Flier* did not escape the reef, she could drop anchor to hold the bow into the waves, thus overcoming the chance of a capsize.

Crowley had been nudging *Flier* thus for twenty minutes when a report on the maneuvering-room fire reached him on the bridge. A large tool chest, mounted on a wall, had fallen to the deck from the jolt when the submarine grounded, and a screwdriver from it had landed so that it shorted out two electrical terminals. Sparks from that short had ignited some rags, and the two men in the maneuvering room were able to quickly extinguish the blaze.

That was good news for the skipper. And now, some more relief: The sub seemed to be turning in a favorable direction, heading southwest, or into the surf—not quite an about-face from its original course, but promising, nevertheless.

Crowley decided to settle for what he had. He ordered that an anchor be set to keep *Flier* from being driven further onto the reef. Seamen James Cahl, Clyde Gerber, and Kenneth Gwinn were on the anchor detail. They moved forward from the gun deck behind the bridge and began climbing down a steel ladder to the foredeck, along with George Banchero and Waite Daggy, the line handlers. Tagging along was Joseph Lia, a torpedo man who had been allowed on deck just to get some air.

The foredeck of the submarine looked, from the base of the conning tower, like a long, large log. One minute it was naked as the bow was lifted by a wave, seawater cascading down the rounded sides. Then the bow plunged again, the deck covered in a swirling froth. As a lifeline, the sailors had only a flimsy fence on each side of the deck, comprising a single strand of cable supported by occasional posts. With small walls of green water from the onrushing surf breaking over *Flier*'s bow, the six men grabbed one or the other cable and started forward. Wading against the current of the surf as it raced around their thighs, they reached the forward gun mount, where the two lifelines joined a single strand leading to the submarine's bow and the anchor controls.

The process of dropping the 2,200-pound anchor involved men on deck and men inside the submarine. Cahl carried a wrench to do his part of the work. The rest had their hands free to hold on to the cables. There were levers to be moved and gears to be turned once they reached the bow. Then the anchor chain would be allowed to run free, the weight of the anchor pulling the chain from the boat.

Lowering the anchor required precision and clear communications in any situation. In this case, with the howl of the wind and the roar of the waves, it demanded unspeakable courage. The men knew when they climbed up the ladder in the conning tower and opened the hatch to the bridge that the risks were grave. As was typical of submariners, they went by habit. Most of them went without life preservers. There was a reason. When a submarine traveled on the surface, crewmen on deck had to be able with only a moment's notice to scamper below and seal the hatch above them should the captain order an emergency dive. A life belt caught on a piece of ship's hardware could leave a sailor stranded above the closed hatch, doomed. Do you risk getting tossed overboard without a flotation device, or getting snagged outside a diving sub by that device?

On this detail, only one man—Banchero—had strapped a life belt around his waist.

The other crewmen had made a deadly mistake. Two sailors—Lia and Cahl—had reached the anchor gear just short of the bow, and the others were somewhere behind them. In the roar of the storm, Lia and Cahl did not hear an officer on the deck call them back. Daggy and the others heard and began a retreat, leaving Lia standing on the starboard side of the lifeline, opposite Cahl, who, poised to begin work, had one hand on the lifeline, the other holding the wrench. It was then that a huge, green wave bore down on *Flier*'s bow, hitting both men before it hit the others, sweeping their feet out from under them. Lia held tight to the lifeline as the sea washed completely over him. When the water was gone, so was Cahl.

"Man overboard!" Lia yelled, his voice riding the wind back to the bridge.

The wave had swept Gerber overboard as well, and had thrown Daggy back to the bridge, where his head was slammed against the welded plate steel of the conning tower. Some part of the steel had slashed the side of his chest an inch deep, tore a jagged rip in his lower lip, cutting a vein, breaking off three teeth, and knocking four others loose. With his jaw probably broken, Daggy climbed to the bridge and down into the conning tower. A torrent of seawater came with him. As he passed them, his mates—Crowley among them—saw that his blue shirt was drenched with salt water and blood.

Lia, having given the man-overboard alarm, held tight to the lifeline and scanned the water for Cahl, whom he spotted in the surf, already many yards from the submarine, being driven away by the currents and waves. He had a hopeless look on his face, and as he treaded water, Cahl's arms were extended before him, as if in a plea.

Now Lia heard someone on the bridge calling for a volunteer to go into the water, and he headed aft. By the time he reached the bridge, Banchero had already stripped off most of his clothing, was wearing an inflated life belt, and was holding a cork life ring. Banchero made his way along the rear of the submarine and then jumped into the sea. He could see Gerber in the water but not Cahl. He swam toward Gerber, who had no life belt.

The thought of three men overboard weighed in Crowley's thinking, balanced against the safety of another seventy-four crewmen still on board the submarine, which now pivoted on the reef, swinging to the southeast and then back fifty compass degrees to the southwest, at the whim of the sea. The captain ordered the diesel engines started, but he could use them only for short periods. The roiling surf had stirred sand from the seabed, and this gritty water quickly fouled the cooling water needed by the engines. Moreover, Crowley could not use one of the four engines at all. Its exhaust valve had to be kept closed against the onslaught of seawater that, if it entered the valve's port, could flood *Flier*.

Everything had happened quickly aboard the *Flier*. Ashore, it was only 2:30 p.m.—fifteen minutes after *Flier's* first contact with the pilot boat—when Captain Connolly was told the *Flier* was aground. He ordered his operations officer to have all the available tugs and the submarine rescue ship *Macaw* dispatched to help the submarine. Joined by another officer, Connolly then went to the small boat basin and boarded *Macaw* to participate in the salvage operation.

Shortly after three o'clock, under a darkening sky, *Macaw* headed out Brooks Channel. Connolly saw that *Flier* was about 400 feet east of the channel, headed south. *Macaw's* skipper, Lieutenant Commander P. W. Burton, took *Macaw* to the end of the channel and then dropped anchor. The boat swung into the wind, and Connolly stood at the bridge beside Burton, looking aft across *Macaw's* stern and the water between the ship and the submarine. Each time *Flier's* bow rose from the sea, another huge green wall of surf slammed it down, one pounding leading to another. Connolly recalled the last time a sub had grounded at Midway. *Scorpion* had hit the reef on the opposite side of the channel five months earlier, just before the most severe waves of a storm lashed Midway. By getting a line to *Scorpion*, Connolly had been able to pull the sub to freedom. Just two weeks ago, *Scorpion* had returned to Midway, topping off her fuel tanks before beginning her fourth war patrol, proof that a grounding on these reefs need not be fatal.

But *Flier* faced a far graver situation, Connolly believed. If he didn't get a wire to Crowley soon, the surf might push *Flier* sideways to the reef and roll the boat over. Should that happen, certainly the entire *Flier* crew would die.

Normally, Connolly could send a small boat from *Macaw* to *Flier* with a cable that would be used to haul a heavier cable, and then an even heavier one, until the rescue ship and the submarine were connected by a wire strong enough to tow the *Flier* to safety. But the roughness of the seas this time made the use of small boats too treacherous. Connolly saw the truth of this judgment just before four o'clock, with daylight running short, when a line-throwing gun shot a wire from *Macaw* to a fifty-foot motor launch. The crewmen began hauling the line aboard, but the strength of the seas prevented the launch from making any headway, and at one point the boat nearly capsized. The men lost the wire and it drifted away.

Connolly, standing on the rear deck now, noticed that the tugs he had dispatched were having trouble with the seas, as well. If the tugs could not operate, then he could expect disaster with the small launches. Just then, he noticed that the *Macaw*'s engines were revving. He went to the bridge, where the skipper informed him that it was impossible to hold his position in these seas. The idea had been to anchor so that *Macaw*'s stern swung east, toward *Flier*, and then use the ship's propellers to move the stern left and right, guiding the line that would be floated to the submarine. But that was not working.

Connolly had another plan. He suggested that the skipper take the *Macaw* halfway up the channel where it could be turned around and then head back to sea, floating a line as it moved so that the line would drift eastward to *Flier*. Commander Burton told Connolly that it would take only ten minutes longer to go all the way back in to Midway's basin.

"All right, let's go all the way in, then," Connolly said, before going aft again to inspect the preparation of the floating line. He was standing beside the towing engine, which was used to run a huge winch that hauled a thick towing cable, and he was keeping his footing with the rolling of the deck while he watched the crew attach yellow cork buoys to the line.

Things started going wrong aboard the *Macaw* now. As the crew began to reel in the starboard anchor, the surf lifted the ship's bow, drawing the anchor chain tight and snapping it in two places. Burton gave the order to turn the ship around the "Two" buoy at the channel's entrance and head back to the lagoon.

In the wheelhouse, the helmsman was having trouble keeping *Macaw* on course. Herman Ehlers, a quartermaster second class, had been steering *Macaw* for the last six months, but this was only his second round-trip in Brooks Channel, and the 251-foot-long ship was swinging wildly from side to side. His skipper stood outside the wheelhouse on the flying bridge and called course changes to him through an open window. Ehlers repeated each order, but the helmsman had little idea of where he was. He was too busy spinning the wheel and watching the gyro compass. All things considered, he believed he was steering an accurate course.

Burton, however, had made an error in judgment. He had told Ehlers to turn sharply around the buoy when he should have told him to head for the center of the channel before turning in toward the lagoon. This left *Macaw* very close to the buoys on the eastern side of Brooks Channel, the same side from which *Flier* had been washed onto the reef only two hours before. The surging sea and its accompanying current were pushing the ship toward the same rocks, despite Ehlers's attempts to steer straight up the channel. In one dizzying moment, the ship was lifted atop a mount of water and shoved to the right before it came crashing down on the reef, bouncing three distinct times.

On the afterdeck, Captain Connolly found himself in the midst of a heap of men, thrown savagely against the towing engine. When he got to the wheelhouse, he found Burton—who had already tried blasting *Macaw* forward and to the left—giving orders to reverse the engines.

Below the main deck, sailors were beginning to see water flooding various compartments, and within minutes, the water had shorted out the main engines. As night settled on Midway, all the lights inside *Macaw* went out. Seventy-five yards to the east, the submarine that the men on the *Macaw* had set out to rescue sawed violently across the reef in the same surf.

Aboard *Flier*, the crewmen had been updated about the progress of *Macaw*, so they could have been forgiven if, at twenty minutes after five that afternoon, their spirits dropped. Until then, they had been focused not only on the efforts of their rescuers but on keeping *Flier* afloat. At four o'clock, severe leaks appeared where the propeller shafts had passed through the thick steel hull. Crowley ordered that some of the boat's ballast tanks be flooded and others emptied so that the sub would tilt, allowing drain pumps to work. And he set a bucket brigade to work, moving water from the flooded areas to the pumps so that the packing around the propeller shafts could be tightened.

Once the leaking had stopped and the pumping succeeded in moving the seawater back outside *Flier*, the skipper could see that he would be unable to power the sub off the reef. At just about the time *Macaw* was grinding onto the reef to the west, Crowley again ordered that the anchor be dropped. This time, the job was completed. More than 200 feet of chain went overboard, and the anchor detail returned intact this time, each man wearing a life belt, all chastened perhaps by the loss of three shipmates.

To stop the lifting and pounding that the surf was dealing to *Flier*, Crowley again ordered the crew to flood the sub's tanks, thereby settling the boat against the coral.

At four o'clock the next morning, Monday in Midway, Lieutenant James Liddell, Crowley's engineering officer, sat down with the boat's deck log and entered *Flier*'s position: "28-12-31.8 N long. 177-21-09 W headed 203* (T) with heavy seas from 200* (T) pounding ship against bottom," he wrote, his tall athlete's frame rocking with the movements of the submarine. A career navy man, Liddell's level of frustration at being so unceremoniously removed from the war effort by *Flier*'s grounding was unapparent in his report, as was any hint of fear. He wrote: "35 fathoms of chain out to anchor. Pressure hull tight. USS *MACAW* (ASR11) grounded on opposite heading about 75 yards to starboard." He signed the log "J. W. Liddell," as he would for each of the several more days that *Flier* would remain on the reef.

On the next watch, Lieutenant John Edward Casey, known as Ed to his crewmates, had little to tell the deck log. "Aground as before. No change in condition of ship," he wrote.

Outside, the surf was unceasing, the waves still monstrous. But with the anchor out, the men on board could feel confident that their boat would not capsize.

By the time of Casey's report, daylight had come to Midway, and the gale that had blown across Midway the day before had fallen to a gentle breeze of less than ten knots. The surf continued to rock *Flier* and *Macaw*. But soon the rescue attempt resumed. At 10:45 a.m., the crew aboard the *Macaw* began trying to float a line to *Flier*, and at eleven o'clock, they succeeded. A rope "messenger" drifted across *Flier*'s deck and was grabbed by crewmen.

Even if the *Macaw* couldn't move, it could transfer its end of the line to another vessel in Brooks Channel. Shortly after noon, the first heavy steel cable, seven-eighths of an inch thick, was pulled aboard *Flier* at the end of the messenger, and, like threading a needle, was passed through the "bullnose"—a huge single nostril and the sub's bow. The cable was then secured to a cleat on the submarine's deck. By late afternoon, another line had been established between a tripod of steel tubing rising from the rear deck of *Macaw* and the main peri-scope sheer—the tube above the bridge through which the periscope rises—the highest point on *Flier*. This cable could be used to rig a breeches buoy—a sort of chairlift to transport men from the submarine to the rescue ship. The chair, made of canvas and shaped like large trousers hanging from a buoy, would dangle from a pulley that would ride on the line and could be pulled one way or the other by separate ropes. That would have to wait for now, however, as night settled over Midway and the seas began to increase.

As the submarine sawed back and forth on the reef, the ocean floor was not far below. The boat's tail floated over an average of 15 feet of water, while its bow was in 17 feet. With an overall length of almost 312 feet, *Flier* could, with high-enough seas, begin slamming its stern or even its bow on the hard-packed sandy bottom. Time was essential if the boat was to be salvaged.

Removing the unessential sailors from *Flier* began at eight o'clock on Tuesday morning. Crewmen whom Crowley deemed "excess" on the submarine began to line up for a ride in the breeches buoy. A half-dozen men had taken the ride by ten o'clock, when the crew's attention was shifted to bringing aboard a heavier tow wire from *Macaw*. Once that task was completed, all the men aboard *Flier* needed was a towboat that was free from the coral reef.

During Tuesday afternoon, January 18, another seventeen men prepared to ride the breeches buoy. Earl Baumgart, a twenty-year-old sailor from Milwaukee who had been a machinist in the few months between his high school graduation in 1941 and his enlistment in the navy in 1942, was in the middle of the group. Raised near the shore of Lake Michigan, he knew what furious winds could do to water, but this ride to Midway had provided even more excitement than he had expected. Now the spray drenched him as he waited on deck to put his feet through the openings in the breeches buoy. He looked off to the west, toward the *Macaw*, and saw that the crests of the surf passed just below the cable on which the chair would ride. He said a silent prayer, grabbed the chair's harness in his big hands, his long legs swinging free below the seat, and felt the line begin to draw him away from *Flier*'s deck. Unlike a chairlift, drawn between fixed towers bolted to concrete anchors set in granite, the breeches buoy was connected to two ships, each precariously balanced on the same reef, each moving in its own time by the separate ocean swells that broke over them. The chair glided quickly and was partway across the seventy-five-yard gap to *Macaw* when the ship's tripod and *Flier*'s periscope sheer leaned toward each other, dropping Baumgart into the surf. There was nothing the sailors manning the line aboard *Macaw* could do but pull furiously. Baumgart, who was wearing an inflatable life preserver, pulled the ripcord that shot carbon dioxide into the vest. When he was dragged up on *Macaw's* deck, Baumgart's face was framed with the big bosoms of his preserver, but he was alive.

A boatswain handling a forty-foot motor launch impressively brought the little craft alongside of *Macaw*. Connolly and thirty-nine other men climbed down from the ship to the launch, and the boatswain gunned his engine and veered for the channel, riding the surf up the inlet toward the lagoon. Once on land, Connolly talked with a private dredging contractor about the two stranded vessels. Together, they came up with separate formal plans for salvaging the ship and the submarine. Although *Macaw* was the larger of the two stricken vessels and carried a larger crew, Connolly felt that saving *Flier* had to be his priority. The bad weather and lack of equipment precluded rescuing both at once, and returning *Flier* to the battle lines was more important to the war effort, he believed.

When the time came to salvage *Flier*, a two-inch wire bridle would be placed around the sub's gun mount and run through the bullnose. A dredging contractor's barge named *Gaylord* would be anchored off the inlet, and another submarine rescue ship, *Florikan*, would be anchored to the east of the barge. By passing a series of ropes and wires to both *Macaw* and *Flier* from the barge and *Florikan*, the submarine would be poised to lighten its ballast tanks and be yanked from the reef.

Navy salvage expert Commander Lebbeus Curtis, who had been dispatched to Midway to help recover *Flier*, arrived by mid-afternoon on Tuesday and agreed with Connolly's plan. That had to be reassuring, because Curtis had thirty years' experience salvaging ships on the Atlantic and Pacific, from the Aleutian Islands off Alaska to the Philippines and Australia.

Everyone agreed that afternoon to wait for better conditions. The surf and winds were too much, and they would remain that way for three more days. It was Saturday, January 26, before a break appeared in the weather. By then, another fifteen men had been taken to shore. At 7:30 a.m., the heavy wire bridle was sent to *Flier* on the same rigging that had brought Earl Baumgart and his companions off the submarine. At noon, the barge *Gaylord* was on its way out Brooks Channel. The salvage was under way.

Only forty-five minutes later, a navy meteorologist stationed on Midway reported that a sudden shift in weather was coming. Wind, which had been blowing from the northeast, would swing to the west, accompanied by winds of over thirty-five miles per hour. The storm would hit in one hour, the weatherman warned.

It was too late to stop. With more black clouds closing in from the west, Crowley ordered the anchor raised on the submarine. *Gaylord* strained on the cable and *Flier*'s skeleton crew felt the mangled bottom of their boat bump off the reef for the first time in six days. The submarine floated, but it was crippled. Not until hundreds of thousands of dollars' of repairs were made could the boat again try to wage war.

Several days earlier, their boat still caught on the coral reef, *Flier*'s crew had learned of the human cost of the grounding. Gerber and Banchero had been driven ashore by the same mountains of seawater that had wracked *Flier* and *Macaw*. They had survived by clinging to each other and to the life preserver and ring buoy Banchero had taken with him when he had leaped from the submarine's afterdeck. But the limp corpse of James Cahl had washed up on Midway's beach.

Flier hadn't even encountered the enemy, but already it had killed one of its own.

CHAPTER 2

PACIFIC PERIL

The inquiry of the Midway grounding would come later.

First, *Flier*, its skipper, Commander Crowley, and its crew had to make it to Pearl Harbor, where mechanics would evaluate the submarine's damage. Meanwhile, the weather that had thrown them onto Midway's reef had returned, as if to complete the job that the reef had left unfinished. Now on Saturday afternoon, as *Florikan* towed *Flier* southeast past the specks of land that are the northwestern extremity of the Hawaiian archipelago, the seas continued to build, driven by winds even higher than those of a week before. The two boats rose and fell in their own rhythms, straining and then slacking the 500-yard-long, two-inch-thick steel cable that tied them together.

The trip to Pearl Harbor tested the seamanship—and the courage—of the men aboard the *Flier* and the *Florikan,* a ship nearly identical to the *Macaw. Flier* was unable to move under its own power at any significant speed. Turning the bent propeller shafts brought seawater gushing through the leaky seals. Crowley had tested the engines two hours after the submarine was hauled off the reef. He saw that the port propeller could not be used, its shaft severely bent apparently by striking the seabed as the boat rocked on the reef. But the starboard propeller worked at one-third speed, both in forward and in reverse, and he decided the submarine could be operated in an emergency with just the starboard motors and propeller. There remained the unknown extent of other damage that the reef might have caused. Towing was the only option, but it was about 500 miles to Hawaii, and a lot could happen in that distance.

When they finally arrived in Pearl Harbor, the inquiry by a panel of navy officers would test whether the grounding at Midway was avoidable—whether, to put it bluntly, Crowley could be blamed for the costly repairs that his boat now needed, and for the death of seaman Cahl.

Many of Crowley's crewmen were absent from the submarine by the morning of January 22, six days after *Flier*'s grounding. Some, like Earl Baumgart, were simply removed four days earlier as excess baggage and would return to *Flier* later. Waite Daggy had been transferred at eight o'clock that very morning to *Macaw* so he could be taken to the hospital on Midway for treatment of the wounds he had suffered during the first anchoring attempt the prior Sunday. Kenneth Gwinn, Harry Ericson, and Lieutenant Commander Benjamin Adams, the executive officer, had been sent ashore by way of *Macaw* the day before, also for treatment of injuries suffered in the grounding. Clyde Gerber, who had been washed overboard while attempting to set the anchor, and who had made it to shore with help, remained in Midway's hospital. George Banchero, who had jumped in to save Gerber, was also still on Midway, although his wounds were superficial. James Cahl's body had been found only the day before, five days after the grounding. Crowley was told that Cahl had been given a navy funeral, his body buried at sea.

The death of Cahl, grim as it was, and the loss of the injured men from the crew was not devastating. A smaller crew could bring the ship to Hawaii. Still, depending on how long it took to repair *Flier,* more crewmen and officers would probably take assignments on other submarines patrolling the Pacific, further depleting the crew's numbers. When *Flier* was ready to head back out on patrol, there would be empty bunks that needed to be filled. But even as the submarine followed *Florikan* like a stubborn dog on a leash, young sailors were being trained as replacements at the U.S. Navy's submarine school back in New London, Connecticut, where *Flier* had been built.

Three months earlier, in September 1943, Elton Stanley Brubaker, an eighteen-year-old with the face of a child—a boy trying to prove to his strong-willed mother that he was a man—had arrived by train at the New London station and boarded a bus for the submarine base, eager to brag a sailor's boast. The bus rolled east across the Thames River into Groton and then north a couple of miles. Elton stepped down from the bus, slung his sea bag over his shoulder, cocked his hat forward, and headed for his new home, a place informally called Spritz's Navy. Chief Charles Spritz was in charge of all enlisted men at New London, and the respect he received from his sailors was a product of the terror he inflicted upon them. It was Spritz's job to help youngsters like Elton Brubaker understand that submarine warfare is deadly business. In Spritz's Navy, everything was by the book. If cocky Elton thought he knew it all, Spritz would happily inform him—in a voice that could travel from the campus's upper base, where the brick classroom building stood looking west toward the river below, to the lower base, where the submarines docked—just how much more he had to learn.

Elton was an average kid, standing five feet, nine inches and weighing 142 pounds, with a heart-shaped face composed of bunched cheeks, large eyes, and a small chin. He was instantly likable, his syrupy north-Florida drawl the sort of voice that, were the beast listening, could lull a hornet. He had already passed a battery of physical examinations to qualify for Sub School. Soon after he had deposited his bag in a barracks on the upper base, he was given yet another physical examination. He passed, but there was more ahead before he would be enrolled in a class of about fifteen sailors to receive submarine training.

An eighteen-year-old's body can be tough. But what about his mind? He is in the throes of adolescence, still ready to retreat at times under his mother's apron, even while he swaggers boldly away from home.

Elton's mind was filled with just such contradictions. His family could read them in almost every letter he had written home since he had joined the navy in March. There had been hints of homesickness, followed by cocky tales of his most-recent exploits. Almost always, he had girls on his mind.

At first, while he was in boot camp in Jacksonville, about thirty miles from his rural hometown of Palatka, it was Pauline, a St. Augustine girl. He wasn't quite sure how she felt, so he asked advice from his sister, Charlotte, who was in her senior year in high school. "Pauline wrote me a letter and inside had two parts," he wrote. "I want you to read it and tell me what you think about it, whether she likes me or feels sorry for me. (You know what I mean.)"

By April, he told Charlotte: "Pauline hasn't written me in about two weeks and I hope she doesn't write me again because I like her too much. (If you follow me.) If I get hooked I won't be able to do what I want to do. (It sounds silly.) When I get out of the Navy at 21 years old I want to finish high school and then go to college, or maybe to Georgia Tech."

Two months later, as he rode to his next assignment in Kentucky, he was still sure about his education, if not about girls. "We get into the town where we are to change trains about 15 minutes late, so we went up town looking for a bus. While waiting for the bus all the fellows and I went to a carnival. All the fellows found girl friends but, I can't understand it, I just couldn't flirt with them. I enjoyed myself, but I only like one girl and I left her back home. I have decided to study hard while I'm here and I don't think that I'll regret it. I think Pauline likes me enough to wait on me."

Elton finally reached Morehead, Kentucky, where he spent the summer of 1943 in electrical school. The navy was using the facilities of Morehead State Teachers College to train its recruits. That summer, a girl working behind a soda fountain caught Elton's eye. His thoughts of Pauline evaporated at the sight of Ruth Turner. He offered to show her how they made ice cream sodas back in Florida, and within weeks he was telling his mother, sister, and father in separate letters that this just might be the girl for him.

It was with such youthfulness that Chief Spritz and his instructors had to deal. Within three days of the arrival of a fresh batch of prospective submariners, Spritz was ready to wash out the less-than-perfect candidates. Three days after his arrival in Groton, Elton's mind was tested for the first time. With several other men, about ten in all, he was led to a room, constructed as a horizontal cylinder with benches along both sides. The lighting was bright, so the instructor—wearing dungaree trousers but no shirt, as were young Elton and the others—could watch the reactions of each man as the heat was increased and the air pressure in the room was pumped up to fifty-five pounds per square inch—about the same pressure as in a skinny bicycle tire, and equivalent to the water pressure at a depth of 100 feet. The temperature gauge rose toward 130 degrees, and the sweat poured from Elton's scalp, his shins, even his toes as he swallowed repeatedly to relieve the pressure in his ears. If he tried to talk, his voice would begin to squeak. But the instructor, his own voice squeaking, had told everyone to remain silent. Elton was accustomed to heat. He had come here from the flat, sun-baked potato-farming country in northern Florida. In fact, he had just come off leave from St. Augustine, where he had picked up a bit of a head cold.

If he was assured that he could tolerate heat, Elton—like any normal person—was unprepared for the pressure in the chamber, and the question in the instructor's mind as he watched the boy was how well he would cope. The first sign of mental weakness would wash Elton from Sub School. But this boy had things to prove, letters to write. He would not crack. His dungarees were soaked with sweat when he stepped from the chamber, but his cheeks were bunched in a smile that told the instructor what he wanted to know.

The next day, when he took out his official Submarine Base writing paper to send a letter to his father, Elton Brubaker was nonchalant: "The weather is not exactly Florida, but I think I'll be able to endure it," he began. "I have had my pressure chamber test yesterday. It wasn't very hard or difficult."

The pressure chamber was one thing; next, there was the 100-foot-deep diving tank where submarine candidates were introduced to *actual* water pressure. By the end of his first week in New London, Elton had ascended from the very bottom of the diving tank to its top, breathing from a "Momsen lung"—a vest strapped around his chest, containing a tank of compressed air. The feat simulated a proper escape from a submarine that could not surface. He passed this test, as well. But within a few days, as he waited for his testing group to begin real training, Elton was diagnosed with a severe ear infection and was admitted to the infirmary on the upper base. Unable to attend classes, he was suspended from Sub School to make room for another man. He celebrated Thanksgiving in sick bay, resuming submarine training only in December, when a doctor cleared him as healthy.

Elton was eager to return to classes. He was on a mission to prove something. His mother, who taught school in St. Augustine, had not approved when he joined the navy. Never a particularly successful student, Elton had even had to repeat one grade. So when he asked his father, a World War I veteran, for permission to quit high school to enlist, he felt the move would make an improvement in his life. His father supported Elton's enlistment, but his mother was silently furious. A boy knows when his mother is angry. With each letter he wrote to her now from his navy assignments, he assured her that he loved what he was doing. Whenever he scored well on an exam, he reported that to her, too.

On January 23, 1944, *Flier*'s first day at sea behind *Florikan*, Elton was less than three weeks away from the end of his submarine training, his days filled with demanding lessons, his mind yearning for action in the war zone. Soon he would have to let the navy know where he wanted to be assigned. The Pacific Ocean was the submarine battleground. After the attack on Pearl Harbor that brought the United States into the world war, the submarine fleet and the aircraft carriers were the navy's only intact fleets, and it was upon these boats that the navy relied to fight the Japanese. Elton was ready to head west.

At this very moment, *Flier* was heading southeast, away from the war zone, towed by *Florikan* through a growing gale. The stronger gusts streaked the slate-gray sea with a racing white lacework of foam. Crowley had emptied much of the submarine's ballast to make the boat easier to tow. The result could be felt by the men in their steel cocoon as each new wave slammed into *Flier*'s right side, rolling it halfway over.

The tow had begun at about five o'clock on the afternoon of January 22, and darkness soon fell. The long dark hours made little difference to most of the crew, who lived in the glow of electric lamps. Their only sense of the outer world was the submarine's motion, and while the rolling was not comfortable, they could be thankful that there were no head seas ripping into *Flier*'s bow. A beam sea made little difference in their progress of about eight knots, while each water wall in a head sea of this magnitude would have stopped the submarine dead.

At about three o'clock the next morning, the wind and sea increased and changed direction, coming from the west-northwest, or almost directly behind *Flier,* at forty knots, with stronger gusts. Now the submarine, light as it was, could be felt almost surfing on the face of the following sea, its bow dipping and then, as a big wave passed, rising, hauling the steel towline tight. For more than two hours, this rocking continued, until, with the suddenness of a slammed door, *Flier* stopped moving forward.

The cable had snapped, and the submarine was bobbing in place, at the mercy of the sea.

With his vessel wallowing in the trough between the waves and still rolling violently, Crowley had to do something. He started the starboard motors now and ordered the propeller to be engaged. The motor turned its massive shaft and slowly built up its revolutions to a level that could drive the boat. There was no excessive vibration, but when the helmsman attempted to turn the boat onto its course, the submarine was unable to move forward against the sea with enough speed to allow the rudder to steer. The skipper called off the effort and radioed *Florikan.*

It was after six o'clock in the morning when *Florikan* passed within 200 yards upwind from the submarine and released a thick film of oil, a technique used to flatten a rough sea. The towboat then attempted to float a line to the submarine, but the effort failed. Crowley had another idea, and he called *Florikan*'s skipper and asked him to bring the towboat close to the submarine. Then he sent several crewmen on deck.

At the very front tip of a submarine was that nostril called the bullnose, through which a towline could be passed before it was secured farther back on the boat. But to get the line through the bullnose, someone would first have to go all the way forward with a rope, far beyond the nearest lifeline. Then, straddling the bow, he would have to thread the rope through the nostril. When the job was completed, he would bring both ends of the rope toward the bridge. Then, when *Florikan* tossed a new towline to the submarine, the towline could be tied to one end of the rope. Men pulling on the rope could then draw the towline through the bullnose.

Whoever agreed to take on this job had either to be supremely confident or enormously fatalistic. This time, the man selected succeeded in his job. His only security as he rode the bow was a rope tied around his waist and held farther back on deck by fellow crewmen.

Daylight had long since arrived over the gale-swept ocean when a new towline was finally pulled aboard *Flier*. It took nearly two hours, a span during which a half-dozen men braving the onslaught of the seas clung to the lurching bow, hauling lines, wrapping chain around winches called capstans, and trying to set the towline properly. Finally, the towing bridle was shackled to the towline. As the final adjustments were being made by the men on deck, another big wave roared across *Flier*'s bow, and chief gunner's mate Charles Pope, a rough-hewn career sailor, was washed into the sea.

Crowley had learned from Cahl's death, and had required Pope— along with all the other men on deck—to tie a rope around his waist. In seconds, he was hauled back aboard, uninjured, and moments later, *Florikan* resumed its work, drawing the towline tight and pointing toward Oahu.

It took a week for *Florikan* to pull *Flier* to Pearl Harbor. On the morning of Monday, January 31, the day after its arrival, *Flier* was moored to the west side of Berth 3-16 at the submarine base when, at just before eight o'clock, two dozen crewmen who had been removed from the submarine at Midway returned. Among them were Earl Baumgart, the seaman who had been dunked in the breeches buoy, and George Banchero, the hero who had saved his mate, Gerber.

Five minutes after these men stepped on board, a yard tug steered to *Flier*'s side and a harbor pilot boarded. *Flier*'s diesel engines were running, fumes rising in wavy streams from the exhaust ports behind the conning tower. With the pilot on board, the tug began moving the submarine out of its slip. Just before nine o'clock, *Flier* floated over the sill of a dry dock from which, an hour later, the water was being drained, revealing the submarine's damage. Over the next week, shipwrights examined the entire boat and decided it had to go to a bigger shipyard for repairs. They patched the starboard propeller shaft, allowing it to turn without causing leaks. Now the submarine could travel under its own power and at a speed at which it could be steered.

The inquiry began on February 1, aboard the USS *Bushnell*, two days after *Flier* arrived at Pearl Harbor. Commander Crowley entered a room aboard the twenty-nine-year-old submarine tender—named for a submarine pioneer—and faced a panel of three navy captains and one lieutenant commander. His future in the navy would be decided by these four men, all but one a graduate, like Crowley, of the Naval Academy. The order creating the "Board of Investigation" was signed by Vice Admiral Charles A. Lockwood, the commander of all the submarines in the Pacific. It instructed the board members that Crowley would be "a party to the investigation in the status of defendant."

For the next five days, the board members listened to witnesses ranging from lowly seamen to experts in the mechanics of submarines. Crowley was called to testify twice, as were his executive officer, Benjamin Adams; James Liddell, his engineering officer; and several other officers and crewmen, including Gwinn, Lia, Daggy, and Banchero, the survivors from the star-crossed anchoring detail.

At least one of the potential witnesses—crew member Donald Tremaine—was incensed at the position in which he found himself. He told his friend, Earl Baumgart, that Crowley had ordered him to swear, under oath, that Cahl and Daggy were wearing life vests.

Tremaine wasn't called as a witness, but several facts became clear to the board members, including the fact that Crowley had not required his men to wear life preservers, and he only belatedly resorted to tying ropes around them as lifelines when he sent them out on the storm-washed decks of *Flier*. It was also obvious that the skipper had used poor judgment in even attempting to enter Brooks Channel, when he might simply have waited offshore for the storm to pass.

The board members pored over *Flier*'s deck log—the journal that records on an hourly basis what has happened on board; its quartermaster's notes; compass check log; engineering bell book; and signal book. They considered nautical charts of the Midway channel and reviewed pictures taken of the submarine's damaged hull.

When the board had heard all the witnesses, Crowley asked to be recalled as a witness.

"I desire to make it clear that the responsibility of the commanding officer for his ship is fully appreciated by me, and that I am fully prepared to accept the responsibility for the decisions in this instance," the skipper began. "However, there are some factors that influenced my decision that I should like to point out."

Crowley now mustered his excuses: First, neither he nor his navigator had any experience entering Brooks Channel. Also, the skipper noted, the Midway authorities signaling him from shore made it clear that he should enter. It was obvious that the pilot was unable, due to the conditions, to board *Flier*, Crowley told the panel. But that did not suggest to him that *Flier* would be unable to follow the tug back into the lagoon.

And finally, he observed that after *Flier* and *Macaw* ran aground, all traffic in the inlet was halted until the weather improved, suggesting that forces beyond the skipper's control were at work, and were belatedly recognized by the Midway brass.

Having offered his defense, Crowley fielded one more question, and the board then retired for eight hours of deliberations over the next two days. By February 8, the board had finished its work.

Back on Midway, however, *Macaw* was still aground. A week earlier, the same day that Crowley's trial had begun on *Bushnell*, the winds that had eased in the prior week returned, blowing at twenty-five knots, and the ship's captain, Lieutenant Commander P. W. Burton, prepared once again for heavy seas. The winds continued to blow. The surf washing over the stern of *Macaw*, which was stuck on the reef facing toward the shore, made it impossible to work on deck. A change in the wind direction on February 5 had allowed Burton and a few of his men to be taken ashore to rest from their ordeal. They returned the next day, and a new batch was sent ashore. By February 8, the third attempt at salvaging *Macaw* since *Flier*'s departure began. Once again, the barge *Gaylord* steamed out through Brooks Channel, only to retreat to Midway's lagoon. The seas were too rough. The operation was delayed for two more days.

But the sea was relentless, and the winds and surf continued to build. Under these conditions, *Macaw* shifted on the reef several times, taking on a dramatic list as the surf shoved in one direction, the currents in another. On the afternoon of February 12, seas were breaking over the starboard side of the ship, which now had a list of 23 degrees. There was no power aboard *Macaw*. A large air compressor, thrown by the violent seas, had crashed through a bulkhead. Burton—accompanied on board *Macaw* by Joseph Connolly, the Midway commander—ordered all hands to the bridge deck, where the crew had brought the remaining supplies of food and clothing. The spirits of the crew were amazingly bright, even at six o'clock that night when the sea began rising up the ladder to the bridge deck. A leak in a bulkhead below that deck was stopped with mattresses and a brass rail from the navigator's desk. But the water continued to rise, reaching the coaming around the pilothouse.

The seas had now become enormous, with thirty-five-foot breakers crashing over the reef and *Macaw*. The steel of the ship groaned under the pounding of the surf. The crewmen and the captain huddled inside the pilothouse as the ship rolled on its side again and again, seemingly on the verge of capsizing. Green water buried the pilothouse, and the sea poured in through a single port kept open for breathing air.

And the water was rising inside the pilothouse. By two-thirty the next morning, only a foot of air space remained between the top of the water and the pilothouse ceiling, and when the boat rocked, even that space became flooded. Burton ordered the pilothouse door opened, but when sailors tried to move the "dogs"—levers that held the watertight door shut—they could barely budge them. Finally, with a mighty shove, the door opened, and Burton told his men to get to the foremast. He waited with Connolly for the last man to depart. Then, together, Burton and Connolly went topside. They could see several of the men on the foremast, but that is all they saw. The next wave swept them from *Macaw*'s deck.

Connolly made it to shore, but Burton drowned that night, along with four of his crewmen.

The grounding by Crowley of *Flier* had cost the lives of six men. The *Macaw* was wrecked and unsalvageable. And *Flier* was crippled and would need months of repairs before it could contribute to the war.

Navy justice is efficient but not instantaneous. It would be September 1, 1944, before the Secretary of the Navy would approve the findings and recommendations of the board of investigation. Admiral Lockwood had the final navy say on those recommendations. When he signed off on the investigation, Lockwood declared that Crowley had "committed an error in judgment in attempting to enter Midway channel." But, he added, the "exigencies of the service which influenced his decision in the matter, his attempt to enter under the existing unfavorable conditions, is excusable."

Lockwood left Crowley in charge and forwarded his opinion to Admiral Chester W. Nimitz, commander in chief of the Pacific Fleet. One error in judgment, Lockwood believed, was not enough to end a promising naval career.

By that time, Crowley had long since steered the limping *Flier* out of the Pearl Harbor channel and headed it toward Mare Island, California, where it would be repaired.

A substantially higher-ranking panel than the one that cleared Crowley had decided, six months earlier, that Alvin Jacobson should be a submariner. It was the summer of 1943 when two admirals and three captains took their seats behind a long table in a room at the University of Michigan and began studying the files of several university students, Jacobson among them. The students, all of whom had applied for submarine duty in the navy, were left waiting in their seats outside the room. They were all dressed in their Naval Reserve Officer Training Corps (NROTC) uniforms, pressed, starched, and spit-shined. Some no doubt were nervous. Jacobson had no reason to be. He had succeeded at virtually everything he had ever tried. He knew that some of the men with him were superior scholars. That had never mattered much. What he accomplished, he did by hard work, and he had prepared well for this interview.

Certainly the people back in Grand Haven, Michigan, expected "Jake" to go far, whatever he chose to pursue. At Grand Haven High School, he had been captain of the admittedly underachieving football and basketball teams. He was class president one year and student council president another. His hair was blond and his jaw was square and dimpled. His blue eyes smiled easily—not an arrogant smile, but one that knows nothing of defeat. At the age of twenty-one, he was still very much an obedient son. His father, Alvin Sr., was perhaps his most significant teacher. Senior was a pillar in Grand Haven, a local titan of industry whose wealth had helped keep the local country club afloat during the recent Great Depression. With another man, Senior had started a brass foundry many years before and had built the business into one of Michigan's strongest, making toilet-seat hinges, and, when Prohibition ended, beer taps and pumps. Senior had brought Alvin Jr. and his brothers—Charles, three years older, and David, two years younger—into the foundry as laborers when they were old enough to work. They learned the business, from the blasting heat of the molds on up. And they were constantly tutored by their father, not only about work but about an approach to life that would help them to succeed. So while Al Jr. was not a gifted student, he knew he could get results with maximum effort. When the door opened and he was called into the room with the captains and admirals, he felt prepared.

He didn't expect to see all that navy brass behind the table, though. Standing rigidly at attention, he began fielding questions—a blur of them, except one. It came at him like a blindside tackle, one of the officers behind the table nonchalantly asking: "When was the last time you made love to your mother?"

When he left the room, Jacobson could not remember what his answer had been, nor could he guess whether it was the correct answer. Raised by churchgoing Swedes in a town run by the Dutch Reformed elders, he knew nothing about making love to any woman. Was his answer to the question satisfactory? And what about his other answers? The officers behind the table gave no hint whether he would go to Sub School. His only guarantee was that, when the summer was over, he would be in the navy—an officer or an enlisted man.

War demanded manpower, and NROTC cadets at the university had been attending classes nonstop since 1942 to hasten their readiness for battle. Jacobson's class was "graduated" in August 1943 when its members were given navy commissions, and Jacobson then became eligible for Sub School. If they made it back from the war, they would be able to return to Michigan to finish their studies and get their degrees.

The navy held an impressive commissioning ceremony at the university, which Jacobson's family attended. By October, he was assigned to the Navy Base at Mare Island, on the bay, thirty miles north of San Francisco, along with nineteen other young ensigns who had just taken their oaths of office. Mare Island was a playground for a fellow who had grown up in a brass foundry. The base built and repaired submarines and had all the machinery for that job, including a brass foundry that turned out huge propellers, valves, gauges, and the big brass "doors" that opened at the ends of the submarine to let the torpedoes out. The 4,000-acre island surged with the pulse of an important industrial city, where sequoia-like cranes towered over the trenches of massive dry docks, and where 46,000 men and women worked, building not only submarines but, by the end of the war, destroyers and sub tenders, more than 300 landing craft and a handful of small craft.

Dazzled as he was by all the activity, young Jacobson was a bit perplexed. He had thought that, finally, having left the university, he was finished with classrooms. But here he found himself in one huge classroom, where his job was to learn every inch of the modern fleet submarine. Every morning, he was on board one of the submarines that was being built or repaired, learning where all the pipes and cables that ran along the arched ceilings and floors of the vessel went and what they did. Afternoons, he was at a desk, drawing diagrams of the air, water, and fuel systems he had inspected just hours before.

"It's a wonderful opportunity and I am very satisfied with the setup," he wrote to his father and mother. "However, it does mean that I'll have about five more months of school."

His father read between the lines. "I know you are fed up on schoolwork, but there is nothing like being prepared," Senior replied. "My suggestion to you is that you get all the information you can while at Mare Island . . . because you will find out when you get to sea and have to issue orders, if you know about the various duties you have to perform, it will be much easier for you to get the respect of the men under you. There is nothing so embarrassing as to issue orders and the men under you know that the orders are wrong."

Jacobson had been at Mare Island for a couple of weeks when his orders came, assigning him to submarine school, beginning January 3, 1944. He arrived in New London about the time that Elton Brubaker was returning to classes with the other enlisted men. Jacobson's first week in officers' Sub School was relaxing. He was amused by the questions the navy psychiatrist asked. He scored well on two parts of his officer's qualification test—the math and mechanical segments— but not so well on the vocabulary test. He found the pressure-tank experience tolerable. Some of the other men were bleeding from their ears and noses. Jacobson remained physically sound, but, as he wrote to his parents: "The pressure made you feel slow, easygoing, and I guess you would call it slap-happy."

After two weeks at New London, training on machines that simulated submarine controls, Jacobson made his first voyage onto Long Island Sound and his first dive beneath the waves.

It was the day after *Flier* ran aground at Midway.

When the inquiry into *Flier*'s grounding was completed and the survey of *Flier*'s condition was finished, it was clear that more work was needed than could be done in Pearl Harbor.

The following Sunday, four more crewmen were returned to the submarine, and on Monday, with their boat bandaged like a wounded fighter, *Flier*'s crew cast off their lines and the boat limped out of Pearl Harbor. Its port propeller was inoperable, and it was incapable of diving. Crowley doubled the lookouts and steered east. At a normal cruising speed of fifteen to twenty knots, a submarine could make the

2,100-nautical-mile passage to San Francisco in four to six days. *Flier* took nine days.

The damage aboard was evident in more than just bent metal. As the boat pushed toward Mare Island's repair yards, a feud was brewing between Crowley and his executive officer, Benjamin E. Adams Jr. By the time *Flier* reached Mare Island, Crowley was convinced that Adams did not want to work. He recommended that Adams be shipped out of the submarine fleet completely. Crowley's request amounted to a career death sentence for Adams, if it was approved.

The day after *Flier* arrived at Mare Island, the submarine was placed in dry dock for extensive repairs. It would take a while to resolve Adams's fate, but it would take longer for the submarine to be fixed. So almost immediately, most of the crew, including Crowley, left for four weeks of leave.

Elton Brubaker had mailed the graduation certificate to his folks in Florida before he had boarded a train headed west from New London. By then, he knew he was destined for some assignment in the Pacific southwest. "Probably be operating from Sydney, Australia," he told his parents. "Keep the home fires burning."

Already a world traveler by his boyhood standards, having spent several months in Kentucky at electricians' school, Elton was nonetheless impressed by the sweep of the land as the train made its way to the coast. Cheyenne, Wyoming, was 15 degrees below zero in mid-February, and it was cold in Utah and Nevada, too. Once the train reached the downhill western slope of the California mountains, the air warmed, the windows in the Pullman car were thrown open, and Elton and the other young men felt springtime wash in. The trackside was blossoming with roses and violets, and when the train reached its destination, the boy was not oblivious to the pretty young women in San Francisco. Then he was taken thirty miles north, to Mare Island.

There, in one of the huge ditches that were the dry docks, *Flier* rested on blocks, its injuries visible to all. Among enlisted men, the word began to spread that this boat, still untested in battle, was jinxed.

CHAPTER 3

MISSING FROM ACTION

There was not much for a sailor to do at Mare Island if his submarine was in dry dock. The casualties of idleness began to mount.

On Thursday, March 2, seaman second class Harry G. Ericson was tried by a summary court-martial, which found he had been under the influence of alcohol and unable to perform his duties. He was guilty, as well, of resisting arrest by the Shore Patrol in the city of Vallejo, within whose limits Mare Island was located. He was sentenced to solitary confinement for thirty days and the loss of $75 in pay, penalties that were reduced by higher authority to ten days' solitary with full rations every third day.

Later, Charles D. Pope, the heroic chief who had been washed overboard in the middle of the Pacific, was found guilty of intoxication and making a nuisance on the street and was deprived of liberty for three weeks. Paul Barron and Robert Surber were guilty of staying on leave three days longer than they were supposed to. Victor Anderson was fined $60 for being drunk and disorderly. And Chester Payne was brought back to the *Flier* and charged by the Shore Patrol with "fighting with a one-legged sailor, fighting and throwing shore patrol into the Napa River."

While some of the enlisted men were ruffians who settled their disputes with fists, the officers used a more civilized method to resolve their nasty quarrels. At two o'clock on the afternoon of April 6, Annapolis graduate Benjamin Adams was transferred from Annapolis graduate John Crowley's submarine. Despite Crowley's recommendation that he was unfit for the submarine service, Adams carried his bags across the island to his new assignment on the submarine *Albacore*, which was there for repairs. In a sense, it was a promotion for the embattled Adams, for *Albacore* had already completed eight war patrols and was well on its way to compiling the best record of any submarine, sinking thirteen Japanese ships and damaging five others. At this point, *Flier* had yet to complete its first patrol.

If the men of *Flier* were growing a bit stir-crazy waiting for some military action, the delay in their arrival in the war zone was a blessing. Every day, improvements were being made in the equipment used aboard submarines. The later *Flier* left Mare Island, the more likely its crew would have better systems on board—tools that could weigh heavily in their survival. Already, the boat was guaranteed to carry torpedoes that would work—most of the time. The same could not be said only months earlier.

As one of two branches of the navy to survive the attack on Pearl Harbor almost intact, the submarine corps was supposed to carry the battle to the Japanese by sinking their supply ships. Convoys of vessels were streaming from Japan's islands, carrying troops and materiel to outposts from what is now Vietnam in the west to the necklace of Indonesian islands that stretch across the equatorial bosom of the western Pacific from Thailand to New Guinea—a string of tropical gems separating the Philippines to the north from Australia to the south. By early 1942, the only land in this area not occupied by the Japanese was Australia. It was the daunting job of the U.S. submarines to halt this advance, to stave off the attack on Australia that was certainly the Japanese goal. But in this effort, the Japanese defenses were not the only obstacle.

From the first days of the war, the men on the subs were hobbled by what to them appeared to be faulty torpedoes. In January 1942, submarines prowling the Pacific sank only three Japanese ships. This brought the total kill for those twenty-eight subs during the first two months of the war to six Japanese ships. At the same time, the navy had lost three submarines. Skippers were not silent about the problems. The torpedoes, called Mark XIVs, were running deeper than they were supposed to, passing well below their targets, no matter how large the ships were. And even when they did hit, they were routinely failing to detonate, bouncing off the steel of an enemy ship with, presumably, a thud.

The navy brass was not quick to address the problems, assuming in many cases that the claims of the skippers were overstated or that the true problem was human error. When Rear Admiral Charles Lockwood arrived in Australia to assume command of the Pacific submarines, he wrote to a friend that the failure of his sailors to sink more enemy ships "is a highly controversial point, but my reading of all war diaries thus far submitted has convinced me that among the causes are: (a) bad choice of stations in that most likely invasion points were not covered soon enough nor heavily enough, (b) bad torpedo performance, in that they evidently ran much too deep and had numerous prematures . . . (c) buck fever—firing with ship swinging when he thought it was on a steady course . . ."

Lockwood could not ignore the reasoned complaints of his only successful submarine captain. James Coe claimed that the torpedoes fired by his boat, *Skipjack*, were running too deep. "To make a round-trip of 8,500 miles into enemy waters, to gain attack position undetected within 800 yards of enemy ships, only to find that the torpedoes run deep and over half the time will fail to explode, seems to me to be an undesirable manner of gaining information which might be determined any morning within a few miles of a torpedo station in the presence of comparatively few hazards," Coe wrote to Lockwood.

Lockwood ordered that a torpedo be fired into a fishing net to test Coe's claim. When the net was brought up, there was a hole at a depth of twenty-five feet, fifteen feet below the depth at which the torpedo had been set. Lockwood reported the results to the Navy Bureau of Ordnance, which was responsible for torpedo design. The bureau replied that the tests were faulty, and "no reliable conclusions" could be drawn. Two months later, in August 1942, the bureau finally agreed that the torpedoes had problems running too deep and gave skippers instructions for modifying their ammunition so that it could be trusted.

This did not, however, solve the second problem—dud torpedoes. Most skippers believed that magnetic exploders, one of the two types of triggering devices on each torpedo, were faulty. (Torpedoes had contact exploders, as well.) A number of skippers had, without authorization, already modified their torpedoes to run more-shallow routes, and yet they still failed to sink enemy ships. Some began disabling the magnetic exploders, also without permission. Lockwood believed in the magnetic exploders, which were designed to be triggered when the torpedo passed into the magnetic field of a ship's steel hull. An explosion in the water below a ship would damage the ship more than the same explosion near the surface, because all the force of the blast would be felt by the ship. In a surface explosion, much of the power would be lost in the air. And the 500-pound warheads on the torpedoes were too small to sink one of the prize targets—the battleships and aircraft carriers—by contact near the surface.

Yet if there was a theoretical reason to favor the magnetic exploders, the evidence was mounting concerning their defects. Twenty-seven patrols by submarines in early 1943—each patrol might be a month or more long, lasting until the fuel or torpedoes were consumed or expended—resulted in only twenty-five sunken Japanese ships. The problem couldn't be corrected, in part, because of rivalries within the navy, long-standing turf battles between sailors and land-locked bureaucrats.

In July 1943, evidence surfaced of another defect in the torpedoes. The contact exploder was not working any more effectively than the magnetic exploder. One submarine, the *Tinosa*, fired fifteen torpedoes—all but one it had on board—at a huge whale factory ship used as a tanker. Eleven were duds, and the ship got away when a Japanese destroyer appeared on the scene.

This time, Lockwood ordered that the torpedoes be tested by submariners in Hawaii. The tests showed that the contact exploders were poorly designed. Lockwood directed his people to fix the problem, which they did in the field, using scrap metal from Japanese airplane propellers found on the island near Pearl Harbor. It was September 1943, a month before *Flier* was launched.

For twenty-one months, the navy's submariners had been putting themselves in treacherous positions in their attempt to sink enemy ships, but, because of their defective torpedoes, they were sitting ducks to depth charges and rammings. By the time Lockwood ordered the improvements, eighteen boats had been lost, along with 825 sailors—including all hands on ten submarines.

Improvements had already been made in the radar used by submarines when the torpedo problems were solved. But early in the war, using a primitive radar that was meant for antiaircraft detection, submariners found themselves in the same position they would create if they broke radio silence. The enemy could use the radar signals to locate the submarines. So skippers relied primarily on human lookouts to spot aircraft.

Then a new generation of radar became available near the end of the first year of the war. This device allowed the sub to search the surface for ships, day or night, giving the direction and distance of the target over a great many miles—something human lookouts could not accomplish.

Further development of radar would benefit *Flier* when it was refit at Mare Island. Despite the improvements in torpedoes, however, one problem with the weapons remained. At times, a torpedo would surface instead of running submerged. Frequently the errant torpedo would take a circular course that would lead it back to the submarine that fired it. By early 1944, no sub had been recognized as a victim of its own torpedo. Yet, the explanations for the losses of a dozen of the twenty-six missing subs were less than credible. In many cases, only the enemy knew what happened.

After the war, the sole survivor of *Tullibee*, when he was repatriated from confinement and labor at a Japanese copper mine, told investigators that his sub sank when it was hit by its own torpedo. The incident had occurred in March 1944, while *Flier* was still in dry dock at Mare Island. Later, on an October evening, the submarine *Tang* sank after one of its torpedoes surfaced and began leaping like a porpoise, turning ever to the left until, despite maneuvers aboard the sub, it struck the rear of the boat. Among the nine survivors was the skipper, who made his report following the war.

"Rang up emergency speed," wrote Richard O'Kane. "Completed part of a fishtail maneuver in a futile attempt to clear the turning circle of this erratic circular run. The torpedo was observed through about 180 degrees of its turn due to the phosphorescence of its wake. It struck abreast the after torpedo room with a violent explosion about 20 seconds after firing. The tops were blown off the only regular ballast tanks aft and the after three compartments flooded instantly. The *Tang* sank by the stern much as you would drop a pendulum suspended in a horizontal position. There was insufficient time even to carry out the last order to close the hatch."

At Mare Island, *Flier* got some new radar equipment. And at the request of its skipper, *Flier*'s forward deck gun was removed and a six-inch, stub-nosed gun was mounted aft of the conning tower. By the time it was ready to leave California, the submarine would have the latest equipment and a well-rested—if antsy—crew.

CHAPTER 4

A GATHERING OF MEN

What Al Jacobson knew in April as he traveled by train across the Midwest on six days of leave was that submarines were sinking in the Pacific. The navy had recently released statistics. Fifteen percent of the boats had been lost, and several hundred men were dead as a result. Submarine safety sparked some gallows humor in Al. "They are having a little trouble convincing some of us that subs are the safest branch of the navy," he had written to his brother a couple of weeks earlier. "However, the first chance I get I would like to go out. What's the old saying about a fool every minute?"

He wasn't foolish, just young, despite the ensign bars on his shoulders. What propelled him was not patriotic zeal alone. In his veins ran the same juice that fuels any adolescent's search for adventure. His thoughts did not harbor the possibility of his own death.

When he left New London on April Fools' Day, Al planned to visit with friends on the East Coast for a couple of days, stop off at the University of Michigan, where some of his heart remained, and then, after swinging by home in Grand Haven briefly, head on to his new assignment, Mare Island. He expected to spend two to three months there, helping to repair submarines, before getting assigned to a ship. But Al had heard that if you arrived early, you might get assigned to a ship immediately. Some of his New London classmates had been assigned directly to submarines, but those boats were still being built and were months away from combat. At Mare Island, Al had something of a gambler's chance to get directly on a boat that was ready for action, so he didn't want to waste time.

Either way—on ship or on shore—Al was pleased with his future. "San Francisco is a great liberty town," he told his brother even before he arrived. "Plenty of women and places to go!"

The train reached the San Francisco terminal on April 13—luckily, a Thursday—and Al headed north to the submarine base. He was two days early. When he showed his orders at the base headquarters, the personnel folks responded with good news. He had been assigned directly to a submarine. He took his bags across the 4,300-acre base and walked up a small gangplank to *Flier,* finally out of dry dock and tied to a pier. It was, he would tell his parents in his next letter, "the best boat that was here."

Flier's narrow corridors and compact compartments were not crowded. The boat had already lost many of its crewmen to other boats, so a fresh, young ensign was welcomed. Al immediately got a job as commissary officer. Technically, this lad, whose mother had done all the cooking and grocery shopping in the large Jacobson family, was in charge of feeding the eighty-six men who would be *Flier's* crew. The job involved planning every meal, buying the necessary food, supervising the storage and cooking, and, critically, making certain the food didn't run out. In reality, the navy would never entrust such a tender fellow with what might be the most important job on the submarine. The real work was done by a chief petty officer.

By day, Al was on the submarine, learning the commissary ropes. The chief had specific ideas, and Al simply listened and absorbed. One thing the chief demanded was that *Flier* be provisioned with Hill Bros. coffee. The brand was roasted in San Francisco, but for some reason the institution-sized cans were not available. So two-pound cans were brought aboard by the case, and the boat's cupboards were filled with them.

Since Al didn't know what he was doing, he depended on the honesty of the chief, who finally convinced the ensign he should buy the best of everything. Not only would he have the funds to do so, but the purchases would come in handy later, the chief explained. Submarines received a higher dollar allotment for food than did surface ships—about $1.20 a day per man compared with 90 cents. And while submariners feasted on steaks instead of chopped meat, the chief promised, once at sea, they would lose their appetites. There just wasn't much physical activity for the men in a submarine. A good chief petty officer is like any good army supply sergeant—he knows the value of stuff, and he knows with whom he can trade. He may find he is short of one item or another, so he has to have a store of other goods available for bartering. The commissary chief explained to young Jacobson that although they would order—as they were required—a certain percentage of ground beef and stew meat with their steaks and roasts, the lesser cuts of meat could be given away to other vessels.

Finally, although Al was responsible for planning meals and overseeing the cooking, it was the chief who supervised *Flier*'s cooks and who drafted the menus. The green ensign dutifully approved the menus. Aware that he knew too little to criticize the cooks, he kept his mouth shut.

It would be two weeks before *Flier* was fit to return to sea, Jacobson learned. Although repairs of the damage wreaked by the Midway reef were completed, work was still under way to fit the boat with the improved radar and the new deck gun. While he spent his days aboard the boat, Al slept at the bachelor officers' quarters on the base, as did the other officers. Ranking officers had their privileges, but there was an easy familiarity in the BOQ among the commissioned men. Al, a product of the yacht and country club society back home, felt very comfortable in these surroundings.

In fact, the young ensign even had familiar hometown faces just minutes away. Paul Johnson, a friend and classmate of his older brother, Chuck, was serving on an admiral's staff in San Francisco. Paul, whom Al regarded as a cousin, and his wife, Charlotte, drew him into their circle, taking him to concerts and inviting him to dinner. It was a nice lingering taste of home.

Everything about the Jacobson home and his upbringing had pointed Al toward the navy. First, there was his birth. Doctor DeWitt, the Jacobson family physician, was leading the Memorial Day parade through the streets of Grand Haven, Michigan, when he got the call that Edna Jacobson was about to deliver her second child. He raced to the hospital and brought Alvin Jr. into the world on the one day when the whole nation looked in unison to its military veterans with thanks.

If the day of his birth—May 30—was not a sufficient omen, there was the place. Grand Haven is on the long, sandy eastern shore of Lake Michigan, a body of water with significant connections to the navy. In 1944, among other activities, the Manitowoc, Wisconsin, shipyard on the western shore was building many of the submarines that the navy was commissioning for the war.

Although much of Michigan in the area of Grand Haven is flat, for eons, lake waves have piled sand in a 100-foot-high berm along that shore. The berm is covered with forests and, in Grand Haven, tidy homes. The Jacobson home, a modest Victorian with steeply pitched gables, was on the eastern slope of the berm, not a long walk from the turn-of-the-century downtown and the public schools. The town was a resort and had been for years, once known as the summer retreat for those in St. Louis, Missouri, who could afford it. The Grand River, which passes through Grand Rapids in the heart of Michigan, empties into the lake at Grand Haven, and legendary Great Lakes freighters and ore ships, then as now, navigated to docks a mile or more inland.

About three miles inland from Grand Haven was the town of Spring Lake and the long lake for which the town is named. On the south shore of this lake, across from the Spring Lake Yacht Club, was the summer home that the Jacobsons built when Al was a boy. From early childhood, Al and his brothers and three sisters had slept every summer night in the cottage's pine-paneled rooms. The floors were carpeted with twenty-seven Navajo rugs, and the walls were decorated with model anchors, spoked wooden helms, and family snapshot collages. During the days, the boys sailed on the cool water of Spring Lake. This was not recreational sailing. Alvin Sr. and Edna were both competitive people, and they would have viewed sailing for fun as frivolous. The boys were expected to race, for racing built character—the sort of character that captains of industry must have. If they were sailing when there was no race, it was to practice their boat-handling skills or to find a better way to trim the sails. The practice paid off. In 1938, Al and three other boys from the yacht club—all of them sixteen years old—competed in Chicago against the best young sailors from the Midwest. They won the regatta and earned the right to represent the Great Lakes at the Junior National Championship in Marblehead, Massachusetts. Sailing on boats unlike those at Spring Lake, they managed to finish second.

Two years later, as Al looked forward to his high school graduation, he and his brothers borrowed an old, wooden cruising sailboat, the *Sea Girl*. Filling the boat with friends and casseroles from home, they set out on a voyage north to Mackinac Island, nearly 300 miles away. *Sea Girl* was a fifty-six-foot-long wooden schooner. It was only fourteen years old, but the boat had been poorly maintained. The boys knew boats well enough to understand *Sea Girl*'s condition, but at three o'clock one afternoon, they cast off and raised the sails in a brisk southerly breeze.

Thrilled as they ran before the wind, the boys covered more than 100 miles in the first twelve hours, and by four o'clock the next morning, they had reached the harbor at Frankfort, Michigan, where they saw a ferry, which carried railcars across the lake to Wisconsin, just starting its trip. To their surprise, the ferry turned abruptly and headed back into the harbor, unwilling to brave the same winds that had been pushing *Sea Girl*. The boys took their cue and lowered their sails, preparing to motor into the harbor. Only at this point did they realize how rough were the seas as they began crossing the steep waves that until now had been gently following them.

They waited then for twenty-four hours, anchored in Frankfort Harbor. The next morning, the wind had moved around, coming from the north, and the water in the harbor was calm. So the boys motored back onto the lake and turned north, into the wind and waves.

Sea Girl had been willing to go with the flow, but these were more-adverse conditions, the boat ramming into waves of gray water that buried the bow. Below the deck, the timbers of *Sea Girl*'s frame were moving. Between the planks that formed the hull, the caulking was shifting. Water was streaming through every crack, and the bilge was filling.

The Jacobson boys were experienced and did not panic. They began working a hand-operated pump and organized their crew into a bucket brigade. Meanwhile, things were flying about inside the boat each time it slammed into another wave. Casseroles were quickly dashed to the floor, and the passengers, several of them not sailors, were terrified.

As they crept north along the now-rocky coast, the boys saw that the flooding was growing worse. *Sea Girl* was sinking.

Al was at the helm, and in the early morning light he scanned the coast until he saw a solitary sandy beach. He steered for shore, running the boat aground on the sand. All hands were safe in Al's first wreck at sea, and with help from the Coast Guard the next day, *Sea Girl* was salvaged.

This was not, however, the first time Al had had bad luck with ladies. He and his best friend, Bob Van Hoef, whom he had known since junior high school and who happened to be on the *Sea Girl* during that voyage, had made a bet earlier in the year. They were both dating girls from their high school class, and the wager concerned which one would be first to get a kiss from his girlfriend. Van Hoef won. If Al, too, had achieved the same tame conquest, he was too much the gentleman to reveal it.

Women and girls had a distinct place in the hierarchy of the Jacobson home. Edna was in charge of the household. Alvin Sr. was the patriarch. The boys worked in the foundry. The girls—Edna May, a year younger than Al, Marylin, five years younger, and Muriel, seven years—polished their father's shoes. Their mother had a clear ranking for those in her family and her community. Her husband came first, followed by the boys, the girls, and the minister. Probably the entire Johnson family came next, because they were integral to the Jacobsons' daily lives and to their livelihood.

Al Sr. had been a shop teacher after high school. In the summers, he was a salesman for a brass foundry in Muskegon. Edna was a secretary at the foundry. When Alvin married Edna, he knew he needed to improve his income, and he felt that he could succeed in the foundry business. He located an existing foundry in Grand Haven and invited his friend, Paul Johnson, who had served an apprenticeship in tool-making, to be his partner. The initial investment in the Grand Haven Brass Foundry was about $2,200, and the products were refrigerator hinges. When they had been in business for a year, the foundry burned to the ground. A local banker, Mr. Sherman, gave them a loan and became a third partner, and the seeds of what would become a multimillion-dollar enterprise were planted. When Alvin Sr. landed a contract to make toilet-seat hinges, the business took off.

In his lectures to his boys, Al Sr. stressed the importance of finding new markets. He was on the road two of every six weeks, traveling across the country, searching for opportunities. When he returned home, he drilled the message into his boys so that by the time they were in the military, it was natural for them to look for hot business prospects wherever they landed. And in his frequent letters from home, their father prodded them, instructed them, and shared his view of the world, which was primarily a business view.

The day after he arrived at Mare Island, Al Jr. wrote home, gave a report to "Daddy and Mother" on what his duties were, and added that, in his trip across the country, "I stopped in and spent a couple of hours with Mr. Berman [a family friend and business associate] when I was in New York. The Vito-Motivator sounds like it has many possibilities. However, I won't have any chance to see if they can be used around the navy yard here because the way it looks now, I am really going to be busy."

A following letter from Al Sr. began: "Dear Junior: I was down to Cleveland this past week, checking up on some new stylecore machines for making small cores at the Brass Foundry."

Other letters carried Al Sr.'s views on a range of topics.

"Campbell, Wyant & Cannon's big foundry went out on a strike, and it is a dirty shame to have these things take place during a war," he wrote. "So when you boys get a chance to vote, be sure to help clean out the White House, as that is where all this stuff starts."

If Dad was fed up with Franklin D. Roosevelt and the nation's other leaders, Son was finding that he liked his superiors on *Flier*. He had been told by an older officer that John Crowley, the commander, was among the best skippers. And the ensign found it easy to talk with Jim Liddell, who was now the executive officer, or second-ranking man on the boat.

Liddell, for one thing, was a Midwesterner. He had graduated from Northwestern University in Chicago in 1940 with a degree in engineering, the diploma Al hoped to earn when the war was over and he returned to Michigan. Moreover, Liddell was a football player at Northwestern—a tackle, as Al had been in high school.

Four years Al's senior, just like Jacobson's brother, Chuck, Liddell had been in submarines since before the war, and had stories to tell. He was on a submarine the day the Japanese bombed both Pearl Harbor and, hours later, Manila, in the Philippines. His submarine hid on the bottom of Manila Bay for ten days, dodging Japanese planes. Three months later, his submarine had participated in the evacuation of two dozen sailors and marines from the island of Corregidor, when American and Filipino troops on Bataan, a peninsula north of Corregidor, surrendered—an incident often referred to as the lowest point in the war for the Allies.

Liddell was tall—about six-two—and solidly built. Some called him baby-faced, but he was also stoic. His reddish-brown hair was thinning, and he was a smoker. He had spent a few months after accepting his engineering degree as a salesman for a cork company. While he had been executive officer of *Flier* for a couple months, Liddell had started as commissary officer, just where Al was now. Liddell told Al that he was lucky to be aboard *Flier*. Liddell, who had been aboard *Flier* when it ran aground at Midway, had served with seven skippers, and he rated Crowley the best.

Not everyone aboard *Flier* shared Liddell's view of the captain. Some of the enlisted men had come to call him Cautious Crowley. If in time the name would prove somewhat ironic, it was not without a sound basis. The sailors who had fashioned the nickname had observed their commander's method of leadership and found it less than inspiring. Crowley's management style was their clue. Rather than dictate from his throne in the conning tower, the skipper almost always consulted with his lieutenants and chiefs before coming to a conclusion. If he knew about his nickname, Crowley no doubt nodded in silent, if grudging, agreement.

Soon after his graduation from the United States Naval Academy in Annapolis, Maryland, Crowley was assigned to flight school in Pensacola, Florida. He did not make it to the end of the training, however. If someone close to him asked why, he had a blunt answer: "I was too cautious."

Crowley liked to know what was expected of him. When the choices were murky, he hedged. He was a perfect fit in the military, where in almost every situation one's duty is to follow orders. This he could do with precision. It was a quality that, on Midway, had gotten *Flier* lodged on a reef because, in order to meet the navy's expectation that he would arrive in that port on a specific date, he simply had followed the directions of the local pilot and entered the channel rather than wait offshore for better weather. But in most instances, his reliance on direction from above in the chain of command had served him well. One only needs to look at Crowley's childhood for the reason.

Both of Crowley's parents had emigrated from Ireland to Springfield, Massachusetts. His father had worked as a laborer in Ireland and, in his new country, found a job with the city department of public works. The elder Crowley had changed his name when he arrived in the United States. His real name was Keochaine (pronounced *KoHANE*). He was concerned that it would be pronounced Cohan (a distant relative was the vaudevillian performer, George M. Cohan) and, as his relatives would explain, the old man had "ethnic issues." So in the new land, he chose to use the name of the richest man in Banty—Crowley the merchant.

The skipper's father was a man whose opinionated bitterness divided him and his wife from family members who joined them in Springfield. He was always at work, so young John Crowley had less of a bond with his father than he did with an adoring and childless uncle. It was the uncle, who had once been a sailor, who influenced Crowley's decision to join the navy. But it was probably the old man who instilled uncertainty in young John, an uneasiness that the son sought to overcome with the regimentation of the military.

By April 1944, Crowley was not only a veteran sailor but also a married man with three children. A daughter, Mary Ellen, arrived the first day of the month in Kansas. Crowley's wife and two older children had moved there for the duration of the war to live near relatives.

Crowley's family aboard *Flier* numbered eighty-five men in April, including four new crewmen needed to operate the new radar and sonar systems. There were nine officers assigned to the boat; the rest were noncommissioned officers and enlisted men.

Perhaps typical of the enlisted men was Earl Baumgart, the Milwaukee kid who had absorbed the dunking in the breeches buoy off Midway. Baumgart, tall as Lieutenant Liddell and lanky, was about a month short of his twenty-first birthday. After his enlistment in the navy in 1942, he had attended submarine training in Key West, Florida, and in New London, before he was assigned to work training other sailors. Then he got a break with an assignment to *Flier*, which was under construction on the Thames River in Connecticut. As an original crewman, he shared many of Liddell's experiences, but he did not share the lieutenant's glowing opinion of Crowley. Baumgart was among those who read Crowley as cautious to a fault.

Baumgart was the youngest child of a production line worker and a homemaker. His mother was in her forties when Earl was born. She had two other sons and two daughters, and the family had a collie named Trixie. The boys and girls all attended North Division High School in Milwaukee, where Earl became captain of the swimming team and joined the cast of the school's production of Shakespeare's *Taming of the Shrew,* only after an English teacher persuaded him. He was average—neither shy nor outgoing, a good student who liked school and studying, particularly English grammar. Outside of school, his only activity before graduation had been delivering newspapers. Once he graduated, he became, in this mecca for beer, a regular with his friends at the local taverns.

If he returned to Milwaukee now, Baumgart would have some stories to tell in those taverns. There was, of course, the episode at Midway. But even before that, after *Flier* got under way on its maiden voyage, the crew had had a scare. Another submarine launched at New London had left for the war in October. *Dorado*, with a crew of seventy-eight, was headed for the Panama Canal but was never seen again. Investigators could not declare a cause, but it was known that a friendly aircraft had dropped three depth charges on a submarine in an area where *Dorado* was supposed to be. When *Flier*'s crewmen learned of the loss, they were terrified. *Flier* made it through the canal, but as the boat crossed the Pacific toward Pearl Harbor, it came under attack from a friendly ship. None of the rounds hit, and *Flier* escaped thanks to rain squalls and a fog bank that Crowley used as camouflage in making his escape.

Baumgart was a motor machinist on *Flier,* and his job was to assist in the maintenance of the submarine. In surface battle, he was assigned as a link in a human chain, passing ammunition to the machine gun on deck. His world was populated by his few enlisted friends and the chiefs who supervised them.

The enlisted men who were not chiefs had little daily contact with the officers, particularly when at sea. The handful who worked in the conning tower or control room, operating the radar, radios, and steering, might be known by name. One man whom the officers all got to know by his face was the steward, who brought them their meals. On *Flier,* this man was John Clyde Turner—one of only two non-white men on the boat.

There was really not much to keep Turner in Powder Springs, Georgia, when he enlisted in the navy in October 1942. He was a twenty-seven-year-old black man with no prospects at home other than working dead-end jobs or tilling the farm that his grandfather, John Turner, had tilled until his death. Powder Springs, a rural community about twenty miles west of Atlanta, offered strong motivation to leave. The family farm on Oglesby Road was twenty acres. There was never an attempt to market what Grandfather grew because there was only enough to feed the family—Grandfather, Grandmother, their daughter, Clyde, and her children, John Clyde and Equilla. Their home was a simple country house, with a hall running down the middle from the front door to the back door, two bedrooms on one side, and, on the other side, the kitchen and a bedroom for company. There was no paint on the walls, no electricity and no plumbing. The Turners cooked their meals on a woodstove in the kitchen. They hauled water from a well outside in a bucket.

Everyone worked the farm except Equilla, whose only chore was water girl for those out in the fields. When the war started, John Clyde had had some jobs off the farm in addition to his work at home. His mother worked in the houses of white people as well as on the farm. The tedium of work was broken on Sundays when everyone walked across the flat landscape of pine and poplar trees, broken by fields, to attend the noon church service at New Hope Baptist Church. The chapel had bare wooden benches in its one room. There was no piano. For music, the parishioners relied on their voices. The voices sounded pretty good, enough to bring your toes to tapping on the wooden floor. When John Clyde looked around, he saw the men all dressed in their one suit, the women in their one dress that they would wash when they got home to have ready for the next Sunday.

It wasn't just the boredom of Powder Springs that moved Turner to leave. If you were black, you had to go to the back door every place you went, and when you stopped at a filling station for gas, you couldn't use the restroom. Segregation meant rejection. The four or five white families who lived near the Turners thought the world of Grandfather Turner. They didn't love him, but there were no problems so long as everyone followed the rules. Perhaps in the navy, Turner would find different rules.

That was questionable. The only black men on submarines were those who served the officers as stewards and cooks. And the typical attitude of officers toward these men was not one of equality. Years after the war, Admiral I. J. Galantin wrote a book, *Take Her Deep!*, about his service as skipper on the submarine *Halibut*. Galantin devoted four pages to a profile of one cook.

The first joke at the cook's expense came when he reported aboard. Asked by an officer what his name was, he replied: "Mr. Mosley, sir.

"Since John Paul Jones's time junior officers in the navy have been addressed 'Mister,' but from this day we had a ship's cook who was 'Mr. Mosley,' or sometimes 'Ol' Man Mose.' He was a stocky, burly man, homely in appearance, as slow-speaking and -thinking as he was lumbering in motion. In the weeks ahead we would learn little more of Mr. Mosley's background than appeared in his brief service record. He was older than the average recruit, and a native of New Mexico, a fact which apparently influenced his cooking. Whatever he cooked, he cooked to a turn—as the boys said, 'Till it turned black'—and sprinkled lavishly with salt, pepper, or Tabasco.

"In a submarine, a cook can't be a sensitive soul. Unlike those in larger ships, his galley is not removed, denied to the ship's company, out of sight from the crew's mess tables and beyond the range of their ceaseless good-humored, derogatory comments. The submarine cook literally stands behind his product in his tiny, hot galley, only an arm's length from the shipmates seated at the mess tables in the after battery room."

The ridicule and the pranks, all predicated on Mosley's lack of sophistication, were relentless, Galantin recalled. "His stolid features never varied as the boys heaped contempt on his cooking or tried to cajole information from him."

As yet untouched by the notion of civil rights, the navy's culture was as predictable as a sailor's uniform. John Clyde Turner, when he got to the *Flier*, would find—even if he failed to anticipate it—the same lack of respect that Ship's Cook Third Class Mosley found on *Halibut*.

And so, Turner left Powder Springs. His sister, Equilla, was about seventeen, his mother was forty-two, and both grandparents were dead. The fields he had worked there had produced little more than the next meal, and the jobs he found in town were dead ends. Certainly in the navy he saw opportunity.

His would not, however, be the same opportunity shared by all the white members of the *Flier* crew.

"As for initial sub school type training, this was a hit or miss proposition and varied from the early part of the war to the later," said

Glenn A. Knoblock, author of *Black Submariners in the U.S. Navy, 1940–1975* (McFarland Publishing, 2005). "In the beginning, stewards generally received little, if any training before joining a boat . . . often it was modified or shortened. However, later in the war (by mid- to late 1943), most stewards that joined the sub force after going through basic training did receive the same training as white enlisted personnel."

Turner enlisted on October 23, 1942, and was assigned to the submarine *Tinosa,* on which he served for five war patrols, according to Knoblock. He then served one patrol on *Cod* before joining *Flier,* according to the author.

"The skippers of *Tinosa* . . . and *Cod* . . . were well-liked skippers and seem to have treated their stewards well, so there is no reason to believe that they did not allow their stewards to go through the qualifying process," said Knoblock, "though it should be noted that some sub skippers *were* prejudiced and did not allow their stewards to qualify, or were indifferent to any training they might have received."

CHAPTER 5

A SECOND CHANCE

One week after Al Jacobson first saw *Flier* tied to a Mare Island dock, the refitted boat was ready for its first sea trial on San Francisco Bay. With a harbor pilot on board, the submarine eased from its berth and headed out through the channel. The pilot left the boat a little after ten o'clock that morning, and Crowley pointed *Flier* to a spot in nineteen fathoms of water off Point Blunt, an island on the bay with a view of the Golden Gate Bridge due west. The skipper ordered the anchor dropped and then gave directions to fire dummy torpedoes from all ten of the sub's tubes—six in the bow and four in the stern. There were no problems with the torpedoes, and all the repairs seemed to be sound. *Flier* returned to Mare Island and the next day, a Friday, *Flier* cruised around the bay and then docked at Pier 31 in San Francisco, like a kid given permission to stay overnight at a friend's house just around the corner. After more tests on Saturday, Crowley headed home to Mare Island. Over the next five days, the skipper handled administrative duties, including disciplining a number of sailors who had stayed on leave too long or were drunk and disorderly.

Early Monday morning of the following week, on May 1, the Shore Patrol brought seaman first class Chester Payne back to *Flier*. It was he who had been fighting with a one-legged sailor and had thrown the Shore Patrol in the Napa River. By eight o'clock that same day, with breakfast finished, Crowley gave orders to cast off the lines, and everyone aboard *Flier*, including Seaman Payne, headed for the submarine's first patrol. At five past ten that morning, the submarine passed under the Golden Gate Bridge and through the net that protected the bay from enemy submarines. As is often the case, fog shrouded the bridge, and *Flier* sounded its foghorn as it passed on the surface into the open ocean. But by noon the fog had lifted, the horn had stopped blowing, and *Flier* was aimed for Hawaii.

Elton Brubaker was already many thousand miles west of *Flier's* destination. His journey began in late February when, along with a buddy from Sub School—Hestel Walker, another eighteen-year-old—he left Mare Island on a refrigerated ship bound for New Guinea, carrying meats and frozen foods for the Allied troops. The trip was uneventful until the ship anchored in New Guinea. There the reality of war was brought into focus when Elton and Hestel saw a navy PT boat shoot down a Japanese Zero airplane. After about ten days in that island nation, the boys boarded an Australian merchant ship, the HMS *Merker*. Once a German cruise ship, the *Merker* had potato bins built on its deck, and Elton and the others slung hammocks inside the bins. It was no idyllic voyage, for the *Merker* was empty and it pounded on the waves of a rough Coral Sea all the 1,200 miles to Brisbane, on Australia's eastern coast. There the boys boarded a troop train, complete with cattle cars, for the arduous 2,200-mile ride across the continent to Fremantle, traversing Australia's deserts in the southern hemisphere's late summer. The train benches were hard. There were three meals a day of mutton stew. The only stops were for meals and to allow the soldiers and sailors to relieve themselves. When the train stopped, aborigines approached, begging for Australian shillings. It took four simmering nights and five blazing hot days to reach Fremantle on the country's western coast, a staging area on the Indian Ocean for Allied navies.

Looking out on the western sea, Elton knew he was a long way from home.

Elton Stanley Brubaker was five months short of his eighteenth birthday when he enlisted in the navy in April 1943. At that time, he was living with his family in St. Augustine. But for most of his life, home had been in San Mateo, a white-sand farming community in flat and rural north-central Florida potato country. There, where the broad St. Johns River winds its slow way northeast toward Jacksonville on the Atlantic coast, the land that was not cultivated was forested in palmetto, pine, and palm trees, and sprawling old oaks on the branches of which grew armies of resurrection fern. Flourishing in the underbrush were colonies of June bugs and palmetto bugs, roaches, ants, and silverfish, and swarms of horseflies and mosquitoes.

There was a screened porch on the front of the small clapboard home where the Brubakers lived, about a mile east of San Mateo's downtown—a general store and post office, school, and citrus-packing business. The family had moved into the three-bedroom home eleven years earlier when Elton was six, his sister Charlotte Marie was seven, and his little brother, Lewis, was four. Until Elton was in high school, there was no electricity. Lighting came from oil lamps. While the screened porch kept bugs outside, nothing kept out the North Florida cold in the winter or, in the summer, the sizzling heat. There was no plumbing. A galvanized tub was used for baths, and the bathwater, heated on the woodstove, was shared. The Brubakers cooked their meals on the same stove, and before each meal, the whole family recited the same prayer: "Bless this food to our bodies and our lives to thy service, in Jesus' name we pray, Amen."

The Brubaker family needed help, divine or otherwise. It was the Great Depression, but Elton's parents faced another hurdle. Emil Scott Brubaker's leg had been paralyzed by a bout of polio in 1927. He could no longer work as a repairman in the rail yards in St. Augustine, so he tried to farm in San Mateo. Nellie May Brubaker was a schoolteacher—indeed, a driven woman who would eventually earn a PhD and become a successful real estate investor. But during the Depression, she was earning $48 a month working in nearby schools. The pay was in scrip, not cash. The state promised that when it got the money, it would pay her the $48. Somehow, the Brubakers managed to eat. There were citrus fruits from the groves around San Mateo, and Emil would cook corn, tomatoes, butter beans, and bacon and serve it to his children over rice.

With their mother living away from home at times to teach in faraway schools, the Brubaker children looked to their father for most of their nurturing. He was the disciplinarian who cut the saplings to use as switches when their behavior required it. He smoked a pipe with a curved stem, and he seemed to his children to be frail. He earned some money picking oranges in season, and he made barrels for storing potatoes as part of the federal Works Progress Administration.

Emil Brubaker knew about the military. He had served in World War I as an army muleskinner in France. His children learned from him not about the war but of the beauty of the gardens at the Palace of Versailles. After that war, Emil worked for some uncles on a farm in Kansas before moving back to Florida. He and Nellie May Cook married in 1923, three years before the polio epidemic. Later, Emil walked with a limp, and the family moved every year, driven by their poverty. They went without an income until an aunt came to live with them in 1929, allowing Nellie May to get a teaching job.

Life was not all drudgery; Brubaker ancestors had moved to Florida in the 1800s, and the family still had property in nearby Federal Point, on the St. Johns River. There was a large tree on the riverbank, and when the older cousins were babysitting, Elton, Charlotte Marie, and Lewis would spend long hours swimming. Even when he was tiny, Elton swam. Swam and flew. A long rope knotted to a tree branch was used by the children to launch themselves out over the St. Johns, whose surface was only inches below the top of the riverbank and the surrounding flatland farm. Elton was fearless as he soared across the water. Lewis adored his older brother and tried to mimic his every move. Charlotte tried to boss them both.

When Elton was in second grade and Charlotte was in third, Nellie May was teaching in San Mateo's one-room schoolhouse. When the other boys picked a fight with Elton, his mother—attempting to show him no favoritism because she wanted to keep her job—would single him out for punishment. Charlotte looked on with a critical eye. Mother was a little hard on Elton, she thought. Viewed from Nellie May's position, she was the primary breadwinner. All of her energy was devoted to teaching, and for the sake of her family, she could not afford to let a perception rob them of their livelihood.

Still, when he reached fifth grade, Elton could not keep pace with the other children and had to repeat the grade. He attacked school with purpose, however, and made it to high school, traveling a few miles west to Palatka, a commercial hub on the far side of the river from San Mateo. He was in the glee club and played the trombone in the band. And he was already a Boy Scout, an activity that gave him a mentor. E. Paul Dunklin, an electrician by trade, was the scoutmaster, and when Elton started high school, Dunklin hired him as a helper. As Dunklin's right hand, Elton helped wire the Brubakers' rustic home, finally putting electric lights where the Aladdin lamps had been. The boy also became fond of Dunklin's daughter, Pauline.

Next thing the family knew, Elton was in the navy's electrician school in Kentucky, and he was dumping Pauline for Ruth Turner. As he made his way across the country, and then the Pacific, Elton let his family know that Ruth would someday be part of the family.

"Do you remember that I asked for a picture of you and Daddy?" he wrote to his mother from Fremantle. "I'm still waiting for it. I would like to have it more than ever now. Ruth Turner is going to send me one of herself, and then when I get a picture of Lewis, I [will] have a complete set, as I already have a picture of Charlotte."

Flier reached Hawaii for the second time in early May, and Al Jacobson was seeing a lot of places that his parents had visited before him. The difference, he noted, was that they had paid for *their* vacations.

Al's visit was not exactly a vacation. Over the next eight days, *Flier* joined other submarines offshore to practice their hunting skills, making coordinated, simulated attacks on friendly ships arriving from San Francisco. On Mother's Day, he wrote a letter to his family, filled with thoughts of home. "Could really use you tonight," he told his mother. "I have to make out the menu for the next week. Am finding out the hard way what the different people don't like." He added: "We have been eating like kings. To have steaks etc. means nothing."

Earlier that day, the crew had had a beach party that Al, as junior officer, was charged with organizing. They barbecued steaks and brought everything else from *Flier* to complete the meal. Al, who had sailed and skied in Michigan, got to try combining those skills on a surfboard that day, and he toured a sugarcane plantation. But his mini island vacation was close to ending a week later. Al, censoring himself so the officials would not have to, wrote to his parents that he would be at sea for "quite some time. Don't get the idea that I won't get mail, though," he wrote.

"Somebody in one of your letters asked how come they call the ship *Flier*, because it doesn't sound like a fish," he recalled then. (Submarines were all typically named for species of fish.) "Well, the flier is a fish. It looks like a bluegill. The same size and shape head and body, but it is a grayish green color. The fish is found in freshwater in Southern United States," he explained.

As *Flier* prepared to depart, Al was struggling with the decision of whether to order 3,000 or 4,000 pounds of potatoes, and in what proportions of fresh and canned. If for Al the war was not entirely a picnic, it certainly had a lot to do with food.

On May 19, as *Flier*'s bow wave rippled out toward the Pearl Harbor entrance buoys and the submarine turned southwest toward Johnston Island, the Allied forces in the Pacific were seizing control of the war that had started for the United States with the December 7, 1941, attack in this very port. Japanese airplanes sank four of eight battleships—the largest navy vessels—and damaged the other four. *Flier* had steamed past this wreckage. The Japanese planes had also damaged three cruisers, three destroyers, and sank or damaged four auxiliary vessels. All of the aircraft carriers were out of port on maneuvers and were spared. Within hours of that raid, which crippled the navy's surface fleet, Japan bombed Manila, the capital of the Philippines, the only U.S. stronghold in the Pacific. Japanese aircraft had destroyed squadrons of airplanes on the ground and many of the U.S. Navy's ships caught in Manila Bay. After Japanese troops landed in the Philippines, they forced General Douglas MacArthur to retreat from Manila to the nearby island of Corregidor, from which he oversaw the retreat of U.S. and Philippine forces to the Bataan Peninsula, west of Manila. MacArthur's subsequent flight from Corregidor and the surrender in March 1942 of the remaining Americans and their Filipino comrades was the low ebb of the struggle.

Since then, under MacArthur's inspired leadership, American and Australian troops and sailors had clawed their way back into the fight. In August 1943, the battle for the island of Guadalcanal, east of New Guinea, had been won, and in November, at the cost of many lives, the battle for Tarawa, halfway between Hawaii and Australia, ended in an Allied victory.

In just the beginning of 1944, Allied forces had landed on the Admiralty Islands and the Marshall Islands, taking the Marshalls in early February and crippling Japanese facilities in the Caroline Islands a month later. In the first move of what would become the strategy to recapture the Philippines, American forces landed on New Guinea in April. The evidence was mounting that the Allies had Japan on the run.

Still, there were hundreds of thousands of Japanese soldiers streaming from their homeland to the Pacific islands, and that meant scores of ships carrying not only troops but also the supplies that could keep the war going. For the men on submarines, this created more opportunities to engage the enemy. And for a change, the submarine fleet was having regular success.

In certain corners of the Pacific, they were getting some help from unexpected—and often unseen—forces. When the Philippines fell in 1942, most of that nation's army—drafted by MacArthur en masse—fell, too. Trapped on Luzon, the largest and northernmost major island of the 7,000-island Philippine archipelago, they became prisoners in Japanese camps.

But a smaller number of Filipino soldiers were on their home islands, not Luzon, when war began. And although they were all summoned to Manila to fight the invaders, many did not make it. Instead, they melted into the mountain jungles and the coastal plains and soon were organized in a lethal guerrilla organization devoted to resisting Japanese authority. They had few supplies. For food, they often relied on rice donations from villagers. And ammunition was also in short supply. If they could capture Japanese soldiers without firing a shot, they did. Then, to save further on ammunition, the guerrillas at times executed their prisoners with bolos—machete-like steel blades that were the universal tool of rural Filipinos. In the first year of the war, guerrillas were responsible for scores of ambushes, a gnat-like pestering of the behemoth Japanese army. The numbers killed were small—a couple of soldiers killed in Baybay, Leyte; nineteen in Sitio—but the result was the unnerving of enemy soldiers.

If the guerrillas, a legitimate agency of the deposed Philippine government, were the islands' national guard, then the bolo battalions, organized by the local Muslim chief, were their auxiliary. Armed with bolos, blowguns, and spears, they served as intermediaries between the guerrillas and the local communities, arranging for supplies, keeping lookouts, and providing communications. In some cases, the bolo battalions were bullies and thugs who took advantage of their position to strong-arm unarmed locals. In other places, their members were a vital link that kept the resistance going.

Out there beyond the International Date Line, where *Flier* was headed, was also a new type of American soldier—men of Filipino descent who had been drafted in the United States at the outbreak of war, and who, recently, had been singled out for the most hazardous of assignments. American officials in Australia had learned of that nation's practice of stationing soldiers called *Coastwatchers* to observe the movement of enemy shipping from the beach. MacArthur's deputies decided to create their own Coastwatchers for the critical area of the Philippines. Those islands bordered all of the thoroughfares that sea traffic could travel from Japan. With men strategically placed across the archipelago, it was predictable that they would be able to relay details of troop and supply movements that could be used to intercept the enemy. Submarine crews would be great beneficiaries of this sort of information, because they would know where to lay in wait for convoys headed for the battle lines.

That was not always the way submarines had operated. Until well into the war's second year, admirals chose to send their submarines to watch ports where Japanese ships were known to dock, in the hope of catching them coming or going. This tactic had proved futile, and its failure encouraged admirals to consider using "wolf packs"—groups of two or three submarines prowling together in search of Japanese supply and naval shipping. Wolf packs were commanded by a senior officer aboard one of the submarines, and their attacks were coordinated to do the most damage. Other boats were simply sent on patrol in designated quadrants of the Pacific, looking for targets.

It was also in 1943 that the navy perfected a new method of decoding Japanese radio messages and relaying the information to submarines. Called Ultra, this system allowed the subs to find convoys crossing the vast southern seas rather than waiting for a lucky break outside a port.

Statistics showed the effectiveness of these changes. In 1942, United States submarines conducted about 350 patrols in the Pacific, sinking 180 ships rated at a total of 725,000 tons. In 1943, the same number of patrols recorded about 335 Japanese ships sunk, or 1.5 million tons.

"In one sense it could be said that the U.S. submarine war against Japan did not truly begin until the opening days of 1944," wrote Clay Blair Jr. in *Silent Victory*. "What had come before had been a learning period, a time of testing, of weeding out, of fixing defects in weapons, strategy, and tactics, of waiting for sufficient numbers of submarines and workable torpedoes. Now that all was set, the contribution of the submarine force would be more than substantial: it would be decisive."

Even the most successful boats were dangerous homes for sailors. In part, this was due to the brazenness with which some submarine skippers attacked the enemy, firing from extremely close range or taking up positions with no escape route.

In the seven months since the October 18 commissioning of *Flier,* nine submarines had been lost, along with 647 men. In seven of those cases, all hands were lost.

Wahoo was the first in that span, disappearing sometime in October, on its seventh patrol. In its first five patrols beginning in August 1942, the boat sank 27 Japanese ships, or 119,100 tons, the measurement that counted as much as any. On its third patrol, *Wahoo* sank two large freighters, a transport, a tanker, and an escort vessel, and, after slipping into a harbor on the Japanese-held north coast of New Guinea, seriously damaged a destroyer. On its sixth patrol, *Wahoo* ran into a drought—not of targets, but of victims. Prowling the Sea of Japan, the boat fired again and again on Japanese ships—nine attacks in all. But in each case, malfunctioning torpedoes caused no damage. A frustrated skipper, Commander Dudley W. Morton—known to his men as Mush—returned to Pearl Harbor from that patrol and vented his anger by pounding Admiral Lockwood's desk.

"Well, Mush, what do you want to do?" Lockwood asked.

"Admiral, I want to go right back to the Sea of Japan, with a load of live fish this time."

Each of the torpedoes delivered to *Wahoo* was carefully examined and then loaded into the submarine. The boat steamed from Pearl Harbor on September 9, stopped at Midway for fuel a few days later, and then headed west, for the Sea of Japan. *Wahoo* apparently reached its destination. Japanese records of the war say that four Japanese ships were sunk in *Wahoo*'s patrol area. The records also show that an antisubmarine attack was made in the same area on October 11. *Wahoo* and the eighty men aboard were never heard from again.

About three weeks later, *Corvina,* with a crew of eighty-two, left Pearl Harbor with an assignment to patrol as close to the island of Truk as possible. Japanese records indicate that a Japanese submarine found *Corvina* on the surface on November 16, 1943, and fired a torpedo, sinking the American boat with all hands.

Sculpin left Pearl Harbor on November 5 and stopped at Johnston Island to refuel before heading for its assignment: intercepting Japanese ships responding to an Allied attack on the Gilbert Islands. The boat and its crew of seventy-four were never heard from again, and were presumed lost. At the end of the war, twenty-one survivors were released from Japanese prison camps—half of the men who had survived a depth-charge attack on *Sculpin* on November 19.

Japanese records show that on November 23, an American submarine was attacked in the area in the Celebes Sea, in northern Indonesia, by Japanese ships. There was little evidence that the submarine was damaged. *Capelin*, with seventy-eight men aboard, was assigned to that area, but another American submarine, *Bonefish,* saw an American submarine nine days later in a region that was also included in *Capelin*'s assignment. The boat and its crew were never seen again, and the navy included among the possible causes for the loss that *Capelin* had struck a mine.

On January 3, thirteen days before *Flier* grounded on the Midway reef, *Scorpion*—which had suffered the same fate five months earlier—had left Midway for its fourth patrol. Two days later, the boat attempted to rendezvous with another submarine returning to Midway to transfer a crewman with a broken arm. The transfer was impossible in heavy seas, so *Scorpion* went on toward its assigned patrol area in the East China and Yellow seas. Mines had been laid recently across the entrance to the Yellow Sea, a fact unknown to the navy. Nor had any of several submarines that had crossed that water encountered mines. The boat and its crew of seventy-six, who had sunk ten ships in their first three patrols, were never heard from again, and in February were listed as presumed lost.

Grayback had completed a remarkable nine patrols in the Pacific when it left Pearl Harbor in late January 1944 for its tenth patrol. Since the war started, the boat had sunk twenty-two ships and damaged another nine, one of them a coveted Japanese destroyer. Four weeks after beginning the tenth patrol, the skipper, Commander J. A. Moore, reported by radio that the crew had sunk two enemy ships and damaged another two. *Grayback* had six torpedoes remaining. The next day, Moore reported having fired four torpedoes, three of which had hit two enemy freighters. The skipper was told to return to Midway. Japanese records show that a day later, a Japanese airplane saw a surfaced submarine and sank it with a direct hit. Moore and his crew of sixty-nine were lost.

On February 4, when the inquiry into the grounding of the *Flier* was in its fourth day in Pearl Harbor, the submarine *Trout* left that port for its eleventh patrol, sailing northwest for a fuel stop at Midway. The day after *Macaw* sank in tumultuous surf on the Midway reef, *Trout* and the seventy-one men aboard sailed out of Brooks Inlet past the wreck and resumed their westward trek, never to be heard from again. Japanese records suggest that the boat was lost in a battle after sinking one ship and badly damaging another on February 29.

In early March, while *Flier* was still at Mare Island, *Tullibee* left Hawaii with sixty-nine men aboard. One survivor later told how a torpedo running in a circle had sunk his boat.

One week before *Flier*'s May departure from Pearl Harbor, the submarine *Gudgeon* had been given orders to return to Midway from its twelfth patrol. Then on May 11, Headquarters had radioed the boat again, altering *Gudgeon*'s assignment. The message required that the skipper call back to Headquarters by radio, but he failed to reply.

Gudgeon was built at Mare Island and was named for a small, freshwater fish, but the submarine was quite at home in the salty sea. Its achievements during the war had been anything but small. In eleven prior patrols, the boat had amassed an incredible record, sinking twenty-five Japanese ships and damaging another eight, ranking it fifteenth in kills among all American submarines. *Gudgeon*'s first patrol had begun in Hawaii four days after the attack on Pearl Harbor. A month later, *Gudgeon* earned the distinction of being the first United States submarine in history to sink an enemy warship when the boat's torpedoes destroyed a Japanese submarine. By May of 1944, *Gudgeon* had been in the battle for two and a half years and had few equals in the navy's submarine fleet. The boat's seventy-eight-man crew had begun its twelfth patrol in April when it left Johnston Island, a tiny refueling depot west of Hawaii. Those men were never heard from again.

Gudgeon was not reported as presumed lost until June 7, 1944, so as *Flier* headed for the front, its captain and crew were unaware of the latest loss. As events would later prove, such information would likely have played little part in tempering the aggressiveness with which *Flier* pursued enemy ships. Finally, John "Cautious" Crowley had a boat and some sailors with whom he could make a dent in the Japanese war machinery. After the Midway debacle, he also had something to prove, and his men had something to learn. In battle, Crowley was anything but cautious.

CHAPTER 6

WELCOME TO THE WAR

Crowley wasted no time on his way to the war zone. The stop at Johnston Island for refueling, two days after leaving Pearl Harbor, took less than three hours. That included time for a pilot to board the boat outside the Johnston inlet and to guide the submarine up to the fuel dock. As the diesel fuel was loaded, the pilot asked, then begged, Crowley to take him along on the patrol. There was nothing for the man to do on the tiny island, and he felt he was going mad. Crowley patted the man on the back but left without him, and at 6:30 p.m. on May 23, *Flier* was on its way west once more. Two days later, as the submarine submerged, the crew took note that they were passing the International Date Line. They threw away the May 26 page from the calendar—a date in which they spent almost no time.

Memorial Day, Al Jacobson's birthday, was uneventful except that he was fed first among the officers, a tradition on the submarine. And the next day, a few hundred miles east of the Philippine archipelago, lookouts saw a Japanese airplane and *Flier* dove, successfully avoiding notice. In the ten days since they had left Pearl Harbor, the crew of *Flier* had seen Jacobson, the newest officer on board, crawling around their boat on hands and knees, inspecting every square inch. After all the schooling he had endured, the young ensign was still learning the nuts and bolts of a submarine. To become a qualified submarine officer, he would have to pass an extensive examination sometime after his first patrol. To prepare for the test, he frequently followed the engineering officer, Ensign Herbert A. "Teddy" Behr. Although the same rank as Jacobson, Behr was an old salt. He already had many years in the navy as a chief petty officer, one who got his hands dirty fixing engines. The navy, apparently recognizing Behr's talents, took the extraordinary step of elevating him to the status of commissioned officer, the equal of Annapolis graduates. Unlike most officers, however, Behr was a mechanic capable of fixing almost anything on the boat. Al, the mechanical engineer with the smell of the foundry still in his nose, and Teddy liked each other almost immediately.

Officers and crewmen alike were on duty for two eight-hour shifts every day, with four hours off between shifts. Meals came during a shift. The floating cribbage game—a no-betting diversion shared by officers, and learned aboard by Jacobson—was played between shifts in the wardroom, a small room with a fixed steel table in its center, covered with green linoleum. The wardroom was the officers' gathering place, separated from the forward torpedo room by the mess steward's pantry. Sitting at the table playing cribbage, every officer from the skipper to the fresh ensign could watch, through an open pass-through to the pantry, as John Clyde Turner, their steward, made the coffee and heated their meals, adding special touches to the plain grub the rest of the crew was eating. Some of the officers smoked, and although Al didn't, he was comfortable with his colleagues' fumes. If the boat was on the surface charging batteries, smoking was prohibited here and in the crew's mess. A spark could set off an explosion in the batteries, which were mounted under the flooring. It was at the wardroom table that Jacobson would sit with his mentor, Lieutenant John Edward Casey, reviewing the latest part of the submarine that young Al had studied.

Flier was a fleet-type submarine, designated *SS-250* for its place in the chronology of submarine construction. Almost identical to every other fleet submarine, *Flier* had a pressure hull—designed to withstand the extreme forces of seawater at a depth of 300 feet—surrounded by a steel superstructure that gave the boat its long, sleek appearance. It was the superstructure that had suffered the cracks and distortions when *Flier* was ground by the surf on the Midway reef.

The pressure hull—a series of eight welded-steel cylindrical compartments joined end to end like sausage links, the links connected by watertight doors—had not been damaged, a testimony to the boat's robust construction.

The forward torpedo room with its six tubes for firing those weapons—often called "fish"—occupied the first sausage link. Stepping high through the watertight door at the torpedo room's rear, a sailor entered the next link in the pressure hull, with the steward's pantry and the officers' wardroom on the port side—the right side as you walked toward the boat's rear. Next came the officers' and chief petty officers' quarters on both port and starboard. Al Jacobson and another officer shared a cramped room with a double bunk on the port side. Under all these rooms was a bank of 126 huge batteries that powered the submarine when it was submerged. The third pressurized link contained the control room, where the crew managed most of the functions of the boat. Here were the two big spoked wheels that sailors turned to tilt the diving planes—pairs of wings on the front and rear of the submarine that, by the angle of their tilt, caused the vessel to rise or dive. Here also were a congestion of brass and glass gauges, long-handled levers, valve wheels, tubes, cables, phones, and bells, all mounted on the inner side of the pressure hull where it curved from the steel deck on one side, overhead and down to the deck on the other side.

Welded to the top of the control-room pressure hull—like another, small sausage link somehow out of sync with the rest of the submarine—was the conning tower, where the skipper would stay for most of his duty when the boat was submerged. The helmsman stood at the big steering wheel at the front of the conning tower, taking directions directly from the officer of the deck, either the skipper or the executive officer. The two periscopes were manned in the conning tower, and the radar and sonar operators were among the half-dozen men crammed into this little space. A watertight hatch opened in the conning-tower floor, and a steel ladder descended to the control room. Another hatch in the conning-tower ceiling led to the bridge, where Commander Crowley spent his time when *Flier* was on the surface.

To the rear of the control room in the row of links came the after battery compartment, where the crew's galley, mess hall, and sleeping quarters were aligned above another bank of 126 batteries. The fifth and sixth links in the pressure hull housed four enormous diesel engines, which ran when the submarine was surfaced, generating electricity both to run the motors that propelled the boat and to charge the batteries. The seventh pressurized link contained the maneuvering room, where two sailors sat at two panels, each with a bank of ten levers the size of—and resembling—shovel handles. Above the levers were two dozen gauges, all used to monitor and control the four powerful electric motors that turned the two propeller shafts.

Finally, the after torpedo room was in the eighth pressurized link. Here were four more torpedo tubes through which *Flier*'s weapons could be fired.

In all, there were tens of thousands of parts that, when pieced together, comprised the submarine, a lot of details for a young ensign to memorize. For Jacobson, being on shift might mean he was inspecting these parts. Frequently, it meant he was sitting in the control room, almost below the hatch that led up to the conning tower. Here his job involved plotting the submarine's course. Jacobson was assistant navigating officer, and he and the navigating officer, Jim Liddell, were solely responsible for recording *Flier*'s path across the ocean. When it was his time to plot the course, Jacobson would lower a rectangular table, hinged against the periscope tube, from its stowed position to its horizontal position on top of a thigh-high, egg-shaped gyro compass. Then he would spread a chart on the table. As the skipper or Liddell called out course changes, the ensign would record them, finding the boat's location on the chart and entering that information in an ongoing log that traced *Flier*'s course.

Two days after *Flier* dove to avoid the Japanese airplane, the boat changed course, having received word that the submarine *Silversides* had located an enemy convoy ripe for attack. At four the next morning, Jacobson calculated *Flier*'s position as being latitude 22 degrees 27 minutes north, longitude 138 degrees 7 minutes east, or roughly northeast of Luzon, the northernmost major Philippine island. Crowley held the position for the next ten hours until, through the magnification of the periscope, he spotted smoke—the telltale sign of a ship at sea—almost due north. He estimated that the ship was thirty miles away. By recording the movement of the smoke, he calculated that it was on a southeasterly course. The convoy that *Silversides* had reported was heading in the opposite direction. *Flier* had found its own prey.

On a glassy calm day at sea, as was June 3, 1944, any object on the surface is visible from miles away. A floating log can appear, at a distance, to be the size of a freighter, and a seagull might seem to be a navigational buoy. The slender periscope of a submarine might well be a mid-oceanic telephone pole, or even a tall building. Consequently, great care had to be taken by the skipper of a submarine on such a day, particularly when he knew that enemy vessels were within sight. Crowley and Liddell discussed the situation, and both concluded that while making a successful surface approach on this convoy was impossible, an approach at periscope depth during daylight was also improbable. Jacobson, sitting on a small stool before his chart table and looking toward the port side and the two planesmen, listened as the two ranking officers weighed their options. These were the first words he had heard in a real combat situation, and, like the quarterback's words in the huddle before the big play, they were the sort that could quicken any young man's pulse.

Crowley decided to dive and sneak toward the target ship, hoping to gather enough information to launch a nighttime attack. Two short blasts from the diving alarm—a claxon bell—rang throughout *Flier,* and a ritual aboard the submarine began to unfold. The diesel engines stopped running, and power from the battery banks began turning the electric motors. The huge air vents that brought fresh air to both the crew and the engines were closed, as were the engine exhaust valves. From above Jacobson's head came the sound of the conning-tower hatch to the bridge closing. Looking ahead over his chart, Al could see the bow and stern planesmen—one on each side of the ladder leading up to the conning tower—standing at their huge wheels. The bow planesman began turning his wheel clockwise, to the full-dive position. The stern planesman to his left turned his wheel counterclockwise. To the right of the bow planesman, a board of red and green lights blinked from red to green. When this "Christmas tree" was all green, air was bled into the boat, and one man watched a pressure gauge that showed whether the sub was watertight.

Chiefs were passing orders to crewmen in an everyday voice. If they felt any excitement, the men aboard *Flier* showed only the calm intensity of well-trained confidence.

The dive began just before two o'clock in the afternoon. At 3:30 p.m., with the smoke of the enemy ship still the only visible assurance of its presence, the men aboard *Flier* heard a series of twenty-two distant depth charges. Three hours later, a look through the periscope revealed a vessel—either a submarine or an escort ship—steaming north at high speed, off to the west of *Flier*. Thirty minutes later, at 7:18 p.m., Crowley gave orders to turn away from the target ship and to prepare to surface. Just then, smoke was sighted to the southwest. This was a different target than the first, which by now had moved from its original position to the north and, by traveling southeast, was steaming to the east of the submarine. Crowley decided to go after the more recently spotted ship because *Flier* was in a better position to make a successful attack than it was on the first, and because, having heard the depth charges, he assumed the first ship was already under attack by another submarine.

At 8:20 p.m., *Flier* surfaced beneath a black sky but on an ocean surface brightly lit by the moon. Crowley and Liddell, conferring with some of the other senior officers, decided to work ahead on the starboard flank of the new ship, which was heading northwest toward Japan at about eight knots, around nine miles per hour. Looking west from the bridge, Crowley could clearly see the smoke rising above the silvery sea—eight columns of smoke from as many ships, a convoy ripe for attack by an eager submarine crew. Looking to the east, the skipper could see that, about thirty miles away, the convoy that he had spotted first was under heavy attack as it headed south. There, the sky was lit again and again by gunfire.

Then to the west, there was gunfire from the second convoy that *Flier* was shadowing. Perhaps they too were under attack.

In order to avoid exposing their broad sides to torpedo attacks, ships of all navies followed zigzag courses, even when in convoy. The challenge for a submarine crew was to calculate, by observing the progress of a convoy over time, what the baseline of its course was—where, in other words, it was headed. At 10:20 p.m., the convoy that now was *Flier's* target zigzagged directly toward the submarine, a little more than ten miles away. Al Jacobson, who had spent two hours on plot and two hours on the bridge, alternating with ensign Teddy Behr, looked toward the approaching convoy and was amazed at what he saw—every ship in the convoy silhouetted in the moonlight, each ship's zigs and zags obvious from this many miles away. He could even see when someone on the deck of one of those ships lit a match. Heading directly for *Flier,* though, the enemy skippers could not see the submarine due to its low profile and the distance it stayed away.

Crowley and his officers quickly concluded that the ships had changed their baseline because they were under attack. If they were running away from their tormentors, the skipper believed, these Japanese ships were in for a surprise. He gave the order to dive and begin a radar approach. But a half-hour before midnight, Crowley changed his mind. He had been unable to get *Flier* any closer than about four miles. He gave the order to surface and resume the chase. Making twice the speed of the convoy, the boat circled ahead to the east, intent on finding a spot in the ocean where it could lay in wait for its prey.

The moon set at 3:20 a.m. that morning, leaving the Pacific in near total darkness. A half-hour later, having maneuvered the submarine so that it was almost directly ahead of the convoy, Crowley gave the order to sound the dive alarm once again. With the lead ship of the group again about ten miles away, *Flier* once more began a radar approach. An hour later, the distance between the stalker and its victims had shrunk to just over a mile.

It was 4:47 a.m. when Al Jacobson heard the order passed.

"Periscope depth," Crowley said in an even voice.

Fourteen minutes later, six torpedoes were blasted from the forward tubes, three at each of two large freighters in a column of three ships passing before the submarine like soldiers on review.

Crowley spun the periscope in the opposite direction now, because another column of ships was passing behind *Flier*. The nearest ship was too close for Crowley to fire. A torpedo had to travel a certain distance before its explosives were armed—a distance that was greater than the space between *Flier* and its target. More important, two escort vessels, armed with depth charges and other weapons, were turning toward the submarine. Crowley ordered a deep dive, and the bow planesman cranked his wheel hard. The skipper took one more look around through the periscope. He saw smoke billowing from the first ship. A torpedo had found its mark. The second freighter had turned away and was apparently stopped. By the timing of the explosions that had by now been heard aboard *Flier*, the crew knew that two torpedoes had hit the first ship and another had hit the second.

Now it was payback time. The first depth charges began exploding over *Flier* soon after the five o'clock torpedo attack. Inside the submarine, everything was silent. The boat could not move because movement meant noise, and the slightest sound could be heard by sensitive sonar equipment on the Japanese military escort ships up on the surface. Silence meant no air-conditioning inside *Flier*. The air became thick with humidity, and following the lead of the senior men, Al began peeling off his clothing until he was down to his undershorts. The lights were off, and the only sounds were those of the depth charges. To Al, it was as if he had his head inside a metal oil drum on which someone was beating with a sledgehammer. The closer the explosions, the more chunks of cork insulation fell from the inside surface of the pressure hull.

The last of thirty-four depth charges exploded at 6:34 that morning, just under two hours after Crowley had initiated the conflict. Just before seven o'clock, Jacobson heard the last of the propeller sounds from the escort ships. *Flier*'s men had survived the retaliation. Crowley gave the order to surface, and the submarine's motors began to turn the two big propellers at its rear. When the periscope broke the surface, the skipper saw smoke on the horizon. Crowley ordered another deep dive to load torpedoes in the six empty forward tubes.

The tension had been felt by everyone aboard *Flier*, not just by the green ensign. And the men needed a little humor just now to let off some steam. Someone looked at John Clyde Turner, the officers' black mess steward, and concluded that he had been scared white. All the white men laughed. Someone said it was a good thing the rest of them were white already.

An escort had apparently lagged behind the convoy after the depth-charge attack, because sometime after ten o'clock on the morning of June 4, the menacing ship was spotted racing toward *Flier*. Crowley turned his boat south and fled the scene, waiting another hour before returning to the hunt. Spotting the escort again, he decided to try circling to the west. But after eighteen hours of searching, he was unable to find the convoy. At daybreak the next morning, he decided to return to the scene of the attack. Arriving four hours later, *Flier* slipped through a floating maritime junkyard. There were six lifeboats and the wooden pilothouse of a ship. When Crowley sent some men over the side to inspect the wreckage, they returned with a packet of documents from one of the lifeboats and said they had seen compass equipment in the pilothouse that was made in New York.

Looking down from the bridge at the *Flier*'s handiwork, Al Jacobson saw not just wood and metal. The bodies of hundreds of Japanese men, buoyed by life jackets, were scattered throughout the debris. At least one of the two ships struck by *Flier*'s torpedoes was a troopship. *Flier* had killed 1,200 men on that darkened ocean.

Crowley pointed *Flier* west once more, and three days later, after steaming across the Philippine Sea, the boat reached the Balintang Channel, the central passage through the Luzon Strait, which separates Taiwan to the north from the Philippines to the south. Later that day, with the submarine running submerged, the smoke and mast of a fast-moving ship was spotted ten miles ahead, moving north toward Japan. Its speed was equal to the best *Flier* could make, and it got away. For the next four days, June 9 through June 12, Crowley kept the boat underwater all day long as he steered ten miles north of Calayan Island, one of the Babuyan Islands—among the northernmost specks of land in the Philippines—and then five miles off Cape Bojeador, the northwestern tip of Luzon. On June 12, *Flier* slipped past Cape Bolinao, a hook of land that reaches out from the peninsula that forms the western side of Lingayen Gulf, where Japanese troops first landed on December 21, 1941, to complete the occupation of the Philippines.

Flier was truly deep in the heart of enemy territory.

The ocean off the western shores of Luzon fills some of the deepest voids on the Earth's surface. Only five miles off the beaches, *Flier* was also miles above the ocean floor, a graveyard where boats and the bones of their sailors could perhaps lie untouched forever. This was not on the minds of John Crowley and his men. They fully expected to send as many Japanese men and ships as they could down to this burying ground.

The next day, June 13, promised to be a lucky one. At one o'clock in the afternoon, *Flier*'s crew saw, through the periscope, the smoke from ships following the submarine from the north as it skirted the shore. Crowley ordered the helmsman to turn the submarine around and, with the boat still submerged, the crew began preparations for its second battle. Ahead of them lay a military bonanza, a convoy of eleven ships and at least six escorts. As they drew closer, it was clear that this big flotilla was hugging the coast, its escorts keeping offshore from the transport ships, like a gentleman walking a lady down a sidewalk, protecting her from being splashed from the gutter.

Again the sea was as smooth as a pool of oil. Crowley remained in the conning tower as he pressed *Flier* in on the convoy, but he kept his periscope observations brief. In the control room below the skipper, and throughout the submarine, there was silence as the men anticipated the coming attack, each sailor poised in position, the whole crew a jungle cat suspended in the moment before the pounce. In the control room, the planesmen turned their wheels without a word, synchronized in the effort to hold the boat level and keep it at the depth that Crowley had dictated. Waiting for the next course change, Jacobson gazed across the control room, watching the depth gauge and the dials that showed the angle of the boat and of the two sets of planes. He saw the competence he had grown to expect, a comforting order in the quiet.

And then he saw trouble. The stern planesman was struggling with his wheel. Calling out a warning to the control-room chief, the planesman grabbed a crank handle mounted near his wheel and, bracing himself, strained to move the planes as the submarine went into an unintended dive.

The bow planesman spun his wheel to counteract the tilt that the stern planes had already given to the boat, and the chief, his voice urgent, ordered all hands to the rear. Men from the forward torpedo room began hustling one after another past Jacobson's chart table, stepping through the high, oval, watertight door at the forward end of the compartment and climbing out through the similar door at the rear. Those who couldn't leave their posts—men like the green ensign—froze in anticipation. Miles of pitch-dark ocean lay beneath them, and *Flier*, with no help from the enemy, was headed there.

Among those moving to the rear was one sailor who raced around the rest. His job was to find out what was wrong in the after torpedo room. The planes, attached to the boat outside that final sausage link, were operated by a hydraulic system. A pump might have gone or a hose might have ruptured. Whatever the problem, it needed to be fixed immediately.

In the control room, the chief waited for his man's report. But without any explanation, the hydraulics suddenly began working. Then, just as quickly, they once again failed, and the stern planesman strained at his crank. Behind him, young Jacobson had a ringside seat to the struggle, but no immediate job to do. It was clear to the ensign that this was a serious matter, but if he felt fear, he also felt confidence in the boat, its crew, and the skipper—a sense of the rightness of things, an assurance, perhaps connected to his god, in the outcome. Finally, at 2:18 p.m., power mysteriously returned to the stern-plane controls. After six minutes of uncertainty, the stern planesman returned from his crank to his wheel, and *Flier* resumed a steady, level course.

Crowley now discussed strategy with Liddell, Ed Casey, and the other senior officers. The convoy they were stalking was within a mile of the lush jungle coast of Luzon, and between those ships and the submarine were the half-dozen escorts. An attack clearly would not be successful if launched from offshore. There were too many escorts protecting the convoy's flank. The alternative, Jacobson heard the officers say, was to speed across the convoy's path ahead of the lead ship and, a half-mile from the coast, launch an attack on the long, unprotected steel of the cargo ships. There would be no escorts on that side . . . until the first torpedo hit.

Crowley was cautious no more. Bristling with a warrior's courage, he gave the order to race across the convoy's path, the naval equivalent of running down a dead-end alley.

At just before three o'clock, with *Flier* facing toward shore, Crowley ordered all four stern torpedo tubes fired. One by one, the fish were blown out of the tubes by compressed air and began running toward the 10,000-ton tanker that was just passing on its southern voyage. As soon as the torpedoes were fired, Crowley ordered the ship turned around so that the forward torpedoes could be aimed. A small freighter was less than 100 yards off *Flier*'s bow when the sub completed its turn. That was too close for an attack, so Crowley shifted his aim to a ship less than a mile away in the convoy column closest to shore. Before the skipper, using the periscope to aim, could give a bearing to the sailor manning the torpedo arming and aiming device, the sonar man in the conning tower, wearing headphones, heard two hits on the tanker, followed immediately by a huge explosion. The word was relayed throughout the submarine—*Score!*

In the haste to get set up for the next target ship, the diving officer, misunderstanding an order, ducked the periscope. Blind under the ocean's waves, Crowley ordered a deep dive without firing the bow torpedoes. He knew that the escorts would be heading to where *Flier* was backed against the shore, and he knew there were not even seconds to spare. Behind him in the conning tower, Crowley heard the voice of the sonar (or sound-) man. Escorts were approaching from several angles. Then more bad news. The stern planes had failed again. Down in the control room, the stern planesman wrenched his crank, struggling to pull the boat from its dive as the first depth charges fell. By the sounds coming from the propellers of the escorts, the soundman could tell that all six vessels were in on the attack, like a pack of dogs against one lonely cat.

The cat had to move, but it needed camouflage. The escort ships on the surface could tell where the submarine was only if it made sounds. There were no devices for "looking" at the ocean floor, only the sonar that could, like radar, read the echo from a sound wave and microphones that could listen for ship noises.

Crowley needed to keep moving and keep the stalking escorts guessing where *Flier* was. But this required running the boat's motors, and that could be done only when the attacking ships were also moving, because their own movement would hide the sound of the submarine. The deadly game had begun, and once again the heat started to build inside *Flier*. The escorts would fall silent and every movement aboard *Flier* would cease. No one walked or talked. They closed their eyes and simply breathed in the thick air. Then the escorts, apparently having decided that the submarine was in a certain location, all began moving toward that point. Crowley would quietly call out orders for a course and speed, and in the bottomless ocean, *Flier* would make a right-angle turn and glide to a new location. At his chart table, Jacobson recorded each new course, the speed, and the length of time the boat moved, and then plotted on the chart where they stopped. He gave this information to Crowley so that when the next move came, the skipper would know how to avoid the rocks of shore, and where to head for safe, deep water.

Twenty minutes after the torpedoes had been fired, everyone on the boat heard a loud rumbling explosion from the general direction of the Japanese tanker. Jacobson listened to the conversations coming from the conning tower. The soundman reported that he heard noises similar to those of a ship breaking up, but these sounds came between continuing blasts from depth charges. Again and again the Japanese escorts—probably destroyers—swung toward *Flier* and rolled off another batch of barrels that sank to a predetermined depth before exploding. Sometimes they were nowhere near the submarine. Other times, they seemed to be directly overhead. Cork rained down from the ceiling then, and in each of the segments of the pressure hull—each one now sealed from the rest by closed, watertight doors on which the locking levers, called dogs, had been jammed in place—trickles of sweat, driven both by heat and fear, fell from eighty-six nearly naked men. The sweat on Crowley's chest streamed around a chain necklace from which hung a small crucifix, etched with the words JESUS NAZARE-NUS, REX JUDAEORUM.

One of the men appeared to be unmoved by the dangers that now preoccupied the rest of the crew. John Clyde Turner needed to keep the officers fed, so he busied himself in his pantry, between the officers' quarters and the forward torpedo room, working as if the next meal was the most crucial concern on board the submarine. In the course of his chores, Turner decided he needed something from the refrigerator. *Flier* happened to be motionless at the time, waiting for the next rush of the escorts. You could have heard the breath of a mouse. The sound of a refrigerator door opening was, to the men in the forward torpedo room, as loud as if the claxon had been tripped. Several of them—no doubt driven by their own inexpressible fears—opened and vaulted through the watertight door, tackling Turner. His life was theirs to take, and their intentions were obvious. Officers raced from the wardroom to restrain the attackers, whose own scrambling had probably made more noise than the opening of several refrigerator doors. In moments, everyone returned to his place to wait for the next round of depth charges that he knew would come.

The pounding continued all afternoon. Each man inside *Flier* could keep his own score as the number of depth-charge runs rose past twenty, thirty, forty—with no end in sight. At one point, an escort was heard directly overhead, as if running straight up the submarine's spine. The ship unleashed its explosives only after it had passed the boat, but there was no spontaneous sigh of relief because the next swing could be the lethal one.

At 7:15 p.m., Crowley grew impatient. *Flier* had a dummy torpedo stored in the after torpedo room. It was filled with explosives, set to detonate after the torpedo had traveled a specific distance. It also held a tank of oil. At the skipper's command, the crew fired the torpedo from a stern tube and the fish ran out a thousand yards before its blast was heard inside *Flier*. The concussion and the huge oil slick that soon appeared on the surface looked and sounded to ships on the surface like evidence of a sinking submarine.

In minutes, the depth-charge attack ceased. It had been five hours since Crowley had started this engagement. Now the skipper was convinced the escorts were finished, and he gave the order to surface. Once the hatch to the bridge was opened and the commander had climbed the ladder, Jacobson followed, eager to escape the stuffy confines and stinking perspiration odor of the control room. To his surprise, he found that now the scent of fresh air was actually offensive.

June 13 had ended okay. None of the 105 depth charges dropped by the Japanese escorts had found its mark.

Night fell off Luzon, and later, *Flier* headed south once more, hoping to pick up the convoy, which was probably headed for Subic Bay, the main shipping port near Manila. In the middle of the night, as *Flier* ran on the surface, lookouts above the bridge spotted smoke on the horizon. But a patrol plane flew over and *Flier* turned away, unwilling to risk the continued pursuit.

For the next four days, the submarine prowled around the islands near Manila, submerged during the day and then surfacing at night. Young Jacobson was thrilled to see the silhouettes of Corregidor, Bataan, and Manila's shoreline, knowing that the enemy soldiers there had no idea *Flier* was so close. He hoped with a youthful eagerness that some vessel would stray out on the water and present the submarine with a target. Having tasted the kill, he wanted to sink another ship.

He would have to wait five days.

Ed Casey was officer of the deck on June 22, standing watch in the conning tower as *Flier*, following its daytime routine, ran submerged. Around dinnertime, Casey spotted five columns of smoke in the southwest, about fifteen miles ahead. This was the eighth time on its first patrol that *Flier* had encountered enemy ships. The crew had destroyed two enemy ships and damaged another, but there had been many more missed opportunities. Listening to Casey's report was young Jacobson, who had the duty of diving officer—the man responsible for ordering a dive should it become necessary. The ensign hoped, as he heard Casey's description from the periscope, for better luck this time.

Casey, an agreeable family man, slender but athletic and quiet, was Jacobson's mentor. He had bet Jacobson earlier in the day that if he saw any targets, the inexperienced kid would order a dive too quickly, ducking the periscope. Jacobson won that bet, and Casey was able to observe the changing compass bearing of the enemy convoy's smoke. The smoke was heading right for *Flier*. Casey consulted with Crowley, who decided to wait for dark to make a surface attack on the convoy. Soon the soundman heard the sonar "pinging" from the convoy's escorts as they searched for trouble. Now Crowley was handling the periscope, taking regular bearings on the convoy, and Jacobson had moved to the chart table to plot the enemy's course.

Darkness had settled on Apo East Pass when *Flier*—which the day before had been directed to intercept the Japanese fleet as it sailed north from Mindanao—surfaced about seven miles behind the convoy, which was zigging and zagging four miles off the coast of Mindoro Island. On the surface, the submarine began a circular sweep, called an "end-around," up the western side of the convoy, and Jacobson reported to the bridge and took up the post of junior officer of the deck, standing to the rear of the bridge on the after cigarette deck. Looking east, he could see the whole convoy and each of the ships' movements.

Flier raced north, and by eleven o'clock that night had reached a position to attack the convoy, almost in front of it on its left flank, about six miles away. Crowley now turned his boat and, driving toward the leading ships, the submarine slipped inside of the destroyers escorting the convoy. Jacobson's job during the approach was to keep the crosshairs of a set of binoculars, temporarily resting in a deck-mounted stand, trained on the target ships. The cradle supporting the binoculars could be pivoted in any direction, and there was a mechanical connection between the cradle and the "torpedo data computer"—the device that programmed the course for each torpedo.

Below the binoculars was a pistol grip with a trigger. As he adjusted the bearing of the crosshairs, Jacobson's finger rested lightly on the trigger. Crowley, standing on the bridge forward of Jacobson, had settled on two freighters out of the nine ships in the convoy—the first one large and the second one medium-size, and both at the lead of the nearest convoy column. Unnoticed, *Flier* moved to within a mile of those ships, scooting in front of the escorting destroyers, and Crowley told Jacobson to fire when he was ready.

If a soldier can be trained to think of the enemy as a target, rather than one or more human beings, the destruction of those lives becomes more of a mathematics problem to be solved than a moral question to be pondered. Admiral I. J. Galantin addressed this phenomenon in his reflections on his World War II submarine service: "Naval warfare had evolved to the point that sailors no longer saw their enemy as people; they saw only the steel or aluminum vehicles in which their enemy sailed or flew, trying to bring their own weapons to bear. The ships or aircraft were the enemy of one's own ship; *they* were the enemy . . .

"Submarine war was even more detached, its special horror comparatively new to history, its action generally remote from human experience. Though our sinkings of enemy combat and cargo ships sent thousands of men to their deaths, this was but incidental to the real purpose—the strangling of an empire through cutting off its oil, its food, its raw materials."

On that black night off Mindoro, Al Jacobson pulled the trigger once. A torpedo shot silently underwater from *Flier*'s bow. He pulled again. Another torpedo followed the first, speeding toward the larger freighter. Again he squeezed his hand and a third torpedo was on its way.

Now he turned the binoculars slightly south. The smaller freighter was in the crosshairs. He pulled the trigger once, twice, a third time, and *Flier* swung sharply away to return to the safety of the open ocean. Looking back at the convoy, Jacobson saw geysers of water rise in the blackness—two from the big ship and one from the medium-size one. The sound of a second torpedo hitting the second ship came through the warm night air. With each hit, the orange flash of an explosion lit the target ship, and, at this close range, Jacobson could see objects flying up into the air—all of it junk to his eyes.

The shooting had begun at 11:23 that night. In only a few minutes, the two target ships were dropping out of the convoy, and then the smaller one sank. Although but one part of a coordinated team, the ensign at the trigger could take direct credit for the steel and flesh that disappeared before his eyes under the waves.

The escorts, now with only seven ships in their convoy, began hunting *Flier,* dropping depth charges where they thought the boat was submerged. But the submarine was on the surface, stealing away in the night at high speed, just far enough away to keep the convoy in sight but not close enough to be spotted by the escorts. Having fallen to the stern of the convoy, Crowley wanted another shot, and so he did another end-around up the western flank of the seven ships and their escorts, and at one minute after midnight, the convoy zigged right toward *Flier.* The saltwater waves splashed over the submarine's bow as the skipper ordered full speed ahead and the predator raced in for another kill. Jacobson was still on deck, hands on the binoculars, a wad of gum in his mouth. When the boat approached an escort, he heard Crowley order the engines slowed so *Flier* could sneak by. Once inside all the escorts, Crowley poured on the power and the submarine went for its next target.

There were only four torpedoes left in the forward torpedo room, and the skipper dedicated these to the ship that now led the convoy, a medium-size freighter. From the bridge, Crowley relayed the compass bearing to the freighter. At the same time, the radar operator relayed his own observations on the distance to the ship. When the submarine was in a firing position, Crowley gave Jacobson the order to fire, and the ensign squeezed his trigger four times. Jacobson knew how long it should take the torpedoes to reach the ship, and he timed their invisible progress with the rhythm of his gum chewing.

There was silence, and like a gunslinger who learns he has fired blanks in a shootout, Jacobson began to worry. A few tense seconds passed before the flash of two explosions lit the rear of the target ship and the sound of a third blast was heard.

By incalculable luck, *Flier* had inflicted damage on two ships. While the skipper had been giving bearings on the lead ship, the radar operator was figuring the distance to a second, closer vessel. All of the torpedoes might well have missed the target, but two had followed a course that found the rear of that ship. The third torpedo had passed behind the ship, but here the luck came in for *Flier.* Seen from the submarine, another ship in the convoy overlapped the first and had the misfortune to be directly in front of that third torpedo.

Crowley swung the boat around, hoping to do more damage to the convoy with torpedoes from the stern tubes. But by now, the escorts had located *Flier.* Crowley called down to Liddell in the conning tower, asking where on the radar the widest space was between the escorts.

"I think course 205 degrees," Liddell yelled back.

"Put on all the power we have and head out on course 205," Crowley shouted.

The escorts were searching wildly as *Flier* raced toward them. From the deck of the surfaced submarine, Jacobson saw one looming out of the darkness, on a course almost parallel to the submarine but headed in the opposite direction. Both boats were moving at full speed, and when they passed, there was no hint that the escort had seen the submarine. *Flier* plowed ahead into the safety of a dark sea, and the ensign looked back to see the ships at which he had fired, smoking heavily and apparently sinking.

It was about two hours after midnight when *Flier* made another dash between two Japanese escort vessels for a second attack on a still-floating but burning freighter two miles closer to shore. When they cleared the escorts, the men on *Flier*'s deck saw their target ship sink—their fourth victim, if they were counting ships. If they were counting men, no one could guess the score.

By now, the rest of the convoy was many miles to the north. Two hours later, the submarine dove so that the crew could take a rest after the long night of fighting. Although the boat remained submerged all day on June 23, the crew knew they were being hunted. Pinging could be heard from several directions, and at two o'clock that afternoon, several patrol planes were seen through the periscope, circling. Later, a group of antisubmarine ships were up there, searching. After dinner, a destroyer headed toward *Flier*, and it was clear the Japanese believed a submarine was still in the neighborhood. Crowley turned the boat away from the destroyer so that the stern tubes, which held *Flier*'s four remaining torpedoes, were aimed at the destroyer. But the menace never came within range of the torpedoes, and eventually turned away.

One young ensign had had enough and sighed with relief.

CHAPTER 7

STRANGERS IN THEIR NATIVE LAND

Earlier on the same night that Al Jacobson first became a triggerman in the eastern Philippines, the setting sun 300 miles to the west was hidden by dense clouds. Just after nightfall, an early monsoon rain began to drench Ramos Island, a small patch of low-lying real estate hugging the northern coast of mountainous Balabac Island at the edge of the South China Sea. Now, in the dark, four men stepped from the Ramos jungle and began wading beside a *kumpit*—a shallow-draft open native boat with a hull shaped from thin wooden planks. The men were American soldiers. Two of their comrades had gone ahead of this group to scout out a new location about an hour's boat ride to the northeast on Mantangule Island. The men in the kumpit brought with them the group's remaining supplies—all that they had not, in their first fifteen days of hiding here in a territory bristling with Japanese soldiers, lost or bartered away to pay natives for their labor.

Strategically, Ramos Island had been an excellent location for these soldiers, whose job was to hide in the jungle and spy on Japanese shipping and troop movements. Ramos provided a clear view of the shipping lanes that Japanese vessels would use to cross from the South China Sea into the Sulu Sea—the big pool encircled by the major Philippine islands. But the mission of these six men was clandestine, and they had come to believe in their short time on Ramos that the local folks probably could not be trusted to keep their secret. Mantangule, they hoped, would solve that problem; only a couple of miles farther from the North Balabac Strait channel than Ramos, it would offer them an unobstructed view of the enemy's seagoing traffic. Mantangule had the advantage of being isolated from Japanese troop encampments. Ramos Island, five miles across at its widest point, and so flat that the one tiny tree-covered mound at its center stood huge as Gibraltar, clung beside Balabac Island like a toddler to its mother, the two separated by the narrow and easily crossed Candaraman Inlet. Balabac Island, about fifteen miles long with a hulking alpine backbone of brooding blue mountains, was home to Balabac City, only five miles to the south of Ramos. The city was the headquarters of 140 Japanese soldiers. Master sergeant Amando Corpus, the man in charge of this American detachment, had decided the enemy was too close. It was time to go.

Corpus and his five men had volunteered for their isolated assignment on the western fringe of the war zone. But not just any soldier could volunteer. It was insufficient that you were a patriot. For this duty, the most significant qualification was your ancestry. All six of the men were Americans with Filipino ancestors, and they looked the part.

Sergeant Carlos S. Placido was from Laguna Beach, California. Sergeant Ramon F. Cortez, called Ray, was also a Californian. Sergeant J. Reynoso, whose nickname was Slug, was from Iowa. Corporal Teodoro J. Rallojay, called Butch, enlisted in Los Angeles, and Technician/5 R. D. Dacquel was from Pomona, California. In the segregated army of the time, they were members of the Filipino Infantry, and they became, under General Douglas MacArthur's command, an American version of a long-standing Australian military specialty known as Coastwatchers.

In simplest terms, Coastwatchers were spies. From their hiding places, they were responsible for sending radio reports to MacArthur's headquarters, 1,700 miles across the Southwest Pacific in New Guinea, giving the number, type, and size of ships they saw. The movement of Japanese troops, airplanes, and supplies was valuable knowledge for the military commanders planning the Allied war effort. And that effort—or the part of it aimed at the Japanese—was now focused heavily on the Philippines, which MacArthur had promised to retake.

To the eyes of these commanders, Corpus, Placido, Cortez, Reynoso, Rallojay, and Dacquel *looked* like the locals, which should have helped them blend into the countryside. If they spoke Tagalog, the dominant language in Manila, they probably did not speak the specific dialect used on Ramos—one of more than seventy Philippine dialects. So the minute they opened their mouths, they revealed themselves as foreigners.

The six men had been brought together at Camp Tabragalba in eastern Australia, and they began their journey toward Ramos the same May day that *Flier,* finally beginning its first patrol in earnest, had stopped at Johnston Island for fuel. Before the Coastwatchers boarded a plane for western Australia, one Colonel Whitney met them.

"God bless you, boys," Whitney said. "Good luck, and I will see you in Manila."

Then an army major boarded the plane with the six for the two-day flight to Perth. A navy truck awaited them in Perth. The Coastwatchers were told not to mention to anyone that they were army personnel, and they were directed to change from army to navy uniforms. The truck took them to a submarine—*Redfin*—which left Fremantle and steered north. Two days later, while *Redfin* stopped at a northern Australian port to take on more fuel, the Coastwatchers practiced rowing inflated rafts and then tried making nighttime landings on a beach.

For the next nine days, *Redfin* picked its way through the equatorial string of islands that is Indonesia and then slipped up the eastern side of Borneo. It was seven o'clock on the night of June 8 when the submarine surfaced in choppy water about 700 yards off of Encampment Point on the eastern side of Ramos Island. The Coastwatchers were brought to the bridge, and although it was dark, they could see the distinctive Ramos outline and that of Balabac to the south. Offshore to their left was another island with two big lights. Among themselves they guessed that the lights were from Japanese outposts.

The rafts were inflated and the first one was lowered to the water, only to be swamped by the waves. Packages from the Coastwatchers' one-year supply of food, clothing, and equipment had been loaded in the raft from *Redfin*. The stuff was in tins wrapped in gunnysacks, and these tins were swept overboard and bobbed away in the swift current. The men scrambled to retrieve as many as could be found in the dark. Finally, sergeants Corpus and Placido took Ray Cortez and Butch Rallojay on the first trip ashore. The raft spun in the strong current, and the surf broke over a ten-foot-wide coral reef, which the little raft cleared only with a struggle. The four men pulled the raft ashore and temporarily piled their supplies on the beach. Then Corpus and Placido paddled the raft back to the submarine for more supplies. After more than two hours of shuttling, all six Coastwatchers were ashore, and *Redfin* had dissolved into the darkness of the Sulu Sea.

Before dawn could expose them, the Coastwatchers, who had worked all night, had gathered their supplies and hauled them the 100 yards from the beach into the jungle, where they fell asleep on the ground, exhausted. Two hours later, daybreak roused them, and, having made some breakfast, they pitched tents and buried some of their supply tins as a cache. For the next day, they huddled close to the coast, making tentative forays into the jungle and along the coast with its occasional mangrove swamps, where the deadly mangrove snakes hung from branches awaiting prey. The following day, Dacquel disappeared on one of these reconnaissance efforts. It was the middle of the night before he stumbled back into the camp.

Four days after they had arrived—the same day that the men aboard *Flier* were enduring their marathon depth charging—the six soldiers moved their camp inland a few hundred yards. They had hoped to occupy the little hill at the center of Ramos, but that was still miles away. During a rainstorm the day before, they had gathered fresh drinking water and had bathed. Life was becoming somewhat more civilized. The following day, Corpus went on a solitary reconnaissance and was gone for four hours. When he returned, he had a Moro—or Muslim—companion.

Until now, the Coastwatchers had ducked whenever they had seen humans in the jungle. Now, talking with the man, they learned that there were about 300 residents on Ramos. The man claimed that he was an escapee from a Japanese prison camp in Puerto Princesa, the major city on the long, skinny island of Palawan, whose southern tip was only a dozen miles north from Ramos. The man told of seeing 300 Americans at the camp, working on a landing strip. They were emaciated, their clothing, rags. He described the politics of Ramos and Balabac, giving the Coastwatchers a new feel for the land of their ancestors, a nation of more than 7,000 islands and perhaps hundreds of languages.

Taken as a whole, the Philippine archipelago—with a little imagination—resembles a dog, sitting on its haunches facing left, its head tipped back as it howls at the moon, its forelegs braced in front of it. There are more than a dozen large islands and thousands of smaller ones. The large ones give this "dog" its general shape. The head is the northernmost large island, Luzon, and Lingayen Gulf on the island's northwest is its mouth. Mindoro, south of Luzon, is the dog's front shoulder. The dog's body comprises the Visayan Islands—Masbate, Panay, Negros, Cebu, Bohol, Leyte, and Samar. Its haunches and rear legs are Mindanao in the southeast. And its forelegs are the long, slender island of Palawan, to the west. Ramos and Balabac together are the dog's front paw, almost stepping on Borneo—a huge island to the south that is part of Malaysia. The Sulu Sea is a 300-mile expanse bordered by Palawan to the west, Mindoro to the north, and Mindanao to the southeast.

The Philippines, first visited by the Chinese and other trading peoples, was reached by European Ferdinand Magellan in 1521. He was killed in the southern islands trying to win friends and subdue rivals among the locals. By 1944, the locals could be divided into three general groups: the Muslims, whose ancestors had arrived from the west by way of Malaysia well before Magellan; the Christians, the product of 400 years of evangelizing missionaries; and natives, aboriginal people who lived on the coast as fishermen or in the dense mountain forests as hunters and gatherers.

Sergeant Corpus's new Moro companion was only the first from his community to reach the Coastwatchers' camp. Soon, others came and would hang around until the Americans gave them clothing, medicine, cigarettes, needles and thread. On a day when *Flier* was diving off Manila Bay and young ensign Jacobson was admiring the audacity of his captain, Sergeant Corpus dispatched two Moro messengers—one to the head of the Moro community, and another to the owner of Ramos Island, Rufo Samson, asking for a meeting. Samson was ill and could not attend, but the chief of the community—the Coastwatchers had come to call the residents a tribe—arrived and was asked to take a message to the mayor of Balabac City. The next day, the chief returned with a message from the mayor. It was too dangerous to set up a camp on Ramos, the mayor said, urging the Coastwatchers to move to another island. The mayor warned the Americans not to trust any of the "non-Christians" because they might, unwittingly, spread the word that the Coastwatchers had been seen.

Corpus and the others considered the mayor's advice and then gathered the Moros who were in their camp, asking them to go home. Giving them blankets, a roll of khaki, and most of their saltwater soap, the men explained that their rations were getting low. By now, they had in truth discovered that much of what they had brought with them had been ruined. The tins that had been wrapped in burlap leaked, a fact that went undiscovered for days after the landing. When the tins had floated in the surf, they had taken on seawater. Termites or white ants had invaded one can of provisions. And a tin of pesos they had brought with them was destroyed. The locals, believing the Coastwatchers were rich Americans, had expected top dollar for their work, but cash was now running short.

That Sunday, one of the Coastwatchers brought out a Bible, and as the book was passed around, each man read from it aloud. But if they felt the time had come for prayer, the Coastwatchers still were slow in responding to the mayor's warning. They worked for several days, again moving their supplies. In nearly two weeks ashore on Ramos, they had yet to attempt sending a radio message to Headquarters. They had been too busy securing their supplies and now moving them again.

Also, they had had nothing to report. That changed on Wednesday, June 21, when at just before five o'clock in the afternoon, they looked offshore and saw an armada of thirty Japanese cargo ships, escorted by a heavy cruiser and destroyers of the Japanese navy, heading into North Balabac Strait from the South China Sea. Still, the Coastwatchers made no report, because their radios were still packed in their tins.

It was two days later when Corpus and three others climbed into the kumpit to follow Placido and Dacquel across the 300-foot-deep North Balabac Strait to Mantangule Island.

With but 1,746 pesos left, the men still decided they needed to spend some cash to hire three Ramos locals. They wanted a trail slashed into the heart of the island's jungle to a spot they had chosen for a camp. Butch Rallojay looked on as Corpus opened the money box from which they had paid their help. This time, the help—locals named Musarapa and Johahini—were standing around and saw the pile of pesos in the box.

"I am opposed very much to flashing all that money," Butch wrote that night in a diary he was keeping in a small, spiral-bound tablet. "But I can't do nothing. With so much money with us that people know about, I get the creeps."

When the trail was made, the Coastwatchers began carrying sixty-pound loads across the beach coral and through the jungle to the camp. Each round-trip took five hours. At that rate, it was going to take a week just to haul the supplies inland through the chatter of monkeys and the steaming jungle soaked by monsoon rains. They hired more locals and paid them, which meant spending more of their dwindling supply of money.

All of the moving had left no time for the Coastwatchers to either observe Japanese activities or to communicate with MacArthur's headquarters. When they reached a small clearing on Mantangule Island that seemed like a logical campsite, the men unpacked their radios, ready to go to work. Now they found that the equipment, like everything else in their supplies, had been soaked during the first landing. There was rust on the radios and the charging devices, and everything needed to be dried first and then repaired.

To add to the problems, Sergeant Corpus became depressed. Gathering his men the next Monday, he told them that he felt like excess baggage because he had no skill to help fix the radios. They tried to comfort him, but he simply had lost heart and asked Sergeant Placido to take charge. Placido ignored his leader's suggestion, but the other men—despite their words of encouragement for Corpus—had lost respect for the sergeant. Bit by bit, their words changed and their eyes shifted to Placido, imploring him to take charge. Butch watched his companions with concern. Everyone now had an opinion and no one agreed. There were arguments about what work they should be doing and whether their camp at the center of Mantangule was too large. Butch wrote down his concerns as he lay in his hammock, strung between trees in a jungle so dense that from his bed he could see none of the other hammocks, only the mess tent about twenty-five yards away.

Mantangule Island was uninhabited. Looking beyond the encircling coral reef from the island's western tip, the men could see the shipping lanes and, to the southwest, Balabac's big mountains that towered over the Japanese encampment. But they only had visibility on those days when the monsoon clouds had lifted. When the rains were heavy, Mantangule was completely isolated from civilization.

The Coastwatchers were not without friends in this land, however. They had been told by MacArthur's people that on Palawan, to the north, a well-organized guerrilla force was battling the Japanese. Their orders were to contact the guerrillas and an American on Palawan by the name of Edwards. They carried a message for Edwards. His daughters were alive and well in the United States.

Communicating with the guerrillas and Edwards was not a simple matter. The southern tip of Palawan was only ten miles from Mantangule Island, but between the two were one forested island and an intricate maze of coral reefs, the paths between whose crowns was as tortuous as a lawyer's logic. And the guerrilla headquarters was even farther away, at Brooke's Point, more than sixty miles up the hostile eastern coast of Palawan, a mountainous jungle of raw beauty on whose land and in whose water lurked some of the world's deadliest beasts.

Palawan's saltwater estuaries and freshwater streams, their mouths notching the coastline, were home to saltwater crocodiles that could grow to thirty feet long and that feasted on dogs and water buffalo. Further inland, pythons that also reached thirty feet in length slithered through the jungle, and cobras and asps could be found anywhere inland from the beach. Monitor lizards, of a large-enough size to snatch a baby or a small dog, clung to tree branches, prepared to dart after their victims. And everywhere, mosquitoes carrying malaria swarmed in clouds, their tiny wings beating a malevolent, whining tune.

Palawan's rural residents—the Muslims and natives—managed most of the time to evade these natural hazards. The Christians, the majority of whom lived in the larger villages and towns, were no less threatened by the wildlife. Crocodiles were everywhere, as were snakes and mosquitoes.

In these war years, a cross section of the population was found in the guerrilla movement, and these men were forced to survive in and be aware of the hazards of the jungle. But the Coastwatchers—despite their appearance—were not attuned to this environment. They were outsiders, as much as the Japanese invaders. They had some training in survival, however, and they had their good sense, so they moved cautiously and avoided the dangers of the land.

Captain Nazario B. Mayor had, since the beginning of the war, been one more deadly hazard for any unfortunate Japanese soldiers who dared to land on Palawan. Mayor was the guerrilla leader on Palawan, and his men fought with guile and ferocity, using their knowledge of the land and their few weapons to terrorize their victims. They held no prisoners. Nor did they waste their few bullets. When they captured a Japanese soldier, they would sever his head with a bolo rather than shoot him. They would leave their victims for other Japanese soldiers to find, the horror of these corpses serving as fair warning—keep off this island!

Mayor was a Christian who was born in 1901 on Sibuyan Island in the Visayan group. As a teen, he went to the United States with an uncle and attended high school in Kansas. At sixteen, he volunteered for the National Guard and was on his way to the front lines when World War I ended. He returned to Kansas, finished high school, and enrolled in the University of Kansas as a civil engineering student. He worked as a porter out of St. Louis on the Union Pacific Railroad to pay for his education. It was there, at a Filipino Association party, that he met Mary Loudon, also a student. Her father was an American veteran of the Spanish-American War who had settled in the southern Philippines and married a Filipino woman. When Mayor proposed, Mary said she would marry him only if he returned to the Philippines. He followed her home and found it was a good deal. Mary's father, Thomas Loudon, had established a profitable lumber business on the island of Bugsuk (*BOOG-sook*) , just northeast of Mantangule Island, and he hired Nazario Mayor to work beside him. During the following decade of peace, Mayor was promoted to captain in the U.S. Army Reserve.

When the Japanese attacked Manila, Mayor left Bugsuk and boarded a ship headed for the battle lines. A Japanese plane bombed the ship, which was traveling close to the coast off the northern Palawan island of Araceli, and Mayor survived by swimming ashore. He made his way back to Bugsuk, but soon received orders to report to Brooke's Point to recruit guerrillas. He left Bugsuk and later wrote a letter to Mary, which she read to the children one night at supper. Their father told them he was being hunted by the Japanese. If the enemy came after Mary and the children, he wrote, he would not surrender to free them because to do so would jeopardize the resistance movement.

Mary had five children with her in the Loudon home, a tranquil place shaded by palm trees on a spectacular, curved white-sand beach on the southern coast of Bugsuk. The view was of vibrant blue-green water and a chain of nearby islands, between which on a good day could be seen the mountains of Balabac. The house was built with bamboo walls and floors and a thatched roof, as were all structures on the island. But unlike the tiny huts in the nearby native village, the Mayor home had three bedrooms, a large living room, and an office. Bamboo shades hung over the open walls to keep the sun out, while letting through a mild tropical breeze that swept in from the ocean. Rainwater was collected from the roof in a concrete cistern beside the house. The kitchen was off to another side, under a lean-to roof, and cooking was done over a wood-burning pit. Pungent wood smoke scented the air all around the house.

Thomas Loudon had moved here from Balabac, where he had begun his lumbering business. Family lore said that his wife and two of their daughters were massacred on Balabac by Muslims who, seized by religious fanaticism, wanted to rid that island of Christians. Loudon escaped the massacre with his daughter Mary and had lived on Bugsuk since. It was to this paradise that Mary returned from the United States with her fiancé.

Now her husband, Nazario Mayor, had been gone from Bugsuk for a few months when a native runner arrived at Mary Mayor's door with a warning: The Japanese were coming the next day. Mary rounded up her children—Robert, the oldest, who at twelve was now the man of the house; Alfred, sixteen, a cousin; Frank, nine; Mary Ann, four; and her sister, Coney, two. The baby, Thomas, was less than a year old. With the help of some natives, Mary and her brood hiked north into the jungle along a narrow trail that crossed the length of Bugsuk. The air under the canopy of 200-foot-tall mahogany and ipil trees was thick with humidity, hot and still, but they walked in shade, the sunlight penetrating the high branches only now and then. Underfoot, the trail was paved with sharp, old coral.

Mary kept her children moving, and by the end of the day, having walked ten miles, they reached the northern shore of the island. A native boat was waiting for them, and soon they were gliding under the shelter of mangroves, the trees' stilt-like roots awash in salt water. Here, snakes hung from the branches, and only a tarp over the boat kept them from dropping directly onto the heads of Mary and her children. The boat moved on to another island, where it stopped in another mangrove swamp. The natives and the boys, Robert and Alfred, built a shelter on the bank of the swamp, which was washed into the sea when early monsoon rains came. For two weeks, the natives helped feed Mary and her children, and when snakes would drop from the branches, they would hack them in two with their bolos. Finally, Nazario, having learned of his family's evacuation, arrived. It was time for the Mayors to move to Brooke's Point.

The major landowner at Brooke's Point was, like Thomas Loudon, an expatriate American. Thomas Edwards had come to the islands as a teacher following the Spanish-American War and the subsequent battle between Filipino nationalists and American occupiers. The Americans had lost several thousand soldiers, while the nationalists lost several hundred thousand, leaving the land more hospitable for Americans interested in helping to improve the lot of locals. Among the arrivals in a land that had been evangelized for hundreds of years by Catholic monks were Protestant missionaries and secular teachers.

A staunch Christian, Edwards married a Filipino woman from Mindanao, a Muslim. He retired from teaching to develop a sprawling coconut plantation in the coastal plains between Brooke's Point and the inland mountains, as well as a sawmill, a logging operation, and other businesses.

Edwards had been the major employer in town before the war and, as a result, was the most important resident of Brooke's Point. But now there was another authority. The guerrilla chief, Nazario Mayor, had begun recruiting guerrillas—terrorists, really, if you were Japanese—in early 1942. He had drawn to his side Christians and Muslims and even some foreigners. He had welcomed into the guerrilla movement Vans Taivo Kerson, a citizen of Finland and a deep-sea diver and salvage and explosives expert, trapped in the Philippines by the war. Before there was a guerrilla force, Kerson had gone from village to village, gathering weapons and organizing the men to resist the Japanese. Mayor inherited the nucleus of Kerson's guerrilla band, and Kerson became Mayor's ally.

After his family had spent two weeks in the mangrove swamp, Nazario Mayor brought them to a home on the beach near Brooke's Point, knowing that they would not be entirely safe there. The Japanese would attack on occasion, and then the family would have to retreat into the foothills. But the danger of malaria inland was the greater hazard.

Mayor deposited Mary and the children and, leaving his son Robert in charge, went back to work, harassing the enemy. When a contingent of Japanese soldiers would come ashore to patrol the area, the guerrillas would shadow them and, when they had settled in for the night, slaughter them. Or they would set up a defense on the beach, well concealed, and through the creative use of explosives—gunpowder salvaged from Japanese mines that floated ashore, packed into hollowed bamboo logs to simulate serious ordnance—they would fool them into retreat.

Supplies were always scarce for the guerrillas. Mayor used another volunteer group—a bolo battalion—to collect supplies and weapons from the public. Armed with bolos and blowguns, spears and bows and arrows, these volunteers on occasion would strong-arm the public, extorting property or material for their own benefit. On better days, they carried messages and stood as sentries. Their chief, Jolkipli—his title was Datu—was an honorable man who would not tolerate hooligans. The people of Brooke's Point had stories to tell on that score. Respecting both Jolkipli and Mayor, they were willing to deal with the bolo battalion to keep Mayor's terrorists fighting against the Japanese. In their third year of war, isolated from the outside world, the guerrillas were all the people of Palawan had.

In this land of their fathers, the Coastwatchers would come to rely on the guerrillas, as well.

CHAPTER 8

THE WAGES OF WINNERS

Low on fuel and having used all but four of his torpedoes, Commander John Crowley radioed submarine headquarters in Fremantle, Australia, asking permission to return from patrol. The sound of the skipper's voice in the radio room Down Under was as stunning as words escaping a closed grave. The Americans had decoded a Japanese message that reported a submarine had been sunk in *Flier*'s patrol area. Crowley's call turned despondency to celebration. Apparently *Flier*'s dummy torpedo with its explosion and oil slick had fooled the enemy.

The submarine had plenty of food on board, so with Ensign Jacobson's approval, the chief adjusted the menu for the next dinner. The "going home" meal offered the crew a smorgasbord with four types of meat, fresh vegetables, strawberry shortcake, and all of it they could eat.

Crowley, however, was still hungry for targets. He had those four remaining torpedoes. The skipper clung to the periscope during the day and scanned the horizon through binoculars from the bridge at night. But other than some sailing ships and floating debris, the *Flier* was alone at sea.

For the next five days, *Flier* continued south, leaving the Sulu Sea near the easternmost peninsula of Borneo, then crossing the Celebes Sea—still sliding along the eastern Borneo coast. Enemy ships and planes could be expected any place, at any time. Japanese soldiers still held much of the jungle-covered countryside, and General MacArthur had yet to take control of either the skies or the seas. The submarine crept south through the Makassar Strait, separating Borneo from the island of Celebes, and then began its dash across the Java Sea, which stretches east and west just below the equator between southern Borneo and the main chain of Indonesian islands. Still ahead lay narrow Lombok Strait, east of Bali, and then the Indian Ocean, separating Indonesia from Australia. There was still a chance to use the final four fish in *Flier*'s tubes.

By the end of May 1944, it had been more than a month since Elton Brubaker's friend, Hestel Walker, had left Fremantle aboard the submarine *Rasher,* a time during which the Florida boy had suffered through shore duty without finding a sea berth. He and some friends had thrown a beer party for Walker before *Rasher* began its fourth patrol. ("We drink beer only," he had assured his family in a letter he scribbled off earlier that day. "When I came out here the beer hurt my kidneys because it was lots stronger than that in the States, but I'm getting used to it now.")

Both Elton and Hestel had been assigned to a submarine tender, *Orion*, when they arrived in Fremantle. The tender was tied to a dock, and at any one time up to a half-dozen submarines would nestle against the ship's other side—side by side—allowing *Orion*'s crew to go back and forth to whichever sub they were helping return to duty. The *Rasher*'s crew was on its two-week rest-and-recuperation (also referred to as R&R) leave when Elton and Hestel arrived on *Orion*. Elton went to work on *Rasher* and Hestel on *Puffer*, which was also berthed against the tender. Hestel seemed to be getting the worst of the deal. Every day for the first few days, he was sent into one of the fuel tanks welded to the outside of *Puffer*'s pressure hull, and there he would spend the day scraping away a protective film so that the tank could be used to hold seawater as ballast. Elton's job on *Rasher* was more conventional for a sailor who had been to electrical school: testing the electrical circuits throughout the submarine to assure they were working properly, and replacing jury-rigged repairs with by-the-book wiring.

Ironically, when *Rasher*'s crew returned from R&R, it was Hestel who was signed on as a new member of the crew. A disappointed Elton wished his friend well and returned to work, living on *Orion* and spending each day preparing submarines for the front lines.

There had been plenty to do to keep Elton's mind off the almost-daily departure of submarines, none with a bunk for him. Right after Hestel left, Elton was enrolled in a new school. He was earning As and Bs, and he thought he might have a chance to attend gunner's school. "You can see more of a fight from topside," he explained to his sister, Charlotte. "I think that I have really learned to study," he wrote to his parents. And now he began boasting that he was going to leave the navy after the war and graduate from college—probably Georgia Tech.

If he wasn't helping to provision a submarine, hauling sacks of potatoes weighing more than he did, Elton was thinking about Ruth Turner, or planning what he would do on liberty. One day, he rented a horse in town and rode it to a park high above the city. The view down from the hill was pretty, and the weather—even though it was early winter—was balmy. Most of the time when he was on liberty, he located some beer to drink, and once he found himself restricted to the ship after he punched a fellow in the nose.

By the first week in June, *Rasher* had returned to Fremantle. Hestel Walker went on R&R, staying in a hotel on the beach in nearby Perth. Elton joined him one night and they drank gin squashes. Elton was happy to see his friend, but he was longing for sea duty. Now Hestel had sea stories he could tell his envious pal, who really wanted stories of his own.

Hestel told his friend about how *Rasher* had headed north for Darwin, Australia, when it left Fremantle in late April. The submarine, Hestel found out, had finished three patrols before that one and had established itself as a successful submarine, one on which any sailor would be proud to serve. The first lesson Hestel had learned was to let the chief know you had a specialty. For three days at sea, he found himself standing watch on lookout, hanging on to the side of the radar tower as the submarine cruised along the surface at night. This duty ended only after the chief realized Hestel was trained as an electrician. Now he was a "belowdecks man," standing watch inside the submarine, dealing with engine and pump electrical problems.

As a fireman first class, the same rating as Elton, Hestel was assigned to check *Rasher*'s huge banks of batteries. One electrician would go down into the battery well—either through a hatch in the floor of the officers' quarters, or one in the crew's quarters. With a hose and nozzle, like a gasoline pump nozzle, he would crawl across a grating over the batteries, filling the battery cells with water. There were nine electricians and one chief. Like everyone else on the submarine, they stood four-hour watches with three hours off.

Always belowdecks, Hestel only heard from others what was happening on the surface. It was, he could assure Elton, a grim story at first.

After refueling and stocking up on supplies at Darwin, *Rasher* headed for the battle zone. There was no shortage of targets, but after twelve days at sea, the submarine's commander, Captain Laughton, had fired all twenty-four of his torpedoes, sinking only one vessel. The torpedoes—relics, apparently, from earlier in the war—ran in circles, dove too deep, or hit the targets but failed to explode. Hestel got word they were headed back to Darwin. They didn't stay long, simply loading another supply of torpedoes—the last eighteen left at the time in Darwin. Again they headed north, through Makassar Strait and into the Celebes Sea. This time, the torpedoes worked, Hestel told Elton. They fired all eighteen torpedoes and sank three more ships.

That was worth a gin squash toast if any story was.

As *Flier* crossed the Java Sea on the last morning of June, its crew still eager to fire the remaining four torpedoes, Crowley, standing on the bridge, spotted a sailboat and decided to investigate. The skipper ordered the gunnery chief to fire some twenty-millimeter rounds across the bow of the sailboat, and after the burst, the sailors dropped their sail. With two crew members on deck armed with machine guns, *Flier* pulled beside to find a typical Indonesian fishing boat. The navy men boarded the fishing boat, nudging one of the sailors with the machine guns. The man signaled that he would willingly board *Flier*. Then, leaving his primitive wooden vessel, he climbed to the bridge of the submarine, indicating as he went that there were no Japanese on the sailboat. He was led down the steel ladder into the steel, brass, glass, and artificial light of the submarine, and Crowley ordered his men to hand some supplies to the other ten fishermen still on the sixty-foot sailboat. Delivering canned pork tongue that no submariner would stoop to eat, as well as fruit, vegetables, and cigarettes, they told the men they were free to go. Following standing orders, they took the one man with them for interrogation by navy intelligence officers in Australia.

Native fishermen, it was assumed, knew who was doing what at sea just as small-town mailmen know everyone's business. The new guest aboard *Flier* was given a bunk in the crew quarters, and through sign language the crew began to question him. One of the first things they learned was that he and his shipmates were Muslims who could not eat pork. In return for his good nature, the crew taught the man to say "All marines are lousy," aware that when they docked it would be a marine who escorted him from the submarine.

The following day, July 1, *Flier* reached narrow Lombok Strait, the passage between the islands of Bali to the west and Lombok to the east. There were two antisubmarine ships patrolling the strait, so Crowley waited for dark. The patrol boats would go together from one side of the strait to the other and then return. After sunset, Crowley asked the radar operator where the patrol boats were and learned that they were clearly visible on one side of the strait. The skipper gave the order to partially submerge *Flier*. This left the deck above water so that the diesel engines could drive the boat at full speed, yet left the submarine with a much smaller profile than were it fully surfaced. Then Crowley gave the order for full speed, and *Flier* dashed behind the Japanese patrol.

Early the next morning, with the light of a new day, the submarine surfaced and Al Jacobson, standing watch, could see the Bali beaches and mountains off to starboard. To his eye, the beauty of the island suggested an equal beauty among its native women. He was, after all, a young man who had been at sea for more than a month.

Once in the Indian Ocean, the submarine kept going past Darwin, arriving in Fremantle on July 5 with only 100 gallons of diesel fuel left, enough to run for two hours. *Flier* drew alongside a submarine tender where shore crew lowered a gangplank to its deck. The entire *Flier* crew, dressed in their denims and white sailor caps, assembled topside for the first time since they had left Hawaii. Then Captain McLean, the commander of Submarine Squadron Sixteen—and Crowley's immediate boss—arrived with several other high-ranking navy officers. With the crew standing at attention in three ranks along the starboard side of the bow, and with a waterfront backdrop of other submarines moored beside other tenders, McLean went down the line, shaking hands with every sailor and officer as two photographers snapped pictures for naval records. Crowley and *Flier* had returned—in and of itself a happy surprise for the brass, who, due to the intercepted enemy report, had assumed it lost—and had come back as heroes, with four ships, or 19,500 tons, sunk and two more ships, or 13,500 tons, damaged. *Flier* had sailed 5,888 miles to get to the war zone and covered 1,750 miles in that area before steaming another 2,914 miles to Fremantle. They had consumed 113,000 gallons of fuel and twenty-two torpedoes in getting the job done. Now, after a detailed briefing on the status of the war effort, they were due for some fun.

Fremantle and Perth are adjacent cities on Australia's western coast, washed by the Indian Ocean. For the United States, Fremantle was a base for submarines only, and the commander of all submarines in the Pacific, Rear Admiral Ralph W. Christie, had his headquarters there. He saw to it that his officers were treated well between patrols. Resort hotels in downtown Fremantle were reserved for them. Each officer—just like each enlisted man—was given a case of beer. Each bottle held twenty-four ounces, so the case was expected to last for a while. The hotel room and the meals at the hotel were free. Once the case of beer was consumed, the men were responsible for slaking their own thirst.

In addition to beer, the officers could get all the booze they wanted. But there were other forms of recreation. Young Jacobson lounged by a lake, played golf, tennis, and badminton, and went horseback riding (although the horse threw him). He could go sailing if he wanted, but the boat was old and he was spoiled by the racy sailing scows on Spring Lake. He had hunted some back in Michigan, and now he joined a few other men every other day who were taking guns from *Flier* for hunting. The game was rabbits, kangaroos, and wallabies, and the range was the rolling hills outside of town. They would take boys from a local orphanage on these outings, teaching them to shoot. The farmers on whose land they hunted were pleased to have the rabbit population thinned. And for a few days at least, the submariners were happy to be on solid land.

There were parties, as well, and girls for dancing. At one dance, Jacobson met a young woman from Jakarta, Indonesia. This was not just any girl, and her story illustrated how this war left no one—from the lowest peasant to society's thin privileged crust—untouched. Her grandfather, perhaps the European equivalent of Henry Ford, was one of the owners of the Dutch electrical company, Phillips. Her family had fled Jakarta when the Japanese invaded, and now she was a driver for Admiral Christie. Whenever he could, Jacobson spent time with the young woman, and before it was time for *Flier* to leave, she asked him to look up her grandfather in New York City when he got back to the States. He assured her he would.

After two weeks in port, the R&R was over, and the ensign finally picked up a pen.

"You know the old saying, if you want something done, give it to the busy man. Well, that has been very true in my case with regards to letters. For the last two weeks I have had nothing special to do, but I couldn't find the time to write. Now while I am [as] busy as [I] can possibly be, loading the ship, I write. It is safe to say this will probably be my last letter for a while. Have to go back and start earning my pay again," he wrote.

Al told his father that he enjoyed getting a copy of a letter Senior had written to his older brother, Chuck, about events at the family foundry. Then he suggested that his mother make carbon copies of all the letters the family sent to each of the sons—Chuck, Dave, and Al—and send the copies to the other sons. "That way, you would only have to write 1/3 as many letters. Also, remember the pictures; the ones I received have already been shown to everyone on the ship."

He wrote about his rabbit hunting, noting that a .30 caliber rifle didn't leave much of the rabbit when it was shot. He told his father that the Australian spirit in the face of war was upbeat, and he reported how a local foundry was working. He said he was sending his mother an Australian lambskin rug "so when you get up on a cold morning you will have a nice warm spot to put your feet."

He wanted to know the details about the news in one of the letters that had been waiting for him when he had reached Fremantle—that his sister Mary was getting engaged.

"I can't say much more because tomorrow will be another big day and I should get some sleep," the ensign told his family. "I'll say good-bye for now, and will write again when we get in. Above all don't worry, because we have the same officers, crew and the best ship in any navy. So for another month or so, God bless and keep you all."

All Elton Brubaker knew about *Flier* was that one more submarine had tied up in Fremantle. A week after Crowley's men arrived and went out on R&R, Elton had submitted another request for sea duty. "I think this time it will go through," he wrote to his family with less than total assuredness. One night, he had an invitation from an Australian family to visit them for tea. He couldn't go because all the men on his ship had been restricted, but he would have liked to. "It takes my mind off the navy for a few hours," he wrote his mother. "I go to these people's homes and they like for us to feel at ease."

Clearly, despite the bragging he did about his grades, Elton was tired of academics. "I have made out a list of the number of hours that I have been in navy schools and it amounts to 1,306 hours," he wrote. "That is a lot of time to put in school. Do you think I could get some high school credits out of this? It is harder work in the navy school than in a public school. I am having my division officer get this out of my record, then I want you to see Mr. Crookshank and find out what the score is."

He had a word for his brother, Lewis, who was about to graduate from high school. "Tell that brother of mine, for goodness' sake, keep the hell out of the navy."

Letters from home had told him the family was moving to a newer home in St. Augustine. He asked his father to draw him a diagram of the new place, with rooms and furniture, and he wanted to know which room would be his when he came home.

Still, he was happy with some aspects of navy life. The men around him were great. "One thing I learned quick in the navy, race and religion isn't the thing that makes a person—it's the person that counts. As a matter of fact, this paper belongs to a 'wop' that I am writing on, the ink that I'm using belongs to a Jew, and this pen I borrowed from a fellow who is a Holiness by faith. The whole lot of the boys are O.K. There are some Protestant boys here that I would refuse to let my sister go out with, so you see, my point is clear."

Two weeks after *Flier* had docked—about the time the boat's crew was returning from R&R—Elton finally got the word he was longing for. He was now assigned to *Flier*. Hestel Walker was just coming off two weeks of R&R and beer drinking, and he found his friend happy as a kid just promoted from JV to varsity. Elton wrote home the same day. "Dear Mom," he started, "By this letter you will know that my address has changed; yes, and it's just a good bit of luck for me." He did not elaborate, but went on to tell his mother of a letter he had received from a girl back in Florida whose brother was serving in Europe. "Mrs. Dupont was afraid that Frank was in the invasion force, but they had a letter from him and he is still in England. Those boys are really going to town over there, and I'm sure the war over there will be finished in short order," he wrote. "I'm glad that I'm getting to swing into action myself."

The landscape of the war had shifted constantly, moved by actions huge and minuscule, each event a piece of the overall mosaic that would become history.

D-day—the invasion of the fortified beaches of Normandy, France, by 160,000 Allied troops—had taken place six weeks before Elton Brubaker's world was dramatically changed with his assignment to *Flier*. Just as he had suspected, the daring landing in the face of German gunfire was to lead to the end of the war in Europe in eleven months. Victory against Japan would take more time, but there were signs that progress was being made in the Pacific.

In February, U.S. Army Air Corps planes destroyed a convoy of Japanese ships off New Ireland, and Allied aircraft sank most of another convoy in the Bismarck Archipelago.

March brought the sinking of a Japanese troopship on its way to the Marianas, by the submarine *Sandlance*. And a naval bombardment of the Palau Islands east of the Philippines destroyed 150 airplanes, 6 Japanese naval vessels, and 100,000 tons of shipping.

In April, the navy shelled the island of Truk, smashing another 120 airplanes.

By July, Japanese leaders were sufficiently distressed that they demoted their top admiral.

While these events were making headlines, the world at large was unaware when, on the Philippine island of Mantangule, Sergeant Amando Corpus decided that he would make a journey north to Brooke's Point, the guerrillas' headquarters, without his men. It was July 1, the day that *Flier* was slipping through Lombok Strait on its way to Australia. Corpus told the five other Coastwatchers that he would contact the guerrilla leader, deliver the message to the Edwards family about their daughters in the States, and hire a boat. He brought some medicine, cigarettes, and magazines with him to trade for help from the natives.

The men who stayed behind kept busy, even when Independence Day came. Placido worked with the radio sets and the battery charger, which was coated with rust. The others busied themselves burying equipment that they did not need. They worked through lunch, finally stopping late in the day for biscuits, jam, and coconuts. Then they worked again, stopping only when, unannounced, they were visited by Cirilo Sunson, a local man who brought them cooked chickens, rice, and eggplants, their first solid meal in days.

Two days later, a monsoon unleashed its fury on Mantangule, the slanting rain drilling through the jungle foliage, almost stopping all work. The men managed to bury some supplies in the sand near the beach. Placido continued to labor over the radios. Finally, one radio showed some life. He swore at the rusted charger, a curse that seemed to work. On July 7, the Coastwatchers for the first time contacted General MacArthur's headquarters, more than 3,000 miles away in Australia. The signal was weak, but Placido reported where the group was staying and their condition. When Headquarters attempted to respond, their message was garbled. And then the radio quit.

Placido would not give up. The next day, when the other four were out of camp, he toiled over the radios. He had finally managed to charge a battery when suddenly, three strange men came into the jungle clearing. If he was startled, he was soon pleased. The police chief of Balabac, Vicente Aizo, who had heard rumors that some Australian soldiers were on Mantangule, had brought Sergeant Pasqual de la Cruz from the guerrilla outpost at the southern tip of Palawan. The chief also brought George Marquez, an American soldier from Oakdale, Illinois, who had escaped from Manila in December 1941 and had been hiding in the jungle and working with the guerrillas ever since.

With the working battery, Placido turned on a radio and managed to receive a signal from the *Philippine Hour*, broadcast from Australia. The three guests were delighted, hearing radio for the first time in nearly three years.

Sergeant Corpus returned to the island on July 10 as Dacquel and Butch were covering the Coastwatchers' tracks and Slug and Ray were burying the last of the unneeded supplies. He brought with him Nazario Mayor and a few of his guerrillas. Mayor told the men he was surprised to see them still alive because the whole Balabac area was infested with enemy soldiers. Acting once again as the leader of the Coastwatchers, Corpus decided that the group should abandon Mantangule and establish a base in Brooke's Point, under Captain Mayor's protection. Placido resisted. He could keep trying to contact Australia from this island and would have a better chance here than in Brooke's Point, he argued. But the rest of the men liked Corpus's plan, and so they all once again dug out their hidden supplies. The next day, the deputy governor of southern Palawan, Datu Jolkipli, arrived with four native boats, apparently summoned by Captain Mayor. Once again the Coastwatchers' supplies were loaded aboard and, towed by one of the boats that had an outboard motor, the flotilla headed north, their two craft zigzagging along a path between the coral reefs that only a local would know.

CHAPTER 9

MINES AND MARINERS

The submarine *Darter,* which was launched in New London a month before *Flier,* would, in time, end its career the same ignominious way *Flier* had begun its first patrol—stranded on a reef. But on the same day that *Flier* was sneaking south between Borneo and Celebes, *Darter* was a few hundred miles to the east, in the Spice Islands, the world's primary source of clove and nutmeg—an idyllic place in peacetime where, in any season, the air is perfumed by exotic plants.

The idyll had disappeared. This was war, and *Darter* was looking for Japanese ships. At three o'clock that afternoon, as the submarine patrolled submerged, its crew got lucky. A group of Coastwatchers hiding on the islands reported that the large Japanese minelayer, *Tsugaru,* escorted by two destroyers and a scout plane, was headed for the submarine. *Darter* got close, pointed its bow at the ship, and emptied the six forward torpedo tubes, scoring two hits on *Tsugaru.* The crew heard the sounds of the ship breaking up before the first of twenty-four depth charges began raining on them from the escorts.

Darter's daring and success were impressive, but its accomplishment was somewhat like killing the hornet that has already stung you. *Tsugaru*'s deadly work laying mines had been accomplished much earlier. And it would bear fruit.

Japanese forces had, in the first two years of the war, sown the ocean south of Palawan, near Balabac, with a field of mines. Naval-mine warfare relies—just as land-mine warfare does—on a simple axiom: If you know where the mines are and your enemy does not, you can pass through that real estate while your foes, should they attempt it, risk death. The Japanese Southern Expeditionary Force had seized the Philippines, Indonesia, and Malaysia in 1942. Controlling all the sea-lanes, the force was able to plant mines where Allied ships would have to pass.

But currents and storms can move mines, and so the Japanese commanders decided in December 1943 that it was time to refurbish their minefields. *Tsugaru* was assigned this work and left Palau on March 24, 1944. When it reached Balabac Strait, it set a number of mines, and then it headed south for Balikpapan, on Borneo's Makassar Strait coast.

Allied intelligence operations knew of the first minefield laid near Palawan. They had not yet learned of *Tsugaru*'s seedlings near Balabac when, on June 22—a week before *Darter* found *Tsugaru*—the submarine *Robalo* left Darwin, Australia, headed for the South China Sea. *Robalo*'s orders involved sinking Japanese ships—except hospital ships and small fishing boats. (Some submarines, such as *Redfin*, had less-confrontational assignments, rescuing downed airmen or landing spies or Coastwatchers.)

Robalo was commanded by Lieutenant Commander Manning M. Kimmel, a sailor with a family name to defend. His father, Admiral Husband E. Kimmel, had been commander and chief of the Pacific Fleet and of the U.S. Fleet when the Japanese attacked Pearl Harbor. Husband Kimmel was, at the time, blamed for the navy's losses and was relieved of his command.

Despite his extensive naval heritage—one grandfather also was an admiral, and Manning was a 1935 graduate of the Naval Academy—Kimmel's success on *Robalo*'s last patrol had been limited. The first-time skipper reported that he had sunk one tanker in the South China Sea.

Kimmel had been aboard submarines since before the war, and he knew the Philippines, particularly the world traveled by the upper echelons of Manila society. His wife had delivered a daughter in a Manila hospital while he was stationed aboard a submarine there, and he had dazzled the local tennis world, winning tournaments easily when he was ashore. A few months before the Japanese attack that drew the United States into the war, he was reassigned to join the new submarine *Drum,* which was under construction. After a few months on *Drum,* Kimmel was promoted to executive officer of the submarine *Raton,* and then took command of *Robalo.*

By June 1944, as *Robalo* steamed north from Australia, Kimmel had served aboard submarines as long as most other sub commanders. Despite the disappointment of his first patrol with *Robalo,* he set out now with enough credentials to get the job done. And his boat was ready.

Willis A. Lent, a navy commander who had served as training officer while *Robalo* was in Darwin, was impressed with the general efficiency of the officers and crew members, and with Kimmel's service on five prior patrols. Lent went along one day when the crew practiced firing torpedoes outside of Darwin. The captain and his crew were ready for battle, he concluded.

The boat was just as fit as the crew, another navy officer decided. *Robalo* had been climbed over, crawled through, tweaked, tightened, tested, and thoroughly inspected by a relief crew, assisted by the submarine's own men, for twenty-three days. Kimmel told the refit commanding officer, Lieutenant Commander Maurice William Shea, that he was happy with the shape of his boat. It had been sound-tested for flaws in the steel (none were located), and its degaussing had been found adequate. All ships were degaussed—meaning, they had their magnetic fields neutralized—by moving them into a special slip, so they would not attract mines designed to be drawn to them by magnetism. Shea's very thorough testing even included *Robalo*'s battery ventilation system, which he found to be in excellent condition.

So after meeting with Admiral Christie, Kimmel was sent on his way with eight officers and a crew of seventy-three men, of whom fifty-two were qualified submariners. Christie had reminded Kimmel—as he did every departing captain—of the need to remain vigilant against enemy submarines throughout his patrol, including the return trip when the men might let down their guard. He had asked Kimmel if he was satisfied with his boat and his men. The answer was: Yes, sir.

Kimmel had on board detailed instructions on the route to follow to get to his assigned patrol area in the South China Sea. Admiral
Christie selected the route based on several considerations, including
the shortest distance, the need to keep submarines separated to reduce
the chance of a sinking from friendly fire, and the desirability of diver-
sifying their routes so that the Japanese could not predict where they
would go. In selecting a sub's route, Christie would also consider the
possibility of enemy attacks on the submarines, whether the phase
of the moon made nighttime travel hazardous, and the likelihood of
encountering enemy ships that could be opportunistically attacked by
the submarine while it was traveling to its assigned patrol area.

Robalo's route took Kimmel along a path through the Indonesian
islands that looped northeast from Australia, crossed the equator, and
then ran across the southern part of the Sulu Sea near Borneo. At some
point, *Robalo* would cross the track of *Flier* as Crowley steered south
from his first patrol. To get to Kimmel's assigned patrol area in the
South China Sea, his submarine would have to travel through Balabac Strait, that narrow passage between Mantangule Island and Ramos
Island, where the submarine *Redfin* had landed the Coastwatchers in
May.

Christie believed that due to their depth, most of the waters through
which he had sent *Robalo* could not be mined. He knew, however, that
the navy faced the possibility that the Japanese would be able to close
some of the passages in and around the Philippines, and would "make
every attempt" to do so. The options facing the enemy were many,
the admiral realized. Sonar buoys, radar detection equipment onshore
and at sea, patrol vessels and airplanes, underwater nets, and cables
and mines were out there, waiting for careless skippers.

Among the places where mines were most likely to be found was
Balabac Strait, the admiral thought. But he concluded that while
several channels through the strait probably held mines, there was a
swath a mile wide and 600 feet deep that should be safe for shipping.
A reference book at use at the time, *The Coast Pilot*, declared: "Nasubata Channel is five miles wide between Roughton Reef and Comiran

Danger Bank with depths above 100 fathoms in the fairway. This is an excellent deep-water channel and a considerable amount of 'straits' shipping rounds Cape Melville and passes to the northwestward of Comiran Island into the Sulu Sea. In navigating this channel, it is only necessary to guard against the effects of the tidal stream which, when combined with the surface current set up by the wind, sweeps with considerable velocity at times in the general direction of the prevailing wind."

A mine anchored in water 600 feet deep would be ineffective if there was too swift a current. It was a simple matter of geometry and physics. The floating mine would attempt to go with the flow, but its anchor at the end of a chain nearly as long as the water was deep would hold it back. Without a current, the mine could be rigged to float at the correct depth to be struck by a passing ship. But in a strong current, the mine—moving in the direction of the water—would swing on its long anchor chain in an arc, down toward the bottom of the sea, toward a depth that was well below the hull of a passing ship.

Christie had some other information that gave him comfort in telling Kimmel to go through Balabac Strait. Submarines had made ten trips through the passage since February. *Robalo* itself had come through the area on April 22, and as recently as May 8, the submarine *Crevalle* had gone the same route. In the course of the war, forty submarines had cleared Balabac Strait successfully. Christie was certain Kimmel could bring *Robalo* through, as well.

Ten days after leaving Darwin, *Robalo* crossed the southern limits of the Sulu Sea north of Borneo and aimed for Balabac Strait. At eight o'clock that morning, Kimmel gave his coordinates in a message to Australia. The numbers placed him on the eastern side of Borneo. Kimmel also had the unpleasant duty then to report that a Japanese battleship, an aircraft carrier, and two destroyers had gotten by him.

At eight o'clock that night, *Robalo* entered Balabac Strait on the surface. Kimmel was on the bridge. Nine other officers and crewmen were on watch topside as well when a sudden explosion to the rear of the bridge rocked the boat. The ten men were thrown into the water and the submarine sank in less than two minutes.

Four of the men found each other in the darkness. Samuel Tucker, a twenty-one-year-old Massachusetts boy who had graduated from Harvard University a year before, was a fresh ensign on *Robalo,* serving as commissary officer. Floyd Laughlin, twenty-seven, was a petty officer, also from Massachusetts, who had ten years in the navy and was assistant navigator. Mason Poston, twenty-nine, a petty officer from Pensacola, Florida, had volunteered for the navy after Pearl Harbor was attacked. He had entered submarine school about the same time Elton Brubaker arrived, and, like Elton, was an electrician. And Wallace Martin, twenty-two, the third petty officer, had graduated from high school in Illinois the May before Pearl Harbor and had just joined the *Robalo* as a signalman.

As they gathered their wits in the warm ocean water, Tucker, Laughlin, Poston, and Martin called out and found several other men. Now they realized that all but the skipper and five of their shipmates had ridden the submarine to the bottom after the explosion. They were aware, as the night wore on, when two of those six slipped beneath the waves and never returned. Then three more crewmen disappeared in the darkness. That left Kimmel and these four men.

In the distance, a light was flashing and, moved by the current, Kimmel and Ensign Tucker stayed afloat and together, drifting toward the beacon. Poston and Martin, separated from the skipper and ensign, kept each other going through the dark hours. Laughlin was but a voice in the night, and then he was gone.

At about midnight, Kimmel disappeared, and for the next thirteen hours, Tucker managed to float until he washed ashore on Comiran Island, on the southern side of Balabac Strait. He had survived seventeen hours in the ocean. Staggering up the beach, Tucker found Poston and Martin, who had made it to the island two hours earlier. An hour later, Laughlin crawled ashore. He told the others he had last seen Kimmel a couple of hours after sunrise. They had stayed together for a while, but Kimmel had been exhausted and barely able to swim. The skipper, floating on his back, had disappeared, Laughlin reported.

At about this time, the wind changed direction and the current grew stronger. Conserving their strength, the four stayed on the beach for the next three hours, watching the water for Kimmel or any other survivors. But none came.

Then they set to work. Scavenging from what was available on this tiny speck of land, the men built a crude shelter and gathered coconuts, which they broke open. The meat was inedible, but it was monsoon season and the rain was predictable. They gathered rainwater in the shell halves and were able to drink. The next day, the men looked west from Comiran and could see Balabac Island with its massive, jungle-covered mountains. If they could get there, no doubt the food would be more abundant. So they began building a raft.

At eleven o'clock on the third morning, having seen no other survivors from the submarine, the four men boarded their raft and began paddling toward Balabac. The nearest beach was ten miles to the west, across the swift current of the Nasubata Channel. For twenty-two hours, through the driving rain of that day and the pitch darkness of the following night, they urged their little raft onward, struggling against the current now, only to be swept ahead by it later. At nine o'clock the next morning, they landed on Balabac near a river. They walked along the beach until, after about two miles, they reached a coconut grove. Here the nuts were ripe, and for the first time in four days, they ate. Then they headed into the hills, where they spent the next night. When the sun rose on July 8—just as Al Jacobson and his friends from *Flier* were settling in at their resort hotel in Perth, Australia—the *Robalo* survivors began moving once more. It was nine o'clock that morning when a patrol from the Japanese Naval Garrison and Defense units captured them. If they thought they had survived the worst, they were about to discover that their ordeal had only just begun.

Word was spreading across Balabac, from one small village to the next. In time, the guerrillas on Palawan would hear rumors of the submarine survivors. By then, the survivors would be gone from Balabac, taken to the notorious prisoner of war camp at Puerto Princesa, more than 100 jungle miles north of Captain Nazario Mayor's headquarters in Brooke's Point.

Sergeant Corpus and the Coastwatchers were on Mantangule Island on the day the *Robalo* survivors were captured. But the six spies had little contact with the outside world, and would not hear about *Robalo*'s sinking for many weeks. Indeed, one day later, the Coastwatchers would pack up and leave Mantangule Island for Brooke's Point.

By then, the *Robalo* men were beginning to experience the degradations of life as prisoners of war. The questioning had already begun before they left Balabac, and continued when they reached the prison camp, perched on a seaside cliff in Puerto Princesa, the largest city on Palawan. They could expect beatings at the hands of their interrogators and, at times, other kinds of torture. Although the Geneva Convention required them to give their captors only their name, rank, and serial number, these men would be grilled for hours about the smallest details of their submarine, as well as the grand social, economic, and psychological impact of the war back in the States.

"What course were you following?" an interrogator asked.

"What were the ranks of the officers on board? Their names? The names of your shipmates?

"What are the movements and plans of the Pacific submarine force for operations against Japan?

"How are the submarines in the Pacific organized and equipped?

"What are the American submarines' secret marks and codes?

"How is America's war spirit?

"What is the impact of the war in the American homeland?"

Many of the questions were answered in time. The Japanese learned the difference between the old and new American submarines. The answers from the *Robalo* survivors read like the navy's textbook on the fleet-type submarine, including such arcane details as the current consumed by the electric motors in a submarine, the cost of each torpedo, and the effective radius of the surface radar units.

But the prisoners were not reliable. The Japanese interrogators realized that in some cases, the men were lying. So the captors planted a stool pigeon among the survivors, and that spy gathered more information. In a report based on his findings, Japanese officials wrote: "The prisoners are unhappy in confinement, and are uneasy about the treatment they will receive in the future. They believe firmly that America will win the war, but they fear that POWs will be shot when the American forces return to the Philippines, and they intend to escape."

Those who tried to break out were never treated gently. One survivor of the Puerto Princesa camp told of seeing his captors force four men, whose crime had been talking with natives and possessing several cans of corned beef, to hug a coconut tree.

"A Japanese would stand behind him with a wire whip approximately three feet long and severely lash him with all his strength across the center of the back. This lashing continued until the Japanese could swing no more. Another Japanese then stepped up with a pole approximately six feet in length and maybe two to three inches in diameter and severely beat the men across the buttocks until they too could swing no more," the survivor testified.

Perhaps it was a euphemism for one of their methods of questioning. The official Japanese report at Puerto Princesa said the *Robalo* survivors had been "pressed" for information concerning submarine bases in the Philippines, but had given no details.

"Since these men have intentions of escape, it is necessary to be on guard," the report concluded.

Rather than lose these prisoners, the Japanese arranged to send them to Manila aboard the ship *Takao Maru*, for further questioning.

Whatever their fate, it could have been no more horrific than what awaited the men who remained at Puerto Princesa, the place where all prisoners caught near Palawan were taken by the Japanese. The prisoners in this camp worked to build an airstrip a few miles north of the camp. From early morning until late evening, they hacked out the jungle vegetation—thick vines and towering trees—with only picks and shovels. Once the jungle was cleared, the men worked with one five-minute break per hour building the airstrip. Those who faltered in the sweltering sun were beaten. By October 1944, the prisoners were building revetments, dugouts, and gun positions for the planes and troops that would use the strip.

Then Allied bombers began attacking the field. The American prisoners who were officers asked their captors to provide air-raid shelters for them. The camp commandant ordered five shelters built near the prisoner barracks, each less than five feet deep. Three were trenches with thick covers and only one entrance. Two others were small holes, designed for three to four prisoners. Once inside one of these shelters, the prisoners had to sit with their knees pulled up under their chins to make room for their comrades. The Americans argued that more entrances were needed, and eventually, two entrances were made for each trench.

A double barbed-wire fence encircled the entire camp at Puerto Princesa, which stood between a Catholic cathedral and a fifty-foot-high cliff that descended to the northern shore of Puerto Princesa Bay. The air-raid shelters were in the center of this compound, some with one entrance on the cathedral end and another at the cliff end. The smaller shelters still had but one entrance each, and this was too small for more than one man to climb through at a time.

The bombing runs continued into December, and the commandant of the prison camp, seeing the work on the airstrip destroyed by the raids, grew incensed. By December 14, he could take no more. At two o'clock that afternoon, all the prisoners, having been brought in from the airfield, were standing in the air-raid shelter area. Japanese soldiers were stationed around them with rifles and machine guns. Some of the prisoners noticed that a pair of American P-38 airplanes were circling two miles overhead. The Japanese lieutenant in charge began yelling, and the guards ordered the prisoners into the shelters. Hundreds of American planes were coming, they screamed.

"No sooner had we got under cover when I heard a dull explosion and incessant yelling and laughing and the shooting of machine guns and rifles," marine gunnery sergeant Douglas William Bogue testified after the war. "I immediately stuck my head out of the entrance of my shelter to see what was taking place. The first thing I saw was a black pillar of smoke coming from the entrance of A Company shelter. In the few seconds that I had my head up, I was able to see the following events:

"It appeared to me that approximately fifty to sixty Jap soldiers, armed with rifles, hand grenades, light machine guns and buckets containing gasoline, with torches, were attacking this A Company shelter. With these buckets of gasoline they were thrown into the entrance of A Company shelter, then a lighted torch was thrown in to ignite the gasoline; and, as the men were forced to come out on fire, they were bayoneted or shot or clubbed or stabbed. I saw several of these men tumbling about, still on fire, and falling from being shot."

In all, 154 prisoners would die that afternoon, some of them slaughtered when, having escaped the burning pits, they dove over the cliff, only to find more Japanese soldiers there to shoot them or kill them with bayonets.

"The Japanese soldiers participating were yelling and in such a manner that it seemed to me as if they were enjoying their task," Bogue testified. "This Lieutenant Sato (the man in charge) was running about with his sword out, giving orders, urging his men on."

Bogue, like some others, made a dash for the cliff and, after fighting off some Japanese soldiers, hid in some rocks near the bottom of the cliff. He testified he could hear the sounds of explosions and the screams of dying prisoners and could smell their burning flesh. He eventually escaped by swimming the two miles across Puerto Princesa Bay, crawling ashore and heading into the thick jungle. It was there that Bogue eventually met some guerrillas, who sheltered him until the war ended.

The men of *Robalo* were not among the few survivors of the Puerto Princesa massacre, nor were any of them recorded among the dead prisoners. Whether they were all aboard *Takao Maru* when it left Puerto Princesa harbor, and whether the ship ever reached its destination, is unclear. But none of the crewmen of the submarine *Robalo* returned home from the war.

CHAPTER 10

BACK TOWARD GLORY

There was no rousing send-off scene as in the movies, where the grim, pipe-smoking admiral calls the dazzlingly handsome, rock-solid submarine commander in and says: "Walt, it's up to you now. Go out there and get 'em!"

John Crowley, a thirty-five-year-old man with the physical contours of a dumpling that camouflaged his steely courage, made several visits to Admiral Christie's headquarters in Fremantle in the final days of July, 1944. But these meetings were with Christie's subordinates, not with the admiral. And the skipper was by no means free to ad-lib his way through this war. Detailed orders for *Flier*'s second patrol had to mesh with instructions given to scores of other submarines. All those individual orders had to dovetail with naval maneuvers now being orchestrated all across the Pacific. Above all, Crowley's assignment had to fit within the schemes that General MacArthur—who in April had moved his headquarters from Brisbane, Australia, to Hollandia, New Guinea—was hatching for retaking the Philippines on his way to conquering Japan.

Murray J. Tichenor, a navy captain, was Christie's operations officer. He had a subordinate, Commander Jensen. These two men were responsible for planning the coordinated use of all the submarines at their disposal at the end of July. When Tichenor and Jensen had developed a preliminary plan, they took it to Christie, who, when he was satisfied, gave his approval. Jensen wrote the individual "operations order"—the assignment for the upcoming patrol of a boat such as *Flier*—taking into consideration how that submarine's work could contribute to the overall plan.

Once he had received the plan for *Flier* from Jensen, Tichenor—who was constantly in discussions with Crowley and Jensen—reworked the proposal. Crowley by then had also been talking with Christie's intelligence officer. They had discussed what the intelligence people had learned that might help Crowley out on the open sea. Among other things, they talked about Japanese ship traffic routes and the experiences of other submarines on past patrols.

The final operations order for *Flier* was passed through the chain of command to Christie, who gave his approval. That done, Crowley was once again briefed by Jensen and Tichenor, and his written, top-secret orders were handed to him. For *Flier*'s second patrol, they instructed the skipper to cruise in the South China Sea, a vast rectangle of ocean 600 miles across between the Philippines on the east and Vietnam—then called Indochina—on the west, and extending from Borneo in the south 800 miles to China in the north.

Crowley was to reach his patrol area by nearly reversing his route south a month earlier from the Sulu Sea to Australia: heading north across the Indian Ocean, squirting through Lombok Strait, dashing across the Java Sea, and then sneaking through Makassar Strait. Then *Flier* was to cross the Celebes Sea and pass north through the Sibutu Passage before once again reaching the Sulu Sea. When Crowley found himself in these familiar waters, he was then to head west, toward Balabac Strait.

This last leg was precisely the route Manning Kimmel on *Robalo* had been ordered to take six weeks earlier.

It was only after Crowley had read these instructions that the admiral called him into his office and gave him a pep talk. The day was August 1, and the orders directed *Flier* to leave the next day.

Crowley was smiling when, on a stage with props designed for the purpose, he gathered the same day with his officers and crew for the photograph that would record their departure. The photographer placed the skipper dead center in the second of four rows of men. An officer was to his left, an enlisted man to his right. Al Jacobson was in front of him, kneeling with Lieutenant James Liddell, the executive officer, and several other officers. Above them, most sailors smiled, many draping their arms around their buddies, with the same mix of bravado and trepidation experienced by fraternity brothers who are just about to graduate from their sheltering university. Mysteriously, in the upper right-hand corner, in the top row of sailors, was a beautiful young woman with long dark hair that fell to her stylishly wide blouse collar, the points of which were splayed across even wider jacket lapels. As the photographer triggered the shutter, she looked down at a young man to her left in the third row. Her expression was beatific as she reached behind the man to rest a hand on his far shoulder. Directly in front of her, a young sailor tilted his head back, chin skyward, as if to get a final look at this gorgeous girl. The boy's ears stuck out on either side and his cheeks bunched just like those of that girl-crazy eighteen-year-old Elton Brubaker. The camera clicked, and the strength of the woman's reassuring smile was engraved forever in the official navy portrait of the *Flier*'s crew, an image that remained unexplained sixty years later.

The next day, a Wednesday, *Flier* and her crew cast off from the dock along with the submarines *Bluefish* and *Rasher.* Elton was excited that he and Hestel Walker, on *Rasher,* were going to sea together. Just before he left, he sat down to write a letter home, knowing that it would be more than a month before he was again in port.

"I don't have time to write but one letter," he apologized, "so this is for the whole family. I hope you understand. I had a letter from Lewis and it seems that he still has the idea about the Navy, but as I have said before, the place to be is in college; tell him that. Georgia Tech or [the] University of Florida is a heck of a lot better than this for an education."

Then the boy spoke to his mother, the one person in the world whom he most wanted to impress, for whose approval he ached. "I [meant] to tell you this before but I know how you feel about the thing which I am about to bring up." He had to ease into the subject, had to prepare his mother. "I have my eye on a girl that I like very much, and if I still think as much of her when the war is over as I do now, I'll take her home to see how you and [Dad] like her. I have already told her about my finishing school and going to college; she is willing to wait for me and work her own way until I have finished my education. I have known her for fourteen months and haven't seen her in ten months. [S]he writes me more regular than either you or Charlotte, so you see, she must care a little about me. Don't go getting mad at me because I'm never taking a girl home to be my wife if you start getting that way.

"This is a long time off and a thing of the future," the boy assured his mother. "You will have a chance to find out what kind of girl she is, and I'm sure you have an idea who she is.

"I can't write again for a long time, so please keep writing, and so long." He signed the letter "Much love, Elton S. Brubaker."

Al Jacobson found that he had time to write one more letter just before leaving. He was at least as eager to please his parents as Elton had been to get his mother's blessing.

"I had a chance to visit the largest foundry they had in the town or in that section of the country," he reported to his father, being coy about his location in order to get his letter past the censors. "However, as is true with everything else here, their equipment and methods were many years behind the times." Then he got into the arcane details of casting brass in Australia.

Before signing off, he reported that the crew had just been awarded combat pins for their last patrol. "They make a big ceremony out of it, which makes you feel important and big so you'll be in good spirits for going back to sea," he commented. "These pins are only given to the officers and crew of submarines that sink a certain number of tons on a patrol, and everybody doesn't get them. So you can see we didn't do bad. Really have to stop now, for [it's] back to sea for me."

Traveling up the relatively safe western coast of Australia, *Flier, Rasher,* and *Bluefish* could remain surfaced. In one day, they had

reached Exmouth Gulf, a large bay about halfway between Fremantle and Darwin. The route from here to Lombok Strait led due north,
so there was no reason for *Flier* to follow the other boats to Darwin.
Crowley could top off his fuel tanks here and be on his way. It was late
afternoon when the submarine reached the dock. Crowley decided
to spend the night. The officers went ashore, trading their cave-like
bunks in the steel-and-cork sterility of "officer country" for the comforts of the bachelor officers' quarters. At the BOQ, they met a contingent of Australian commandos who were in training for a future raid
on the biggest Japanese oil refinery in the southwest Pacific, on Borneo. The commandos had in common with each other an aptitude for
problem solving, a fact that the *Flier* officers discovered as they shared
experiences with the Australians.

Crowley, making conversation, complained that during the refit at
Fremantle, his submarine had not been equipped with a radar reflector. Standard equipment now aboard submarines was a device that,
when towed behind the sub, would make the boat appear to be two
vessels on radar. One of the commandoes said it would be no problem
for them to make a reflector, and by morning they presented Crowley
with their handiwork: an aluminum triangle five feet across, fabricated
from the floorboards of a crashed airplane. The triangle was mounted
on a wooden raft, and the whole thing could be collapsed and stowed
under *Flier*'s after cigarette deck. Crowley thanked the commandoes
and wished them well.

After the crew had brushed their teeth, washed their faces, and
shaved in the one cup of water that the parched Exmouth Gulf rationed
to them, they cast off their lines to begin their second patrol in earnest.
On the way out of the gulf, Crowley stopped near an abandoned ship
and gave his gunner's mate and crew some time for target practice
with the deck gun. Then they headed north once more.

The trip to Lombok Strait was scheduled to take about two days,
but when *Flier* was twelve hours south of the strait, a huge explosion
rocked the boat. If Al Jacobson, relaxed from his R&R in Australia,
thought as he sat once again at the chart table that he had seen everything during the excitement of the first patrol, the concussion that

blasted now through the control room eliminated that illusion. The control-room phone jangled on the wall. It was the forward engine room, reporting that something serious was wrong with one of the four engines. The sailor with the phone relayed the message up through the conning-tower hatch to Crowley, who sent Ensign Behr, his onboard mechanic, to investigate. In a few minutes, Behr reported back. The forward port engine was blown and would need major repairs. Crowley contemplated turning back to Australia, but Behr, the former chief petty officer, told him to hold on—he might be able to fix the problem.

The noise in the engine room of any ship is deafening. Normal conversation is typically impossible. And in the forward engine room of *Flier*, there were two engines—the crippled one on the port side, and the starboard engine, which was running well. Behr could not work with the racket and vibration, so as the submarine resumed its trek toward Lombok, it was running with just the two engines in the aft engine room generating the electricity needed to both run the motors that turned the two propellers and to recharge the batteries.

Behr's challenge was not that of a garage mechanic working on a Ford. Each engine in *Flier*'s belly was the size of a pickup truck and rose from near the boat's keel, up through the engine room's main deck—the deck that ran the length of the boat from the forward torpedo room, through the control room, and back to the aft torpedo room. Each of these massive engines produced 1,600 horsepower to drive an electrical generator connected directly to it and housed under the deck.

The ensign-mechanic set to work with a few helpers, including a new man on the boat, Wesley Miller, a twenty-year-old from Oregon who was a long way from the cattle ranch of his youth. The forward engine room is to the rear of the crew mess and the crew quarters, and every sailor who worked farther back in the submarine had to make his way over the deck between the two engines to reach his station or to get to meals and a bunk. For most of the next twenty-four hours, until *Flier* approached the southern entrance to Lombok Strait, Behr and his detail worked around this flow of sailors. The sea was rough and *Flier* was rolling too much when it was time to do heavy lifting, so the skipper gave the order to dive. Behr had discovered that back in Fremantle, a valve had been improperly closed on a ventilation line, causing fumes to build up inside the engine. The result was the explosion that had rocked the boat. A cylinder liner and a couple of pistons would have to be replaced. The cylinder head would have to be removed using a heavy hoist. All the equipment was on board, so this was a job Behr could accomplish.

But now *Flier* was at the entrance to Lombok Strait. The repairs would have to cease, because Crowley needed all the power his three good engines could provide.

Once more, the skipper kept *Flier* submerged until dark. Then he blew enough air into the ballast tanks that *Flier's* deck just poked above the surface, allowing the engine air vents to be opened. The radar operator in the conning tower watched his screen, tracking the movement of the two Japanese patrol boats that were posted to keep out submarines. When both patrol boats had reached the same side, Crowley, sure they would remain there for a while, gave the order for full speed ahead, and the three working engines gave the submarine enough juice to race through the strait.

After *Flier's* bow had splashed north into the Java Sea, Behr finished his work and *Flier's* repaired engine worked flawlessly. Everyone relaxed.

Perhaps Elton Brubaker did not relax. He was meeting shipmates, hearing stories. After the first patrol, there were plenty of tales to tell, and who better to hear them than an eager young seaman. Probably before he had ever set foot on *Flier,* he had heard that the boat was jinxed. It was the word going around, a story that had its roots in the Midway grounding. Some sailors actually tried to get their orders changed when, in Fremantle, they had been assigned to *Flier.*

Elton Brubaker was not one who flinched from this boat. Happy to be aboard, he stood watch in the control room when he had no chores to do. Here and in the conning tower, everyone was a veteran of at least the first patrol. Charles Pope, the man who had been swept overboard when *Flier* was being towed back to Hawaii by *Florikan,* was operating the radar up in the conning tower, alternating shifts with Arthur Gibson Howell, who had been radar man at Midway. The story of that grounding alone, and of Pope's heroic work to reconnect the *Florikan* towline, were enough to impress a green sailor. In the long hours as the submarine steamed north, the rest of the veterans in the control room could swap tales, from depth-charge attacks to an ocean littered with Japanese corpses, from jammed diving planes to the sounds of an enemy ship breaking up.

There was never a time on *Flier* when a young man was left entirely alone with his thoughts. The boat was designed for fewer than seventy men, yet had eighty-six aboard. This meant that everyone with a rating below first class had to share a bunk. If you happened to be on a lower bunk—particularly the one at floor level—there was little room to turn over when you slept. And if the fellow with whom you were sharing stayed in bed, you had to wait to get your turn.

Cozy as the bunkroom was, and outgoing as Elton had always been, there was every likelihood that he would quickly get to know the men around him. From Earl Baumgart, with whom he shared a fondness for beer, he could learn about the perils of riding a breeches buoy. And Donald Tremaine, a Californian who had been in the navy five years, could give him one seasoned sailor's complaints about the officers of the boat. Tremaine had met Elton and, if he chose, he would tell Elton that the same officers now running *Flier* had directed him to lie to investigators and say that the sailor lost at Midway was wearing a life jacket.

When he heard a story like Tremaine's, one with a moral question, Elton could think back to the Brubaker home in San Mateo, to the bossy older sister and the adoring younger brother, to the mother who more often than not was away from home, earning the family keep, and the father who, when discipline was needed, would walk to the peach tree behind the house for a supple switch. There was an order in that household that could be relied on. If the roles of the parents were unconventional, the reversal was only due to Emil Brubaker's lameness from polio. The reversed roles taught a lesson: When there is trouble, find a way around it. Both Emil and Nellie

May threw themselves with purpose into their respective family duties. And they maintained a moral code which each of their children could identify. God came first, with family right up there. The Brubakers were proud people with a strong work ethic, private and modest, with no ostentation.

Saturdays, when everyone was home and the place was perfumed with wood smoke, was the time when chores were done. Elton and Lewis built a fire in the backyard under an iron pot four feet in diameter. When the water in the pot was boiling, they added Octagon Soap, which they broke into smaller pieces so it would dissolve. Once the clothes were in the water, the boys poked at them with broom handles until their mother decided it was time for her to use the washboard. Nellie May would hang the clothes and, when they were dry, iron them with one of three flatirons that she heated on the wood-burning kitchen stove.

Under a Depression-era program, the family had received forty acres and a mule, and, to prepare the land for raising vegetables and fruit, the boys had helped Emil clear the land with grub axes and Lil, the mule. A stream flowed through the property, which was down the country road from the family home, and the soil near the water was rich, unlike the rest of the sandy earth. Elton knew that the rich soil provided good crops while the sand produced little. There were broader lessons to be drawn from facts such as these—lessons in living. Be productive and be valued. As teenagers, Elton and Lewis were valued as the family woodcutters, felling trees and cutting them to length with a long crosscut saw, then splitting the pieces for firewood.

Before he joined the navy, Elton had proved his work ethic beyond the boundaries of the San Mateo home. In Boy Scouts, he had earned the rank of Star Scout. After working for Mr. Dunklin, the electrician and scoutmaster, he got a job in a little shipyard on the St. Johns River in Palatka, helping to build wooden picket boats, forty-foot-long patrol boats used by the navy. He was a role model as well as a hard worker. Lewis, when he got old enough, emulated his older brother and got a job at the shipyard, as well. Then Elton got a job a dozen miles away in St. Augustine at the Alhambra Hotel, working as a bellhop. The hotel was a bustling place, often filled with soldiers on leave. Elton carried suitcases up to the rooms and delivered room service, all for tips.

It had been about this time that Elton, feeling an adolescent's need for identity, decided people should call him "Al." And he also began smoking a pipe—straight-stemmed, not curved like his father's. His next step in finding himself was joining the navy.

Inside *Flier,* Elton finally became a man, bonded like a brother with the other men, an equal in many respects because the others had to rely on him to do his job, to keep the submarine safe.

At first, Elton's job involved the same hands-and-knees survey of the ship that Al Jacobson, an officer, had conducted. Elton was not yet a qualified submariner, and the only way to achieve that distinction was to poke around the boat and learn everything about it. As *Flier* traveled north through Makassar Strait and headed for the Celebes Sea, he found himself spending all his free time following the same pipes and wires Al had traced three months earlier.

Alvin Jacobson, on the other hand, was now a qualified submariner. This meant that when he was not on watch, he could relax in the wardroom with other officers and play that peculiar game involving pegs and a board that he had learned during the first patrol—cribbage.

Or he could take out the many letters that had been waiting for him when he got to Fremantle. Rereading them made him feel closer to home.

On May 27, the week of Al's birthday, his father had handed his secretary some tidbits of news to be typed. "Charles seems to be very much disgusted and wants to get a transfer," Al Sr. noted of his oldest son. "Here's hoping you run into him out there some place.

"If you remember Carl Johnson from Grand Haven, he has been sent out to New Guinea, and David Johnston is also out there some place. It would be a lot of fun for you undoubtedly to meet some of the Grand Haven boys."

Well, that would not be happening for at least another month, the ensign knew. *Flier* had more than 100,000 gallons of fuel in its tanks, most of which would be consumed before he again touched land.

His father's letter then settled into the predictable.

"You remember Mr. Berman of the Vita Motivator Co. He was here last week conducting some experiments on some new jobs. At the present time we have $432,000 worth of business booked up for these valves and . . ."

The next letter was written four days after Al's birthday.

"Well, how does it seem to be twenty-two?" his father's secretary typed. "We had the usual crowd out to the cottage for Decoration Day, but we certainly missed you boys as there was no sailing." Father said the family probably would not put its sailboat on Spring Lake this summer.

A letter on June 12 from Al Sr. expanded on this theme. "Mother and I took a ride over to the Yacht Club yesterday, and it is absolutely deserted—things look rather upset." If Al could read between the lines, his father was longing for his boys. The next letter confirmed the sentiment. "I was out sailing this afternoon, but it did not seem like old times with you boys around here." Then he went on to mention that "Sister is home and it seems good to have her around. She drove a car full of girls down to Church Conference near Three Rivers today—she got through with school in fine shape."

On this day, Al Sr. was full of news. "Grandma and Helen and Russell and family and Virginia were over today, and Helen had a little hard luck—she got a chicken bone in her throat, and they are having a little hard time getting it out—she cannot lie down and has to sit up—they went back to Muskegon to try to get hold of a specialist to take it out."

Then the father returned to the theme, the emotion that finally was breaking through all the talk of foundries and business. "At home now there is only Sis, Mother and I, so perhaps it will be a little quiet for a week. Was out and played nine holes of golf Friday afternoon—it seemed good. So, when you get a chance to get back to Hawaii, you had better practice a little so we can have a good game when all of you boys get back home.

"As ever . . ."

The ensign knew that back home on the kitchen wall, there was a large map of the world with pins stuck in the places where Al, Chuck, and David were stationed. And in the front window of the two-story clapboard Victorian home with its steeply pitched gables, tall, skinny chimney, and carved pineapple over the front door was an American flag with three stars—one for each son in the military.

Inside that home on Lafayette Street, the mail delivery was the high—and low—point of every day. At lunch and dinner, the family's conversations revolved around the adventures of the boys, except on Saturday when the Grand Ole Opry radio broadcast occupied the dinner hour. Every time the family got a letter from one of the boys, Mrs. Hatton, who lived next door, came over to read it. Her husband was a businessman like Al Sr. He had a leather company. Mrs. Hatton was a homemaker and had been like a grandmother to Al and his brothers and sisters, so she wanted to follow their exploits, keeping track of the pins on the map.

Right now, Al's pin should have been moving north as *Flier* entered the Sibutu Passage, towing its wooden raft and radar reflector by a rope 200 yards long. The trip was going smoothly for most of the men aboard the submarine. When the boat was surfaced, two of the sailors who had started the trip belowdecks now found themselves standing watch, clinging to the superstructure above the bridge, scanning the daytime horizon or the blackness of night for enemy ships and planes.

The first few days out of Fremantle, Earl Baumgart had stood watch in the after engine room, ready to help with whatever chores needed to be done. Perhaps it was because he, a Milwaukee lad with a homegrown thirst, had consumed too much of that good Australian beer. He had to admit that this was a possible explanation for why he found himself reduced from motor machinist mate third class to fireman first class. He had already been busted when a chief told him he looked like he needed some fresh air. The chief assigned him to stand watch topside when *Flier* was surfaced. Baumgart thought the chief was overly sarcastic, and he did not want to give up his cozy assignment belowdecks. But Crowley would not intervene in a decision like this made by a chief. With no help from above, Baumgart was left clinging to the A-frame high above the rear of the bridge. After a few nights of this duty, Baumgart began to enjoy it, even if he still wanted to fight his demotion. Particularly at night, the balmy sea air was refreshing after the confinement of the submarine.

Standing watch on the other side of the A-frame was Wesley Miller. When *Flier* left Fremantle, he had been working with Baumgart in the after engine room. He had helped Ensign Behr repair the damage from the explosion, but a couple of days later, he got word that he would be standing watch topside. Another sailor with a rating senior to Miller had been on lookout duty and complained that he had not been given a chance to get training in the engine room. Outranked, Miller was sent up to peer into the night sky.

He did not complain. But then, unlike Baumgart, Miller had not been demoted. And out there in the darkness, there were enemies to be conquered, medals to win, and glory to be won.

CHAPTER 11

TRAPPED IN THE PATH OF WAR

Nearly seven months had passed since the grounding on Midway when, on August 12, the now-battle-tested *Flier* approached Sibutu Passage like a slugger stepping into the batter's box. On the far side of this strait was the Sulu Sea, nearly 90,000 square miles of unbroken blue water shaped roughly like a baseball diamond. Sibutu Passage was home plate. The opposing team—the Japanese soldiers and sailors—had taken all the land around that diamond two years earlier. They were scattered along the first-base line, a string of islands called the Sulu Archipelago that ended in Mindanao, more than 200 miles to the northeast. More Japanese troops were strung along the islands from first base to second—Mindoro, at the top of the diamond, 500 miles due north. The enemy also held third base—the small island of Balabac to the northwest—as the doomed crew of *Robalo* had discovered. And the huge island nation of Borneo, due west of Sibutu Passage, was thick with supporting troops, like the bench-dwellers in the dugout. Throughout the more than 7,000 Philippine islands and their Indonesian and Malaysian neighbors, the Japanese navy and army were arrayed in what until now had been an almost impenetrable defense. Americans entered the Sulu Sea only by submarine, and when they did, they knew it was kill or be killed in this deadly World Series.

Of course the Philippines was not a land of conquerors alone. Throughout these green islands, men and women—most of whom called the Philippines home, and some of whom were foreign visitors before being stranded here by the war—lived from one day to the next in their vast tropical prison. The threads of their social fabric had, in thirty-one months, frequently become unraveled. Their neighbors were always suspect, and the threat of death was a constant reality. But somehow their communities lived on, clinging to the hope brought by the next sunrise.

As *Flier* circled north and west around Borneo, the six American Coastwatchers who two months earlier had been deposited on Ramos Island were settling into their new community on Palawan— Brooke's Point—and getting to know its people. The trip there in early July had begun at night, with three *bancas*—long, slender outrigger boats—being towed by a fourth boat with a motor. It was still dark when this flotilla grounded on the beach sand at Buliluyan Point, the southern tip of Palawan. In the morning, the Americans drank coffee, an unexpected treat, with their breakfast in the guerrillas' palm-shaded encampment. As the travelers rested under the thatched roof of a bamboo house, the local guerrilla commander, Sergeant Pasqual de la Cruz, had his men slaughter a cow. While they waited for darkness to fall and their journey to resume, they ate a dinner of porterhouse steak with deputy governor Datu Jolkipli and Captain Mayor, the guerrilla leader. De la Cruz told his boss, Captain Mayor, that the Mayor family compound on nearby Bugsuk Island had been raided by the Japanese, who had burned four houses and taken the guerrilla leader's motor launch, which had been dry-docked. This did not surprise Mayor, who had evacuated his entire family from the island two years earlier when the Japanese were about to land.

That night, the four boats, loaded with the Coastwatchers' supplies, headed north once again, and by daybreak they had reached a broad bay on the northern tip of which was Brooke's Point. The bancas nudged ashore and the guerrilla leader's wife invited the six Americans into her home in a coconut grove just inland from the beach in a small village called Buligay. (The guerrilla base camp was a couple of miles south of the town of Brooke's Point.) Mary Mayor fed the Coastwatchers and, although it was daytime, they soon fell asleep.

Sergeant Corpus and the others rose after only a couple of hours, though, and began to search for an ideal location for their radio equipment. As they fanned out from Buligay, they discovered a countryside of breathtaking beauty. The blue waves of the Sulu Sea and Ipolote Bay lapped up on a gray beach where the sand was as fine as ash. The beach curved to the west and south like the edge of a blade without a nick, and looking along the shore the men could see, beyond the arc of sand, green mountains that seemed to tumble down from the heartland. Looking west, even with the coconut trees close at hand, they saw the summit of Addison's Peak, more than 3,000 feet high and sharp as an eyetooth. It had been renamed by Europeans who apparently were unsatisfied with its native name, Maruyog. Behind this green spire, the brooding blue hulks of greater inland mountains rose to the dark monsoon clouds. The greatest of these jungle peaks was 6,740-foot-high Mount Mantalingajan, a nonvolcanic rock that is Palawan's highest point. Coconut trees—the edge of the plantation started by Thomas Edwards twenty or more years ago—began at the beach and crossed the coastal plain, stretching toward the mountains in the west.

The Coastwatchers began to learn the lay of the land and its settlements: Macagua (*MA-ka-gwa*), eight miles up in the foothills, where the Edwardses had their wartime home; Tubtub, surrounded by the coconut plantation, and in the same direction from the beach as Macagua, but much closer; Pangobilian, to the north in the rice paddies, several miles from Buligay (*BOO-li-guy*), and Saraza (*sa-RA-sa*), to the south, in the coastal plain. Each village—and even Brooke's Point, with its 100 permanent homes—was watched over by Addison Peak, whose authoritative presence was a common landmark for everyone on this coast.

It rained the next day, a Friday, but not enough to slow the spreading news that the Coastwatchers had radios. A crowd began to gather in Buligay, outside the Mayor family's home. Perhaps, the locals thought, they would hear some news. Since January, 1942, there had been very little reliable information from the rest of the world.

With the patter of rain on the Mayors' thatched roof above them, Butch Rallojay and Carlos Placido worked on one radio, hoping once again to receive a signal from General MacArthur's headquarters and, with luck, hear the *Philippine Hour* news broadcast. But the radio would not work, and the crowd went back to their villages, disappointed.

The next morning, the men trudged west across the plantation and up the foothills to Macagua, where the Edwards family welcomed them. Like the people on the coast, they too wanted news. On Sunday, after a good night's rest in Macagua, the Coastwatchers again were the center of attention. Since no one worked on the Christian Sabbath, the day was spent in conversation with a stream of curious visitors.

Macagua—or, at least the Edwards property there—occupied not only the gently rising coastal plain but also the first steep sides of the inland mountains. Thomas and Rosario Edwards had located this, their bamboo and thatched-roof evacuation home, a few hundred feet up the mountainside. From their front door, they looked down on terraced rice paddies and the veins of small mountain brooks that joined to form Macagua River, a modest stream. Beyond the rice, they could gaze over the coconut plantation as it spread like a nubbly green afghan to the sands of Ipolote Bay. Theirs was a world almost devoid of the war, except that it was also a life in retreat. They had adult children in the States whom they had not seen for years. They had lost a son early in the war, and had two daughters still in Macagua. They remained perhaps the most prominent family in the Brooke's Point region, but they lived with their backs against the malarial mountains, held in place by the threat of capture by the Japanese. They wanted their freedom, and in a small way, the Coastwatchers' radios could deliver a sense of liberty if only the Edwardses could receive some news. So that afternoon, Butch and Carlos again tinkered with their gear. This time, something connected. There, coming from a speaker, was the *Philippine Hour*, live from Brisbane! The Coastwatchers were celebrities from Saraza to Pangobilian, and from Brooke's Point to Macagua. They had brought light to a community that had been lost in the shadows of war.

Although it was the second-largest community on Palawan after Puerto Princesa, Brooke's Point was in reality an outpost, linked to the rest of the world by shipping alone. There were no roads from here to anyplace, only jungle trails, beaten down over the centuries by the natives whose descendants still roamed this area, dressed in tribal skirts as often as they wore Western clothes. There were no motor vehicles to speak of. All transportation was by horse or *carabao*, the local name for water buffalo. There had been some commerce and, as a result, some employment before the war. There was a school in town, as well as a few shops and some streets that dead-ended at the beach. Until the war, the countryside here was best known as the source of the world's largest pearl, called the Pearl of Allah, a fourteen-pound egg discovered in 1934 in the Buligay River.

Brooke's Point became a dot on the Philippine map when Thomas H. Edwards arrived in 1919, drawn by the fertile soil and the availability of steamer traffic. Harry, as he was known to everyone, had come to the Philippines on the ship *Thomas*, sent by the United States in 1901 to teach the Filipinos English and other subjects useful in trade. For seventeen years, Edwards taught in outlying islands and in Manila. In that time, he married Rosario, a young woman from Mindanao who had been his student, and they had their first child, a daughter, in 1913. Eventually, Harry became school superintendent for Palawan, and the family lived in Puerto Princesa. Then, at age thirty-nine, Harry decided he wanted a new challenge. For three months, he sailed a small boat down the coast of Palawan until he reached a place designated on the nautical charts as Sir J. Brooke Point. Since the Spanish-American War, the Philippines had been governed by the United States, and now Edwards—an American from Benton, Pennsylvania—was granted a government concession to harvest the land around Brooke's Point.

At first, logging seemed like the logical business. The mountains bristled with towering mahogany and other trees, and the transportation was at the beach, where steamers anchored. But in the mountains, Harry caught malaria, suffered from pneumonia, and was away from his wife and child too long. He saw that the gently rising forest between the coast and the mountains was layered in soil made rich by the rains that washed nutrients from the highlands. He hired natives to clear the land and to plant coconut trees, and brought additional workers from other parts of the Philippines, a smart business move because with little transportation, they had few prospects of going home once they arrived. With a stable labor force, Harry expanded his operations. There were 400 head of cattle, a sawmill at the beach in Brooke's Point, and a sari sari store, much like a frontier general store or a coal miner's company store, where his workers could spend their pay. The coconut meat was dried into copra that was sent to Manila by steamship to be processed into oil. Through another government concession, Edwards developed a business tapping almaciga trees for their resin, which could be used in making paint.

The Edwardses made a memorable couple. He was over six feet tall, she, about four feet. Both of them were driven to achieve. She, with the better business mind, watched in her bantam fury over the finances. He, the field supervisor, would rail in imprecise Tagalog at his workers: *Ikaw sa pag atrabaho!* ("You get to work!")

The Edwardses treated their children as they did the rest of the labor. Offspring were expected to work for their keep. Ruth, the oldest, ran the sari sari under her mother's supervision, and kept the company books.

Ruth was twenty-six when a humorously self-deprecating young man began shopping at the store. Jose Santos was a civil engineer with a government job, sent from Manila to oversee the construction of a pier on Ipolote Bay. He pursued Ruth. She gave him the brush-off, but he persisted, finally winning her heart when he played Chopin on the family piano. They married, and in August 1941, they were anticipating the birth of their first child when complications arose. Jose took Ruth to a hospital in Manila, where she delivered Elizabeth. The baby was fine, but Ruth needed medical attention, and the couple was still in the city on December 8, when the Japanese attacked. Together with some other Palawanos, they conspired to get a boat, and, at night, they sailed from Manila, heading for home, Elizabeth clutched in Ruth's arms. After many nights at sea, they turned their boat into Ipolote Bay and the men dragged it onto the beach. To their astonishment, there was not a soul in Brooke's Point.

Two weeks after the Japanese attacked Manila, the leader of the local guerrillas, a man by the name of Sergeant Tumbaga, came to the home of the Brooke's Point municipal treasurer, Eduardo Villapa, and told the family that they and all the other residents had to leave. Villapa gathered his wife, three sons, and six daughters, telling them to pack what they could. The next day, they began life on their farmland in rural Saraza. It was a peaceful life. The family raised crops, enough to feed themselves. They built native-style houses—bamboo poles lashed together in a frame, nipa leaves thatched as roofing, and *sawali*, or young bamboo, hammered flat and woven into mats to make walls and flooring. Villapa continued as town treasurer, his job to sign "scrip," the temporary currency used for trade and for paying the guerrillas. But with all of the stores in Brooke's Point closed, there was no place to spend the scrip. And with the schools closed, there were no classes for Villapa's nine children, or their friends. For children like the Villapas', the school vacation was paid for by moments of terror when a Japanese plane would fly by and they would be ordered to *Run! Run!* and to hide under a coconut tree.

Families fled from Brooke's Point to various outposts, and the more capable—or those who already owned land—survived by planting crops of corn, root plants, vegetables, and camote, a type of sweet potato. They improvised with stones to grind the corn. They could cook on fires as usual, but were told to keep other fires to a minimum so that they would not be targets for Japanese planes.

The Japanese almost never landed near Brooke's Point, thanks largely to the guerrillas' efforts. But there had been, early in the war, a more intimate enemy. Families collected stories about their encounters with the guerrillas and the bolo battalion, whose members were often little more than thugs. The bolo battalion torched one family's home in Brooke's Point after they had evacuated. They demanded medicine from another man, who had been sent by the government before the war to serve as a physician; this man had performed operations without anesthesia, had sewn ears back on that had been severed by bolos, and had delivered most of the local babies.

At times, the early guerrillas and their helpers bullied many of the local residents for their crops and livestock. Angry with these goons, one man—Modesto Rodriguez—met with their leaders and made an offer: five head of cattle, or the equivalent of rice each week for the guerrillas and bolo battalion if the harassment stopped. If it did not, he would join the Japanese.

There were bandits, as well. They were assumed by the Christian town residents to be Muslims. Despite the teachings of their Savior, the Christians had no love for these fellow citizens and judged them all as barbarians. Evidence certainly proves that some of these felons were Muslims.

On one occasion, for example, a band of men armed with bolos approached Jose Santos at his home in Brooke's Point, demanding that he take them to the Edwardses' home in Macagua. He had been warned that the men intended to rob Edwards, and he passed the word along before him. Then he led the gang up through the coconut plantation to the Edwards compound. There, Harry Edwards, armed with a rifle, confronted the men, told them to drop their bolos, which they did, and then lectured them on the rule of law. Edwards reported the men to Datu Jolkipli, upon whose wisdom Edwards had often relied. The datu dealt with the men, to the satisfaction of Edwards and the other Christians.

The complaints against the guerrillas and bolo battalion ended once Nazario Mayor became the guerrilla commander. Now, as long as the Brooke's Point residents managed to evade the Japanese patrols that cruised near the beaches, their only threats came from nature—the mosquitoes inland that carried malaria, and the saltwater crocodiles swimming along the coast and in the Buligay and other tidal rivers. A crocodile had killed a man who had been fishing by the Buligay. Unaware that the animal was near, he probably never knew that the massive tail of the animal had struck him, knocking him unconscious. The beast then took him in its mouth to administer a crunching finish. The crocodile then walked away, waiting a few days until the corpse had rotted before dragging it into the river and devouring the flesh. Later, when the crocodile climbed out of the river, another man killed it.

To combat malaria, there was an extremely bitter root called *makahiya* that seemed to work when boiled—but not always. In every family, there was someone with malaria. Once contracted, the disease returned at will, leaving the victim with cold sweats, high fevers, and, at times, in a coma or hallucinating.

Alexander Sutherland's malaria had begun in Brooke's Point before the war. The Scotsman arrived in Palawan in 1932 as a Protestant missionary. In 1936, he returned to Scotland and married Mary, whom he called Maisie. They sailed back to Brooke's Point and continued the ministry he had begun. Then came the war.

The Sutherlands, like Job in the Bible, seemed to experience every deprivation that the times could inflict. Theirs was a trial shared by many of their neighbors and illustrated the perils of life in Brooke's Point.

By 1941, the Sutherlands had a year-old daughter, Heather, and a three-year-old son, Alistair. All four were infected with malaria, and Alistair was particularly ill. For medical help, the family sailed north to Manila, and when they all seemed well, they boarded a ship and arrived in Brooke's Point in late November. Two weeks later, the war began, and all connection with Manila and the world beyond ceased.

On New Year's Day, 1942, the Japanese air force raided Puerto Princesa. When news of the attack reached Brooke's Point, the guerrilla leader told the residents to evacuate. The Sutherlands gathered a few belongings in their home, which had been built by Japanese carpenters on the beach only a few years earlier. They loaded their stuff into a cart provided by Harry Edwards and began a trek. A native guide led them to Imulnod, a mountain valley village northwest of Brooke's Point. Along the way, they passed the Villapa family struggling with their possessions across the Tigaplan River. Once in the mountains, they settled into a partially finished bamboo hut that, when completed, was rather comfortable. On tropical Palawan, a house needed to provide shelter only from the rain and sun, and a well-constructed "nipa hut" did this quite well. The Sutherland home seemed ideally located, since a branch of the small Imulnod River passed nearby, providing water. But the stream also harbored mosquitoes and malaria.

Alexander and Maisie Sutherland were, in stature, the exact opposites of Harry and Rosario Edwards. She was tall and slender, he noticeably shorter and squarely built. He had been a professional rugby player in Scotland and then an aspiring oil company employee before he decided to become a clergyman. He departed his homeland as a missionary after two years of medical training, and in Brooke's Point, he quickly became the town physician. He dispensed quinine for malaria and anti-dysentery medicine to combat the second most troublesome local illness. He traveled by foot from settlement to settlement. When he had to cross a stream, he would bark like a dog because he knew the crocodiles liked dog meat and would surface at the sound.

In the social order of the town, Alexander and Maisie were the equals of the merchants and other businessmen, a full step above the Muslims, who made up most of the local population, and two steps above the natives. Unlike the merchants and businesspeople, some of whom were Chinese who had fled Puerto Princesa after the Japanese invasion, the Sutherlands had no personal wealth. And unlike most businesspeople in town, who also owned farms scattered across the landscape where they raised crops, the Sutherlands had no land except for their beachfront home. Their job was the introduction of the unaware to the Christian religion, and with medical work as their entrée, they reached out for neighbors to convert. Their income came from church collections back in Scotland, a flow that ceased when the war stopped the steamships.

Evacuation from Brooke's Point presented the Sutherlands with several problems, including lack of food and the threat to their health and personal safety. Occasionally they were given food by their neighbors, but at other times they had to either spend their dwindling cash or barter with household items. The sources of illness were everywhere, and now they were camped beside a mosquito breeding ground.

And with the collapse of all forms of government, lawlessness became a way of life for some neighbors. The locals had a name for it: mundo fever. A *mundo* was an armed bandit who killed to rob. Two groups of mundos were organized near the Sutherlands' home in

Imulnod. The Sutherlands viewed all of their neighbors as wild and savage, and believed they were being watched. They had been told that people thought they were rich and had a cache of money buried near their bamboo hut. They understood that they were categorized with the Chinese, who had become targets of the bandits.

One day, two Chinese men—one of whom had already given the minister chickens, eggs, and a milking cow—arrived at their hut on horses. The men warned the minister that his family and their white friends would be victims of the mundos. Before the men left, they gave the family some cash, the first infusion they had received since the war started. Alexander then made a quick trip to Macagua to warn Harry Edwards, who had a trading post and other interests in Imulnod. Edwards decided to abandon Imulnod, and the Sutherlands—not ready to quit the place entirely because they had won some converts there—moved back to Brooke's Point for what they thought would be a brief visit.

There was no food in Brooke's Point, however, and when some Chinese friends invited them to move north to another village, Punang, they packed what they could and left on two boats loaded to the gunwales, one with a tiny motor towing the other. Traveling in blistering heat, they had almost reached their destination—just two miles away on the far side of a mangrove swamp—when the engine quit. In this festering tropical wildlife sanctuary, they dragged the boats the final stretch.

The deterioration of their voyage predicted the future course of their lives. For the next month, the Sutherlands lived cramped in one small room in a home already occupied by two Chinese families. They were sick with malaria. The food was poorly cooked. The dry season, normally two to three months, did not end, and water became scarce. For drinking water, they hiked close to a mile to a dry riverbed where they dug a hole, into which brackish, discolored water seeped. Their room was in a house on the bank of the crocodile-infested Punang River, and their entertainment, as they sat parched and aching with disease in the suffocating heat, was watching the animals in the river.

After a month, they moved inland to Pinoltol, a settlement upstream on the Punang River. The water supply was marginally improved in this isolated place. Their home was a bamboo hut they built with a roof and walls made of palm leaves. Soon, however, the place filled to bursting with Chinese families fleeing the Japanese. The drinking water was becoming more foul as men and women crowded the waterholes in the river to bathe and wash clothes. Moreover, the Sutherlands' diet was deteriorating. The jungle around Pinoltol provided lots of wild pigs that could be easily speared, but the Sutherlands had finally consumed the last of their flour. Most of their meals—the corn, chickens, fish, and the firewood to cook them—came from trading their used clothing, dishes, needles, and thread—and even their empty tin cans.

Fear ruled the Sutherlands. When word was passed that a Japanese launch had anchored off the beach, the family fled into the hills. Alexander had already located a steep gorge that led to a good hideout. He hustled Maisie and the children up a dry riverbed to the gorge. Then he headed back to town for a rice pot they had left behind. Maisie pleaded with him to stay with her, and when he left, she huddled with the children, weeping because she was certain her husband would be slaughtered. She was calmed by her son, Alistair.

"Don't cry, Mummy," the child told her. "God will take care of us."

It had been a false alarm. The minister discovered when he reached their home that some Chinese refugees, not Japanese soldiers, had come in the motor launch.

But everyone in the little community was on edge. Men patrolled every night, on guard for Japanese soldiers and mundo bandits. When the Sutherlands learned that a boat was preparing to sail south, past Brooke's Point, they got on board, hoping that closer to home they would be protected from bandits, at least, by Datu Jolkipli, the only man in the region with any apparent authority over civilians. The boat set out at dark one evening but was becalmed until midnight. By sunrise, the boat had sailed out of the bay against a strong headwind, just in time to miss a Japanese patrol. The little vessel struggled against the wind for two days before it reached Brooke's Point. Finally, in their beachfront home, the Sutherlands felt relieved.

A week later, Harry Edwards sent three carts and an invitation for the family to relocate in Macagua. They accepted, and for the next eight months, their days were crowded with the ongoing search for food and their struggle with malaria. Alexander roamed the jungle by day, returning at night exhausted with only a few bananas or camotes, some fish or some meat. Malarial fevers repeatedly assaulted not only Alexander and Maise but also their small children. At times, the parents and children were all sprawled in agony on their bamboo floor.

Despite the hardships, the minister found time to hold prayer meetings with the Christians in Macagua, and in some of the nearby native enclaves. He presided over the funerals of three local men who had attended his meetings. They died from malaria and malnutrition.

Food was scarce in Macagua, but medicine was in even shorter supply. Before the war, Sutherland had dispensed a steady flow of quinine and other drugs. Now, if they could be had, these remedies cost 150 times as much—ten pesos for a dose that would have cost seven centavos before the war. The minister began treating his family with potions made from roots, leaves, and bark, but their reactions were so severe that he had to quit even that medication.

It was at Macagua that the Sutherlands first encountered some American soldiers who had escaped from the Japanese prison camp at Puerto Princesa. Three sailors lived with the Edwards family, and three marines lived with the Sutherlands for two months. Their few clothes were in rags when they arrived, and the Sutherlands did what they could to outfit the men. These men eventually left, perhaps hoping to find their way home. But the news came back to Macagua: After a few months, only two of the six were still alive.

Although the sheltering arms of the Edwards family were reassuring, the Sutherlands decided they needed to escape the mosquitoes and malaria of Macagua. So once again they moved, this time going to a settlement closer to the shore. But malaria followed them to Paratungan, a mile from the beach. For three months, Maisie had a fever every day. The person with the lowest temperature on any given day served as the family's cook. At times, that was Alistair, not quite six years old.

At one point, the minister fell into a coma and was unable to recognize his wife or children for a week. When he recovered, he thanked God for his deliverance.

By this time, the Sutherlands' children were dressed in rags. The family had traded away most of their clothes and bedding for food. Maisie had sewn clothes out of an old tent, and for two years they had been without shoes. New Year's Day of 1944 found them barefoot.

"I know that our jungle schooling has not been time lost," Alexander wrote then. "Who can estimate what the Lord's dealings have meant to us, how He has revealed His Word to us in a new way, teaching us to rely more upon Himself and on what He has said?

"And we have learned to know that life can be lived happily and usefully in the midst of daily dangers and when stripped of most of the so-called advantages and comforts of civilization. We have learned to wash our clothes without soap, to light our fires without matches, to live without bread and butter, and sugar, tea, coffee and milk and all the lesser things one remembers having stored on shelves in the distant past."

The Sutherlands looked around and knew that they were not alone in their suffering. The rice crop had failed in 1943, and people in the mountains and valleys were starving, their children crying for food. With four to five months until the next rice harvest, it was uncertain whether these neighbors would survive. Alexander wrote: "Even the best and richest families have to gather roots from the forest to eat, and one old headman nearby told us in our house the other day that but for the few sweet potatoes some of his people have, not a few of them would be dead today."

Somehow through all of this, the Sutherlands, too, had survived. When they could make time, they gave Alistair, nearly six years old, reading and writing lessons, and the boy showed an eagerness for books. And now, living near the beach, there were some new friends to entertain the children.

At the first of the year, a new group of American soldiers arrived in the villages around Brooke's Point. Two quickly died of malaria, and three others who began living with the Sutherlands often were in the grip of fever. When they were well, however, the three became "uncles" to the children.

Uncle Wigfield was William Wigfield of Theodore, Alabama. Uncle George was George Marquez. Both men had enlisted in the U.S. Army in 1940. Trapped with the other Americans when the Bataan Peninsula was captured by the Japanese in 1942, Wigfield, Marquez, and about fifty other soldiers fled into the hills. They made their way by sailboat to the island of Cuyo, north of Palawan, where they joined a group of local guerrillas and stayed until the Japanese invaded about a year later. Most of their comrades surrendered, but Wigfield and Marquez chose their freedom, again sailing south, living off octopus, horse, and monkey meat, rice, and coconuts. At times, they stayed with natives, but they kept moving until they arrived in Brooke's Point.

Uncle Charlie was Charles O. Watkins, a sailor who had been surrendered by his commander in Manila in May 1942. Watkins had been in four Japanese prison camps before he was shipped to the camp at Puerto Princesa. He escaped three months after his capture and lived with natives until he met Wigfield and Marquez and traveled with them to Brooke's Point.

Wigfield was little Heather's friend, spending his time entertaining the toddler. He kept his few possessions in tin boxes, and constantly whittled wooden toys for the children with a pocketknife. Watkins seemed to be enthusiastic about everything, which helped the Sutherlands to keep their spirits up. To him, every event was grand or wonderful.

Another guest in the Sutherland hut was an elderly American civil engineer, Henry C. Garretson, who had first come to the Philippines in 1920 to work for the government. He had owned a business on the island of Cebu in the Visayas. When the war began, Garretson had worked with the army in demolitions and salvage, helping to recover ammunition from some sunken ships. Then he fled into the mountains, heading south to try to get some help for the guerrillas. He made it as far as Brooke's Point, where he was felled by malaria. In the Sutherland household, he was viewed as a welcome guest and a stabilizing influence.

With more mouths to feed—Wigfield, normally a slender 122 pounds, was skin draped over bones—the minister decided to use the spring rains to start a garden in the fertile soil of Paratungan. As Sutherland followed, holding tightly to the handles, a carabao pulled a plow across a plot. Then Alexander planted camote, millet, peas, beans, and peanuts, a gesture of hope in the future.

In the absence of any news, hope came from the guerrillas alone. In all their time in and around Brooke's Point, the Sutherlands and their neighbors had little need to fear the Japanese. The issue of who owned this shore had been settled earlier, the first time the invaders decided to set up camp. The final word was delivered by the guerrillas, with the help of some American soldiers passing through and one of the expatriate residents caught by the war.

Only the wind was moving through the streets of Brooke's Point then; the wind and the rain that it drove. To the Japanese, this ghost town was an appealing place to establish a foothold in southern Palawan. Its harbor was broad and deep and well protected from storms that might come from the north and west. And the town was not far from the narrow Balabac Strait passage to the South China Sea.

The war was not a full year old when a contingent of Japanese soldiers landed on the beach and moved into the deserted town. At the heart of the community they found the elementary school, a one-block square collection of wooden buildings with corrugated steel roofs, the main classroom building facing south across a rectangular courtyard toward the entrance gate, and smaller single-story buildings along the east and west sides of the courtyard. The soldiers moved into the larger building and settled in for the night. The next morning, while the two dozen soldiers were eating breakfast, the guerrillas—Nazario Mayor leading his men, their American allies, and one Finnish native—silently encircled the compound. The attack was precisely coordinated and swift. In minutes, several of the Japanese soldiers were dead. Stunned, the survivors returned fire, holding off the guerrillas as they attempted to retreat from the schoolyard to the beach, where they had left an anchored launch with a machine gun mounted on its roof. One of the Japanese soldiers waded to the boat and climbed aboard, ready to man the machine gun. But a guerrilla—Delfin Magbanua, hiding high in a coconut tree—shot the man. Another soldier tried to climb to the roof of the launch, but Magbanua fired again, killing the second man.

Meanwhile, the survivors were dragging their fallen comrades to a nearby bamboo hut. When all the dead were inside, they torched the hut. Then, firing toward shore, the remaining soldiers retreated to the launch, where a third soldier lay dead with one of Magbanua's bullets in him. Backing toward the launch and firing a fusillade at the shore, the soldiers managed to get aboard and escape.

A few days later, the drone of Japanese planes broke the Palawan quiet, and a few bombs dropped on the town. The municipal building was destroyed. But from the first attack to the last bomb, no resident of Brooke's Point and none of the guerrillas was lost. The Japanese occupation in this corner of the Philippines had ended after one day.

Nazario Mayor wrote his official report of the incident, summarizing: "Enemy casualties—20 killed; our casualties—sore trigger fingers."

CHAPTER 12

CHANGED ORDERS

Flier's general orders, drafted back in Fremantle, became specific on the evening of August 13 as the submarine approached Balabac Strait. The word came around dinnertime, the normal hour for submarine headquarters in Australia to broadcast the war news along with any special instructions for the submarines on patrol. On this, the third consecutive day, there was a message for the submarine *Robalo*, which was scheduled to return from its most recent patrol. The message asked for the boat's location and estimated time of arrival in Fremantle. There was no urgency in the transmission. A returning submarine could easily be a few days late.

There was a message for *Flier*, as well. But the sailor in the radio room—a small cubicle off the main deck to the rear of the control room—knew none of this when the Morse code message began to arrive. The sailor wrote down the jumble of encoded letters that he then handed to an officer. The officer took the notes to a machine that was kept in Captain Crowley's stateroom. Headquarters changed the code for each day of the month, and each officer was trained to use the decoding machine with the most current code found in a book kept in Crowley's safe. The codes and the machine were top secret. If a submarine ever was threatened with capture, the top priority was the destruction of both book and machine. More than one captain had gone down with his ship to prevent the codes from falling into enemy hands.

When the radioman's message was typed into the machine, the officer informed Crowley of the new orders. The submarine *Puffer*, which had been patrolling in the northern Philippines, had encountered a Japanese convoy heading south. *Puffer* had sent torpedoes into several of the ships in the convoy and was now trailing "cripples," the message said. The rest of the convoy, thwarted by *Puffer* from entering Mindoro Strait on the northern end of Palawan, was now traveling southwest, along the western shore of Palawan in the South China Sea. Until now, *Flier*'s assignment had been to patrol the South China Sea, looking particularly for four Japanese submarines making supply runs from Vietnam. The new orders directed *Flier* to go after *Puffer*'s convoy. There was no need for Crowley to change course. *Flier* was already headed for Balabac Strait, and that would take the submarine right into the path of the approaching convoy.

Crowley was energized. The patrol had just begun and already there were targets. The word was passed along by intercom, and the crew knew they were back in the war.

John Clyde Turner was in the process of cleaning up after the dinner meal when the message about *Flier*'s new target circulated. Turner worked in the pantry, a cubbyhole on the port side half the size of the radio room, and except for the motion of the submarine, he might as well have had a job in the galley of a railroad dining car. Every surface was stainless steel. There was a warming oven where he could keep a meal heated for an officer whose watch was not yet over. A coffeepot was always on in the pantry, and Turner had to keep it fresh. His galley had a window that opened onto the forward end of the wardroom table so that he could easily serve a cup of coffee or hand through a steaming dinner plate. There was a sink in which he cleaned the officers' plates when the meal was done. But more than dirty dishes came through the window. Perhaps more than any other man on the submarine, Turner knew about the lives of *Flier*'s officers. In their relaxed conversations, the officers spoke of their homes, their careers, their education, their wives and children. They rehashed their exploits— military and otherwise, no doubt. They revealed, even when not talk-

USS Flier *in friendly waters. On August 13, 1944, an explosion as the boat crossed the Sulu Sea sent* Flier *to the bottom, taking the lives of 78 of its crew members. Eight survived, evading enemy capture and eventually returning to duty. Photo no. 19-M-65326 in the National Archives*

n the violent seas of a January 1944 storm at Midway atoll, the submarine Flier *and the ubmarine rescue ship* Macaw *lie stranded on a reef, their bows pointed in opposite directions. fter* Flier *grounded attempting to enter the Midway channel on January 16,* Macaw *was ispatched to haul the submarine free. Instead,* Macaw *too became grounded on the reef. The epartment of the Navy photos were found among the effects of* Macaw*'s executive officer, Lt. erald F. Loughman. Courtesy of Tim Loughman*

Portrait of the Flier crew taken August 1, 1944, before departure on their second war patrol. Executive officer James Liddell is second from right in the first row and young Ensign Jacobson is fourth from the right. Commander John Crowley, the Flier skipper, is in the second row, above Jacobson and to the left. The young woman near the top row, right, is not identified. Department of the Navy

Commander John Crowley, a 1931 graduate of the U.S. Naval Academy, commissioned Flier after her launching in October 1943 in Groton, Connecticut. He was the boat's only skipper until it was lost on August 13, 1944. Courtesy of the family of Gibson Howell

Alvin E. Jacobson in a 1944 official Navy portrait. Jacobson put on the uniform of an ensign after his commissioning at the University of Michigan. He and other volunteers had not yet graduated when they took their oath of office. Graduation would come following the war. Courtesy Mary Jacobson

The Jacobson sons and their parents in 1944. Alvin E. Jacobson Sr. and his wife, Edna, sent all three sons to serve during the war. Charles, the oldest (second left) went to the Navy; Alvin Jr. to the Navy; and David, the youngest, to the Army Air Corps. Courtesy Mary Jacobson

Elton Stanley Brubaker in a portrait taken in Florida while he was at home on leave before attending submarine school. Brubaker had received permission from his father to quit high school to enlist. His mother, a teacher, disapproved. Courtesy Charlotte Brubaker Johns

The Brubaker family at Christmas, 1942, in Florida. Elton Stanley, on the left, stands beside his mother, Nellie Mae, sister Charlotte Marie, father Emil Scott, and brother Lewis. In four months, Elton would have left school to join the Navy. Courtesy Charlotte Brubaker Johns

Telegram informing Elton Brubaker's family on Sept. 14, 1944, that he was missing in action. The telegram arrived in St. Augustine, Florida, on Elton's 19th birthday, a month and a day after Flier sank. Courtesy Charlotte Brubaker Johns

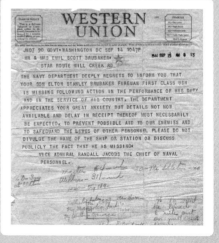

Diagrams from a submarine training textbook illustrating the compartments and outer structure of a submarine in the same class as Flier. Each compartment was made of welded steel and was connected to adjacent compartments by watertight hatches. From The Fleet Type Submarine, Standards and Curriculum Division Training, Bureau of Naval Personnel, June 1946

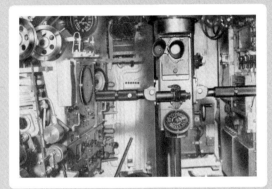

The conning tower of a fleet type submarine similar to Flier, looking aft, and the periscope, with control handles in the down position (right of center.) It was in the conning tower that, when the submarine was submerged, the skipper could use the periscope to view enemy ships. The radar operator's station was in the conning tower, as well. From The Fleet Type Submarine, Standards and Curriculum Division Training, Bureau of Naval Personnel, June 1946

Control room looking forward in a submarine of the same type as Flier. To the left, the chart table—where Ensign Jacobson would plot Flier's course—is folded down onto the egg-shaped gyro compass. The watertight oval passageway to the right leads to the officers' quarters and, beyond, to the forward torpedo room. From The Fleet Type Submarine, Standards and Curriculum Division Training, Bureau of Naval Personnel, June 1946

The precipitous slopes of Mt. Maruyog, also known as Addison Peak, dominate the landscape near Brooke's Point on Palawan Island. The town was the Philippine guerrillas' local headquarters. The peak was among the first landmarks seen by the Flier survivors upon their arrival. Courtesy Samuel Sy-Siong & Bernardita Sy-Siong.

Alexander and Maisie Sutherland with their children, Alistair and Heather, shortly after being rescued from the Philippines. The Scots missionary couple had been in Brooke's Point, Palawan, since the 1930s when the Japanese attacked the Philippines, stranding them with their first two children. Courtesy of Alistair Sutherland and Heather Sutherland Danielson

George Marquez, an American soldier, during World War II. Marquez was serving in the Philippines when the Japanese attacked Manila and Pearl Harbor within hours. He fled into the jungle in December 1941 and helped guerrillas in their fight against the Japanese. Courtesy Larry Legge

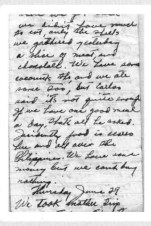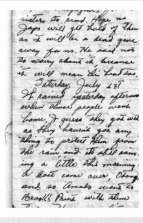

A copy of a page from the diary of Coastwatcher Cpl. Teodoro J. "Butch" Rallojay. Courtesy of Conchita Rallojay

A large commercial fishing boat with outriggers—called a banca—*is anchored off Buligay while a much smaller banca passes its stern. These traditional wooden vessels were in use before and during World War II. The Coastwatchers were transported to Palawan by small bancas. Courtesy Samuel Sy-Siong & Bernardita Sy-Siong*

A dirt road passing through a tunnel of trees in Macagua, the district where Harry Edwards had his wartime retreat. It was along a path like this where the Flier survivors were hauled by carabao cart from Ipolote Bay to the Edwards compound. Courtesy Samuel Sy-Siong & Bernardita Sy-Siong

Seven of the eight survivors of the submarine Flier on the deck of the submarine Redfin soon after their evacuation from Palawan, the Philippines. Those pictured are, from left, front row: James Russo, Wesley Miller, Earl Baumgart, Gibson Howell; back row: James Liddell, John Crowley, Alvin Jacobson. Donald Tremaine was absent due to illness. Courtesy of Alvin E. Jacobson Jr.

ing directly with Turner, a style of living nothing like the cook's own existence back in Powder Springs, Georgia.

There was one other black man on *Flier* named Walter Freeman, who, along with Alvin Skow, a white man, cooked for the crew. Freeman was from Louisiana and he was an excellent cook and baker. He was the sort of man whom any sailor would be wise to befriend. When it came to getting special treats, Earl Baumgart was a genius. Baumgart talked with Freeman and helped with the garbage. In return, Freeman found time when *Flier* was under way to deliver a dish of ice cream or a bowl of cold fruit to Baumgart.

On this evening, Baumgart had lookout duty after dinner, so he donned a pair of red glasses after seven o'clock and wore them for a half-hour before he went to the control room. At eight o'clock, he climbed the ladders up through the conning tower. The glasses, filtering the harsh incandescent submarine lighting, prepared his eyes for scanning the darkened ocean. He was wearing his navy denims and boots. The warmth of a night in the tropics required nothing else. And despite his continuing anger over the way he had been assigned this duty, he was beginning to enjoy the hours he spent standing on the A-frame above the deck, cooled by the breeze as *Flier* made eighteen knots across the surface. On his perch, he escaped the confinement of the submarine, free as a bird on a tree branch. The air smelled of the ocean alone, since the fumes from the submarine's four big diesel engines—all now working well—were expelled through ports behind the bridge, leaving the exhaust in the submarine's wake. The engine sounds trailed aft, as well, and from the starboard side of the A-frame Baumgart could hear the sea splashing off the bow, nearly 100 feet ahead. In the roiling water that flowed along the boat's side, he saw the fluorescence of what he suspected were jellyfish, and in the distance, flashes of electrical storms lit the clouds.

Standing on the port side of the A-frame was Wesley Miller, the twenty-one-year-old from a cattle ranch near Drewsey, Oregon, a land far from the ocean. Miller had joined the navy exactly sixteen months before this night and had spent his time at boot camp even farther from the sea, in Farragut, Idaho. Up on the A-frame, Miller lounged like a sailor on the mast of a square-rigger, his eyes acclimated by the red glasses that he, too, had worn before going topside to scan the water behind *Flier*. He could see land about 8,000 yards away to his right, but barely. The overcast sky shut out the starlight, and the moon had not yet risen.

There were two more sailors on lookout, both high above the bridge where Crowley sat on a stool bolted to the floor behind a thick, neck-high steel bulwark. Ensign Behr was on deck with Crowley and three other officers, who would rotate to jobs belowdecks after their four-hour watch was over.

The conning tower was crowded with its usual complement of officers and crew. Jim Liddell, the executive and navigation officer, stood at the foot of the ladder leading to the bridge so that he could talk with Crowley, whose stool was on deck beside the hatch. Jim Russo stood beside Liddell, helping him with the charts. Arthur Gibson Howell was at the rear of the compartment, operating the radar. Beside him, Charles Pope, the hero who nearly drowned on the trip between Midway and Hawaii, ran the sonar. There was a helmsman, Gerald Madeo, who steered according to Crowley's directions from above, and ensign Phil Mayer was standing by to handle the torpedo data computer should they see some action. Donald Tremaine, a fire controlman second class, was in the radar tracking party as the "talker" who would relay information in case *Flier* made contact with the enemy.

Howell's radar presented him with an image of the nearest shoreline, many miles away. They had traveled on the surface throughout the day and had seen neither Japanese ships nor aircraft, and the radar screen still showed no enemy threats. The night was going as easily as had the day.

Elton Brubaker had finished his meal, and if he wasn't scheduled for his bunk, he had enough duties to occupy him. He still had a long way to go to become a qualified submariner, and that meant a lot of crawling about in *Flier*'s belly. If he had a few minutes to spare, he could again break out the packet of letters that he had been saving, reading the words from Ruth Turner or from home. These letters reminded him of the voices of the people he loved—voices that had to compete with the sounds made by eighty-five other men inside the submarine. He could imagine, if he chose, what was being written from home and what news was being flown to Fremantle to greet him a month or more from now. In exactly one month and one day, he would turn nineteen, a milestone that certified him as an adult—at least, older than most high school seniors. Perhaps they were writing now to congratulate him when he got to port, and to wish him a happy birthday.

Indeed, the letters were accumulating. Lewis, his brother, now worked at the Alhambra Hotel, where Elton had been a bellhop. "We are having a hell of a time keeping help here at the hotel," Lewis wrote in mid-July. "Since I have been here, we have had about eight bellboys, and the third night clerk quit last night. The boss is paying starvation wages as you can't really expect any more than a few weeks of work." Then Lewis reported on a beach party he had attended. "Guess who was there?" he wrote, listing several names, and concluding, ". . . last but not least, Pauline. She asked about you."

Elton's mother sat down in St. Augustine in late July in the family's new home—they had already written to him describing the place. On this day, Mother had been mowing the grass and was hot but proud of the beautiful lawn. "Daddy says sure thing he will draw a floor plan of our house for you and I'll send it on in the very next mail." Charlotte didn't get home from school during the semester break. Betty, the cow, was still giving lots of rich milk, and Mother was making much more butter than the family could use.

"We have been enjoying peaches and cream the past week," she wrote. "I bought a bushel of Elbertas. Won't you have a dish with me right now?"

And just a week ago, Mother had written again. Father had not yet drawn the floor plan, although she planned to nudge him. The family had been offered one thousand dollars more than they had just paid for the house, but Mother had said no. "Daddy is laughing at me. He says this is the first time he has known me to turn down a profit in anything. I know you will like it and I'm so anxious for you to see it."

The mother whom Elton had always tried to impress ached to let him know he was loved. "Do you remember, as I do, our serious confidential talks together?" she asked. "Darling, you have been more than a son to me." His return, she wrote, would be the finest moment in her life.

On this very day as *Flier* was steaming toward Balabac Strait, Al Jacobson Sr. wrote again to all his sons in one letter. For a change, it took him longer to get to the parts about the brass foundry and his sons' expected place as future executives. His mood was wistful.

"This morning we woke up a little early, and looked out the window, and there was a strange boat moored out in front of the cottage; and Mother and I had breakfast in the back yard at the little table under the tree. There are only two of us home now, so it is rather quiet."

After some news of who was where, the father went on: "Jake Pool, who runs the shoe repair shop on Washington Avenue, invited me to go fishing yesterday morning up the River, and we had five bass, using pork rind as a bait on long bamboo poles."

More news about relatives was followed almost with a sigh. "On one of the little peach trees, we picked a small basket of nice pink-cheeked peaches, and they certainly were good."

Prior to nine o'clock that evening, chief radio technician Arthur Gibson Howell got orders to begin operating the radar. During the first patrol, Howell's use of his equipment had been so significant, and his behavior so remarkable, that Crowley had recommended he be awarded the Bronze Star. As the submarine approached the narrow passageway through Balabac Strait, the skipper was pleased he had a man of Howell's ability running the craft's most important piece of navigational equipment.

Al Jacobson was in the control room at the same time, recording *Flier*'s track on the charts. He had just put on a pair of red glasses in preparation for his watch at nine, when he would replace Teddy Behr on deck. Edgar Hudson, a career navy man, was chief of the watch in the control room. Hudson stood at the foot of the conning-tower ladder, keeping contact with Jim Liddell above, whose dialogue with Crowley, on deck, determined where the submarine would go. Jacobson listened intently to every word, alert for any changes he needed to make on his chart. He began hearing Chief Howell's reports of bearings and ranges from the radar. Just as the charts predicted, there was the radar blip of a lighthouse ahead of the submarine on the port side. There were reefs and small islands to starboard. A large land mass—the chart said it was Balabac Island—was straight ahead, and other land masses were beginning to rise above the curve of the earth and appear on radar, many miles away to starboard.

Admiral Christie's orders directing *Flier* through Balabac Strait remained unchanged by the message the radioman had transcribed earlier. Crowley was to take the deepest water route through the strait that he could. In deep water, it was assumed, mines could not be anchored. Specifically, the orders directed Crowley to use the Nasubata Channel, one of eight channels between the Sulu and South China seas allowing east- and west-bound ships to pass through the reef-strewn Balabac Strait. Nasubata Channel was the deepest—more than 500 feet deep in spots—and the broadest, with about five miles' leeway between Roughton Island's reefs to the north and Comiran Island to the south.

As he approached the channel, Crowley had several concerns, as would any skipper. While the ability to navigate safely around natural obstructions such as reefs was always a consideration, in wartime a captain had two more problems to solve. He had to give himself enough room to maneuver if an enemy ship attacked, and he also had to be wary of shallow water where mines could be anchored. Roughton Islands' extensive reefs to the north took away maneuvering room and presented a navigation problem. Crowley, talking the matter over with Liddell through the conning-tower hatch, decided he would try a more southerly route through the channel. If he stayed in fifty fathoms—300 feet or more of water—Crowley believed *Flier* would pass through the channel untroubled.

Admiral Christie's office had given an extremely detailed course, already traveled by the submarine *Crevalle,* and recommended that

Crowley follow that course. Crowley did not believe that the *Crevalle* track was the best approach through a narrow channel with unlighted reefs and unpredictable currents.

Mines were the only military threat Crowley felt he faced that night. He trusted his radar and its operator, Chief Howell, and felt the device could find a target the size of a surfaced submarine—with the possible exception of a midget submarine—at a range of more than three miles. Unless the Japanese had developed a superior night periscope, he believed that on a night as dark as this one, a submarine could not make a submerged attack. And as Howell reported from below what he was seeing on the radar, Crowley was convinced the only things out there in the dark were islands and mountains, a few of which he knew harbored enemy soldiers. *Flier* could make it through.

Chief Howell relayed a constant stream of radar readings to Liddell, who passed them along to the skipper. And Chief Pope, watching the sonar, gave depth readings. With the radar showing the nearest land about 5,000 yards away, *Flier* was traveling in sixty-five to ninety fathoms of ocean when Pope reported a reading of forty-one fathoms. *Flier* wasn't about to scrape bottom, but the depth was shallow enough to raise Crowley's concern about mines. He asked Liddell, a veteran of a Philippine tour before the war, what he thought.

Liddell, the mechanical engineer, had Crowley's trust when it came to all things mathematical. The executive officer had been overseeing the radar and sonar operators as they got navigational fixes on the land every ten minutes, and continuously on the ocean floor. The reports showed that the submarine was exactly where he thought it should be on the chart he had in the conning tower.

By now, Ensign Behr had relieved Al Jacobson at the control-room chart table, and Jacobson was on the after cigarette deck, standing watch below Earl Baumgart, admiring the scenery. Lightning flashed off the sides of distant mountains as the submarine slipped across a nearly calm sea. Teddy Behr, in the control room, was now bombarded with constant updates for the plot from Liddell. Lieutenant John Casey, Jacobson's mentor on the first patrol, was standing watch on the bridge beside Crowley, with lieutenant junior grade Bill Reynolds behind him on the starboard side. Lieutenant Paul Knapp was to the rear of Crowley, watching off the port side. One other ensign on board, Herbert Miner, was the only officer not on duty at just before ten o'clock when Crowley received a report from Howell that the radar showed Comiran Island about four miles south.

With this information, Liddell told Crowley they should continue on course because they would soon intersect with the *Crevalle* track, the route declared safe by the admiral's people.

Crowley was standing in the forward end of the bridge, leaning over the open hatch in the bridge floor to talk with Liddell about taking a new course, when the explosion came. The blast caused the entire submarine to whip to one side and then snap back like an angry stallion trying to throw its rider. Crowley felt the violent motion, but the concussion was without sound, like the thunder from the electrical storms that played their lightning fingers across those distant mountains.

Jim Russo's job had been simply to help handle the conning-tower charts. He was at Liddell's side when the explosion rocked the boat as if it had rammed a wall. Instinctively, he looked down at the hatch to the control room. Something slammed into his cheek below his eye, ripping his flesh like a bullet. A shaft of air was venting straight up from below, blasting out through the hatch to the bridge. Blood was draining down his cheek when Russo felt himself lifted by the column of air, along with Liddell, the 200-pound ex-football-player, straight up to the bridge. Once above deck, Russo—by instinct and without hesitation—followed Liddell, whose shirt had been ripped off by the blast, to the rear of the bridge where, at the railing, they dove into the ocean. When Russo turned around in the water, *Flier* was gone.

Wesley Miller, standing on the A-frame above the bridge, was nearly thrown from his watch but managed to hook his legs over a railing to avoid falling. He was confused. Somehow, he had lost his binoculars, and he was concerned about the discipline that would result. Then there was screaming coming from below and air was blasting out of the hatch in the bridge floor under him. He stood frozen on the

A-frame for an instant, although it seemed longer, until he heard someone yell "Abandon ship!" and saw the bow of the submarine go under.
Then the ocean was swelling around him, dragging him down into its
darkness. The radio antenna had snagged him. Miller struggled to free
himself and then swam and swam, reaching for the surface. Then he
was alone in the water, and the submarine was gone.

Al Jacobson, lost in his reverie, watching the lightning and the
mountains silhouetted in the darkness, felt the blast of air and, curiously, found Lieutenant Reynolds standing on the deck beside him,
complaining that his side hurt. Jacobson told Reynolds to lie down,
and then he crouched over the lieutenant, hoping to help him. He
assumed that an air bank, used to store compressed air for use in diving and surfacing, had blown, and he told Reynolds to lie still. But as
he talked with Reynolds, he saw Ensign Mayer and Ed Casey diving
over *Flier*'s side. Just then, water rose around Jacobson and Reynolds,
and the submarine sank below them, sucking them down with it. The
image in Jacobson's mind was of the two huge propellers at the rear
of the boat, still spinning as they passed him, slicing him to bits. He
struggled to swim up and away from his death. It took a few seconds
before he surfaced in a slick of diesel fuel that floated on warm, calm
seas. Baseball-size chunks of cork from inside *Flier* floated around
him. He could feel them. But there was no light to see what, or who,
else was there.

Crowley, who had been standing to port at the front of the bridge,
saw a geyser shoot toward the sky from the forward starboard side
of the submarine. The next thing he knew, he was standing against
the aft railing of the bridge, near Jacobson. He ran forward to trigger
the collision alarm that was mounted on the bulwark just above the
conning-tower hatch. When he got there, he smelled diesel fuel. He
looked down into the conning tower but it was dark. There was no
time!

"Abandon ship!"

The skipper's yell carried across the deck and perhaps a short way
down into the submarine, where many in the crew already were being
thrown about by the air blast and the flooding that made Crowley's

command superfluous. On the bridge, the skipper felt the shaft of air rising from within the submarine, carrying with it the sounds of rushing water and the screams of seventy-one men trapped inside. Some men were climbing the ladder from the conning tower, just in time because the deck was heading under, *Flier*'s engines still driving it like a train entering a tunnel. Crowley found himself in a raging stream of water as the sea poured around the bulwark and into the bridge, and then he was washed out the rear of the bridge, into the sea.

Chief Howell rode the shaft of air out of the conning tower to the bridge. The sea had already poured in around the bulwark, and it flushed him toward the rear cigarette deck, trapping him against the guardrail. The submarine's plunge carried him deep below the surface before he managed to break free and swim for the surface. The taste of diesel fuel was on his tongue, and having come from the glow of the conning-tower lights, he was blind in the utter darkness. Slowly, though, the phosphorescent light of the sea restored his vision. In the blue glow, he saw the shadows of human heads. He began shouting.

In a matter of just twenty seconds after the blast, *Flier* was gone, and after its passing, the ocean was calm. The dead sailors of the Japanese minelayer *Tsugaru* had once again struck from their graves.

A mine had touched the side of *Flier*—just a glancing blow, but enough to trigger its explosives. The geyser had appeared near the rear of the forward torpedo room. The explosion, quiet as it was on the surface, would have been enough to punch a hole through the submarine's superstructure and one or more of its watertight welded-steel compartments. John Clyde Turner's pantry was right there, across the passageway that led aft from the forward torpedo room. Unless the captain had ordered battle stations for the entire boat, the watertight doors between the submarine's compartments were normally left open. On this night, Crowley had ordered battle stations for the conning tower, but the rest of the crew was not on alert. If the watertight doors were not dogged in place with their big handles, the blast from the mine—having opened a huge hole in *Flier*'s side—flooded the forward torpedo room and the officers' quarters immediately. At the same time, a rupturing of the tanks full of compressed air sent a shock wave through the submarine's ductwork ahead of the flooding water. The seawater raced to the rear, in seconds reaching the control room where Ensign Behr would have been among the first in its path, followed by the bow and stern planesmen and the other sailors handling the various controls.

Standing at the foot of the ladder to the conning tower was Edgar Hudson, chief of the watch. With the explosion and the venting of air up through the conning tower, Hudson was caught like a bug on the stream of a garden hose. As he rose, his body was slammed against the steel above him—the ladder, and the metal around the narrow opening for the conning-tower hatch. His injuries were grave, but somehow he managed to emerge from the bridge hatch onto the deck in time to escape into the flooding sea. No one else from below the conning tower followed him.

Elton Brubaker could have been standing watch in the control room. He might have been inspecting batteries under the officers' quarters or under the crew quarters. He could have been in the mess hall playing cards with his shipmates or in his bunk, daydreaming or sleeping. The boy from Florida who made friends wherever he went could have been almost any place on the submarine, because he still needed to study the boat to become a qualified submariner. And he had by now shown himself to be an eager student. If he was anyplace to the rear of the crew quarters, he was protected from the immediate consequences of the blast because the watertight door at the front of the forward engine room was always dogged shut. But wherever he was—whether among the frantic crewmen screaming in terror, helpless against the rising water that would drown them, or in those still-dry rear capsules between the forward engine room and the aft torpedo room—Elton had to know his time had come. There had been no claxon warning of a dive back in the rear compartments. But the boat had tipped at just the angle it would have for a normal dive. Its diesel engines, which would have been stopped in a dive, were still running and would continue until the exhaust and intake vents were flooded.

What thoughts flood the mind of an eighteen-year-old boy when he believes his life is over, his soul spiraling toward its grave? Is his brain flashing fresh memories of his sweetheart, Ruth Turner—the sound of her Kentucky voice, and perhaps the delight of her young kiss? Does he think of his mother, Nellie May, his boasts to her about his future, and the promises he may never keep? Is there regret that he will never again smell his father's pipe, feel the flattery of his brother's adoration, or the reassuring concern and wisdom of his big sister?

The flooding would stop the engines as *Flier* sank deeper, and the darkness that Crowley had seen when he looked down the hatch from the bridge would spread throughout the submarine. For the men in the rear, there was but one hope to temper their panic—an escape hatch in the aft torpedo room. If they could get the hatch open, then for the first time since their submarine training in Connecticut, they would strap on their air tanks and take their chances floating to the surface.

But what then?

CHAPTER 13

IN THE SHADOW OF DEATH

The darkness was nearly absolute. Al Jacobson could see nothing, but he could taste diesel fuel on his lips. His body felt the warm, wet embrace of the sea as his uniform clung to his arms and legs. All was quiet except for the lapping of small waves.

And then there were shouts, the sounds of a human voice, the first indication to the ensign that he was not alone. He began swimming toward the voice, floating easily in the salt water but slowed by the weight of his shirt, trousers, and boots. The strap of his binoculars was still around his neck, and the glasses floated harmlessly by his chest as he did the sidestroke. *Flier's* sinking had disoriented him, snatching him from the tranquility of a warm ocean night, plunging him into a struggle for survival. Now, order was returning to his thoughts and two things occurred to the ensign. First, he was shipwrecked. Second, back in Boy Scouts he had learned that in a case like this, you should get out of your clothing. He stopped swimming and unbuttoned his shirt and set it adrift, then removed his shoes as he tried to tread water. The shoes sank immediately. Before he shed his trousers, he tried to get his jack-knife out of a pocket, but there was no way he could hold it and swim, so he let it sink, too. With his trousers off, he was left in his undershirt, shorts, and waterproof wristwatch, no more encumbered than when, in summers past, he had fallen off a sailboat on Spring Lake.

Several of the men had responded to the same yell that had drawn Jacobson. Once they were all together, they shared what they knew and tried to decide what had happened to *Flier*. It could have been an explosion in the batteries, but Crowley discarded that notion. The diesel engines had been running and the batteries were idle, not a situation in which they were likely to explode. The other topic concerned who else from the crew had escaped the boat. With almost no light, they could not expect to see other survivors, so their only choice was to call for them. Soon they had gathered more men into their group. A head count was taken. Crowley and Liddell began the roll call. There was Jacobson. Paul Knapp, the lieutenant who had been standing behind Crowley on the bridge, had made it. So had John Casey, who was standing beside the skipper. Bill Reynolds, who had been blown back to Jacobson's end of the deck, was in the water, too, but he was hurting. Two lookouts—Baumgart and Miller—joined the group. From the conning tower, Phil Mayer, the ensign who was operating the torpedo data computer, was counted, as were Chief Howell, the radar man, Jim Russo, who had been Liddell's helper, Chief Pope, the sonar operator, and Gerald Madeo, the helmsman. Chief Hudson, who had been blown up from the control room, was in the water, too, but he was severely injured and was unable to stay afloat without help. Donald Tremaine, from the radar tracking party, was there. Earlier, in the blinding darkness as they floated in the warm water, he had spoken with Elton Brubaker. The young sailor was having trouble swimming, he noticed. And then he was gone, never to be seen again.

A total of fifteen men responded to the roll call. Others might still be out in the darkness, if the stories being told by the men from the conning tower were any indication. Pope and Mayer said they had had to pull themselves forward by holding on to the periscope tubes until they were in the shaft of air, blowing up through the hatches. Somehow, they had ridden the air out to the water. They were not sure how they had gotten there. Others, like Howell, who had escaped from below, had found themselves caught in the guardrail around the bridge deck and had to free themselves from the sinking boat in order to swim to the surface. Perhaps some shipmates snagged like that had been dragged farther away as *Flier* sped forward. If so, they might join the group. For now, in the near-total darkness, there was no urgency to swim away from here. It was almost impossible to know where you were headed.

Like Jacobson, most of the other men had shed their clothing to make swimming easier. But Jacobson discovered that Casey, whom everyone called Ed, and who had been badly injured during the explosion, was still dressed.

"Ed, you've got to get out of those clothes," the ensign told his mentor. As Casey floated on his back, Al began to pull his trousers off. Casey's knife was still in his pocket, and realizing this tool could be valuable, Jacobson took it before letting the lieutenant's pants go. With no way to carry it, Al lost this knife, too. But he kept an eye on Casey, ready to help if he began to struggle. It was clear Casey was only able to swim on his back, and as he paddled, he veered off to one side or the other, apparently unaware of where he was. It dawned on Jacobson that Casey had been blinded during the explosion, and so he decided to stick with him and guide him when he needed help.

All fifteen men were already getting a lift. Not only had they escaped the terrifying death of their seventy-one trapped shipmates, but they had also surfaced on a sea that was unusually docile for this time of year. Summer is monsoon season, and storms can whip the Sulu Sea into a froth. Swimming in those waves would have been exhausting, and the chances of all these men finding and communicating with each other would have been slim. With lightning flashing on distant islands, there remained the possibility that a storm could still come, funneling winds between the mountains. But for now, here on the open ocean, the wind was light and the waves were gentle. As long as each man could stay afloat, he could remain with the group. For the next two hours, as they assessed their situation and developed a plan, that is what the men did.

There was a sense shared by most of the men that they were still part of a military unit. Perhaps this was because of their training, to always follow the lead of Crowley and Liddell. It took time for them to realize that there was no longer a formal chain of command, and that neither Crowley nor Liddell was in charge. The truth was revealed only when various members of the group began to notice something.

One minute they would be swimming in salt water, the next, in a diesel slick. Wesley Miller, not a very good swimmer to start with—he had failed a swimming test earlier in his navy career—noticed that there was a dark cloud on the horizon. But the cloud seemed to be circling the horizon.

It dawned on Miller and everyone else that they were swimming in a circle, going nowhere. Even the skipper had no course plotted. They needed a plan.

The first thing to consider was their location. The skipper and his executive officer knew where they were. Liddell began explaining the options, most of which everyone already understood. There was land on three sides, Liddell said. To the west was Balabac, the largest chunk of land in the vicinity, roughly ten miles away. Each man was aware that the Japanese occupied that mountainous island. They could swim in that direction and with some certainty, due to the island's long shoreline, land on Balabac's beaches. To the south was Comiran Island, less than two miles away. Every survivor could probably swim that far, despite injuries. But there was a problem with this option: Comiran was tiny—only a few hundred feet across. If, swimming in this opaque darkness, they missed Comiran, they would have another forty miles of ocean before they reached land on one of northern Borneo's islands.

The lightning occasionally lit a mountainside to the northwest, but judging from what they could see, that land was about thirty miles away.

And if they headed toward any eastern quadrant, the Sulu Sea threatened them, with hundreds of miles of ocean, uninterrupted by land of any kind.

These were the options Liddell presented, each one unpromising. And none was worth even attempting right now. There were no stars to guide the men, and no moon, only clouds overhead. And the occasional lightning flash on the horizon, while it gave them something of a beacon, left their eyes blinded for several minutes.

But even the strongest among the survivors could not expect to stay afloat forever, and so they adopted two rules. First, they would turn so that the waves were lapping their left cheeks, and then they would swim in the direction they were facing. The course was randomly chosen, as far as young Jacobson knew. Perhaps Crowley and Liddell had a reason. (The wind that moved the waves was coming from the west, for example, and keeping the waves to the left would aim the survivors generally to the north, toward land but away from Balabac and the known Japanese encampment.) But the skipper and his second in command did not share their thinking.

The second rule was Crowley's idea—a death sentence for several of the men, and everyone knew it: It would be each man for himself. The cruel reality was that wherever they were going, it was a long way off. Some of the injured men could not swim the distance without help, and if the whole group waited for the injured, the chances were overwhelming that no one would survive.

Crowley was uninjured, but he was the oldest, at thirty-five, and his physique after several years of sedentary submarine service was not particularly athletic. Crowley could be among the first victims of his edict. But like their skipper, all of the men agreed to the pact, and all fifteen began swimming across the waves, which lifted them a few inches and then gently lowered them in a mesmerizing rhythm.

Jacobson stayed with Casey like a sheepdog, nudging him back toward the group when he strayed. The ensign listened for voices in the darkness, and alternated between the sidestroke and the breaststroke. By now it was around midnight, and the swimmers had been in the water for two hours. For some, exhaustion seemed to lie just beyond the next stroke.

Off to the rear, Miller was having trouble keeping up. He would try to surge forward to reach the group, but his fatigue was overwhelming. In the darkness, he managed to find Chief Hudson, moving slowly. They stopped and talked, and Hudson, treading water, explained how he had been blown up from the control room. No one else from below had made it, he told Miller. And Hudson was not exactly in one piece. While he did not say what was broken or where he was bleeding, he told Miller that he doubted he could swim for much longer.

"I'd like to help you," Miller told the chief. "But I don't think I can stay up very long, either. I'm so tired; I don't think I can stay up more than a few minutes more."

The two men resumed their slow paddling, listening for the sounds of the men ahead, and after a few minutes, they no longer could see or hear each other.

It was about this time that Chief Pope called out in the night for Jim Liddell, asking the distance that lay ahead of them before they reached shore. This, of course, was not the first time *Flier* had tossed Pope into the ocean. Sea conditions were a lot more frightening the last time, though. Then, the waves were twenty feet or more, not a foot, and the winds were blowing at gale force. And that time Pope, the hard-drinking sailor whose bachelor life had been marked by promotions as well as demotions, had volunteered for the trip forward on the deck to save his shipmates by reconnecting the towline from the *Florikan*. Pope was a man of unquestioned courage if not remarkable wisdom.

After two hours in the water, the men still felt little wind. Liddell, pondering Pope's question, knew the entire swim could be fifteen miles or more, but he wanted to be encouraging.

"About nine miles, Chief," Liddell replied.

"Oh, fuck it!" Pope said in disgust. With that, the chief stopped swimming and said no more, his faint image dissolving forever behind the swimmers in the night.

It was not much later that Jacobson, keeping pace with Ed Casey, saw him veer once again. Instead of calling him back to the course as he had done before, the ensign swam over to his mentor.

"Ed, rest a minute, and then just float on your back and put your feet on my shoulders and I'll push you back," Jacobson offered.

"Remember, we agreed every man for himself?" Casey said, refusing his young friend's gesture. But the two of them swam back toward the group, talking as they went. They were joking about a blowout party they had planned to throw in Perth when the patrol was over, and as they talked, they reached the wake of the others.

Ten minutes later, Casey disappeared in the darkness. When Jacobson and the others called to him, there was no response. The lieutenant had chosen not to burden his shipmates any longer.

Paul Knapp had been struggling like Casey, but was keeping in line with the others. Jacobson saw him swim off to the side without a word. The ensign thought little of it until Knapp did not return. Then he realized the courage it had taken for Knapp to separate himself.

As the night wore on, one after another of the men, when they felt they could swim no more, silently turned to the side and disappeared, each man choosing for himself when his time had come.

Among those missing from the file of swimmers now was Wesley Miller. But he was not lost. A few minutes after Chief Hudson floated away, Miller felt a surge of strength. He was euphoric, and felt almost invincible. He believed he could swim forever. But he was no Channel swimmer. While he was swimming at his best, the group pulled ahead. He could hear their voices, and if he shouted, they could hear him. So he settled into a rhythm, pulling himself through the water, paced like the pendulum of a slow clock.

If anyone among the survivors—those at the front, or Miller, the last man—were thinking about the beasts that swam below them, none gave voice to the image. But the reefs of the Sulu Sea were habitat for a vast assortment of large animals. Sharks of every description shared the water with barracudas and rays. Some were harmless, like the white and blacktip sharks, and the guitar sharks. But others were legendary, like the hammerheads and bull sharks, predators that would eat another shark as quickly as they would consume a human being.

If the swimmers were ignoring the carnivores beneath them, it may have been because their minds were filled with the death they had just dodged, and, not that far below the sea, their shipmates already dead inside *Flier*. The thing that now would keep these men alive was their determination to keep swimming.

Nellie May Brubaker's next letter to her son—one that would never reach Elton—began with a complaint. "'Tisn't easy to keep writing letters and never getting an answer," she wrote. "For one thing, without your letters for questions I hardly know what you would like to hear about." So she offered some news. "Lewis just got back from Camp Blanding, where he spent ten days with the State Guard. Myron is home on a three-week leave. Claude will have a three-week leave, too, this month, and will paint his mother's house. And I am making doll clothes for a little girl on the street.

"It was fun, but did I start something. Now all the little girls on the street want me to make doll clothes for them." She continued, "I have been painting. I think it is fun. I have taken all the paint off the refrigerator and am going to do it in white enamel to match my stove. The porch swing I have painted orange like my flower boxes."

But the tidbits of news could not keep her long from her deepest thoughts. "All are well, and speak of you more and more often if that is possible. We will be so glad when the war is over and you, and all our boys, will be coming home. Finish it off as quickly as possible."

The water was warm, soothing. Al Jacobson's face was never submerged. The sidestroke allows the swimmer to breathe at any time, unlike the crawl, where breathing is timed to the second or fourth stroke, and the face is submerged the rest of the time. Once Ed Casey had removed himself from the line of swimmers, Jacobson was alone most of the time, with no one to occupy his attention. He was comfortable in the solitude, and he did not doubt that he would reach land, eventually. The horror endured by the men who went down in *Flier* did not fill him with terror, nor did he worry about his fate should he be greeted by Japanese soldiers when he walked ashore. Throughout his entire life, Jacobson had known only success—a line of achievements based on hard work. He was almost unaware of the concept of failure, and he harbored no fear that he would be unable to keep going, switching from the sidestroke to the breaststroke and then to the backstroke. Others had decided the course, although each man was free to swim where he wished. Jacobson, accustomed to accepting his father's guidance, simply followed the senior men.

Perhaps it was the tranquility of his stroke, which demanded little physical exertion. The mechanics of the sidestroke are perfect for preserving energy if not for achieving speed. The feet kick in a scissor movement that can be as vigorous or as indolent as you wish. And the arms stretch and pull alternately but remain underwater, buoyed into near weightlessness. With none of the distractions fatigue might impose, and with no fears about his future, young Al was being lulled into dreams. The soft lapping of the waves were his lullaby, and his eternal sleep lay ahead in the darkness.

Jolted by the sudden awareness of where he was, Jacobson began reciting the first verse that came to mind: "The Lord is my shepherd, I shall not want . . ."

He could recall Al Sr.'s latest talk about business, his mother's letters about life at home, but the verse continued in his mind. "He leadeth me beside the still waters . . ."

Lightning flashed off a distant mountain, and voices murmured toward him from the darkened ocean. "Yea, though I walk through the valley of the shadow of death, I will fear no evil, for Thou art with me . . ."

Earl Baumgart thought about his brothers and sisters as he swam. Elmer, who was two years older than Earl, was on another submarine, *Skate*. The brothers had seen each other in New London before *Flier* left on patrol. And they had seen each other in Hawaii, when *Skate* returned from its third patrol. Elmer had some combat experiences to share with his submariner brother. In February, when *Flier* was limping back to Mare Island, *Skate* had fired four torpedoes at a Japanese light cruiser, leaving it in thick smoke when the submarine dove to wait out a depth-charge attack. Elmer had told his brother that when they surfaced later, they saw the Japanese ship capsize and sink, a victim of their earlier torpedoes.

These memories drifted through Baumgart's thoughts as he labored with the crawl stroke. He had removed his shoes but had left his blue work uniform on. He thought back to North Division High School, where he, Elmer, and his oldest brother, Norman, had graduated, along with his sisters Norma and Evelyn. He had been captain of the North Division swim team, specializing in "distance" swimming. In the high school swimming pool, a distance event might be the 200-

yard freestyle, which he had won in 1940. His exploits in the pool impressed the girls. Dolores Bocchini wrote in Earl's senior yearbook: "I know you will go far in your swimming activities."

But as he alternated between the crawl and the breaststroke, Baumgart had little hope that he and his shipmates would ever reach shore. And so he repeated a verse that he had learned in his Catholic upbringing, a hymn taken by the navy to be its own:

Eternal Father, strong to save,
Whose arm hath bound the restless wave,
Who biddest the mighty ocean deep
Its own appointed limits keep;
Oh, hear us when we cry to Thee,
For those in peril on the sea!

And he thought about his father and mother, and of his friends who had gone down with *Flier.* He had spent every liberty with Joe Galinac. Joe would have been in the control room when the explosion hit, and Chief Hudson had said that no one had gotten out of there but he. He had been close to Mike Ricciardelli, Ervin Borlick, and A. J. Abrahamson, all motor machinist mates. All were original crewmen aboard *Flier,* and all, he knew, were now dead on the ocean floor.

The overcast sky that had kept the stars hidden was overcome at about three o'clock that morning by the moon, rising grudgingly in the east to give the swimmers a navigational beacon. By now, only nine of the original fifteen survivors remained in the group. Wesley Miller still straggled far behind the main pack but could hear their voices in the dark, and shouted to them to maintain contact.

At about five o'clock, when the first hint of daybreak was tingeing the sky from black to gray, helmsman Gerald Madeo began to panic. He fell below the surface, and after seven hours in the water, no one had the strength to help him. They simply continued swimming, led away from Madeo by the moon toward an unknown destination.

And then the sky brightened, and on the horizon to the northwest were islands, several of them. The seven men who were still together stopped and talked about their options and chose the land that seemed to be closest as their target. Each man would swim toward the island at his own pace. Jim Russo could not contain himself and swam ahead of the others. Jacobson stayed with Baumgart and Howell. Liddell and Crowley were together but some distance away from the rest. Don Tremaine was by himself. And as the sun rose, Miller, who had failed his swimming test earlier in his naval career, was nowhere in sight.

Had the swimmers traveled in a straight line to the north from where *Flier* sank, they would have landed on Roughton Island by daybreak. The island, a coral speck with only a few shrubs, is surrounded by reefs and is perhaps three miles north of their starting point. But local fishermen know that Nasubata Channel, with its 100-fathom depths, has powerful currents that sweep one way and the other with the winds. The waters of the South China Sea to the west and the Sulu Sea to the east must pass through the bottleneck between Balabac Island and northern Borneo when they race back and forth, and the greatest volume of water is squeezed through the Nasubata Channel.

On another night a week before or a week after August 13, the current might have carried the survivors perilously close to Balabac, as it had the four men from *Robalo* who took their chances on a raft and left Comiran Island. But just as the men from *Flier* had benefited from a break in the monsoon weather, so had they found fortune in the flow of the sea. The island toward which they began swimming that morning was more than fourteen miles in a straight line north of where *Flier* sank. But the currents, combined with their determined strokes, had taken them almost that far in the first seven hours of their effort to survive, an unaccounted-for helping hand from fate. And whatever this small island before them now offered, they could assume it was not as unfriendly as Balabac, with its Japanese garrison.

Since there had never been any doubt in Jacobson's mind about survival, he was not surprised to find an island ahead of him, apparently within reach. When he needed a break, he could roll onto his back, gaze up at the rising sun, and do the backstroke, and to refuel his optimism he could daydream about all those successes he had experienced in his short life. He had remained in Boy Scouts until he was eighteen, earning the rank of Eagle Scout and then gathering five more merit badges before he graduated from high school. At Grand Haven High, he had been class president in his junior year and student council president his senior year. He had led the council to change the name for the athletic teams, until then called the Havenites, which to Jacobson meant nothing. He and two friends had wanted the teams to be called the Buccaneers, and they railroaded the idea through the council, leaving an indelible mark on their school. When he decided he wanted to compete in the declamation contest—in which students developed a subject and gave a speech—Jacobson stuck with it until he won. And although the football and basketball teams he led were notorious for their losing ways, he was selected for an honorable mention in the all-conference voting, and was named the state's best sportsman of the year in 1940 by the Michigan coaches.

Aside from his personal accomplishments, Jacobson could think about his brothers, both engaged in the same war that had left him swimming for his life. Chuck had been drafted into the army in 1941 and volunteered instead for the navy after Pearl Harbor, enrolling in the officers' training program. He had been on the light cruiser *Boise* in 1942 during the landing at Guadalcanal when that ship had been severely damaged. Dave, his younger brother, was in training as a tail gunner in the Army Air Corps.

The trio of Howell, Baumgart, and Jacobson kept pace with each other throughout the morning, cooled under the blazing tropical sun by the same glass-clear sea that had warmed them during the night. Slowly, they drew toward their island, probably helped by a change in the tide or the currents.

It was one o'clock in the afternoon when Jacobson checked his wristwatch. The approaching drone of an airplane came from a distance, and when the men stopped swimming to look, they saw a low-flying Japanese craft, coming directly toward them. A half-dozen heads on the surface of the Sulu Sea were too tiny for the pilot to notice, however, and the plane kept going. The swimmers resumed their strokes, their luck apparently intact.

CHAPTER 14

CHOOSING FREEDOM

The jungle island floated in the distance like a thin, green wafer. Little about its shore could be determined, but it was closer than anything else, and distance was important for the men, who by now had been in the water for nearly seventeen hours. Jacobson, Howell, and Baumgart had managed to stay close to each other since they had first spotted land. If there was anyone else afloat, they were no longer in sight. There were only the three and the island.

And then ahead, almost on a line toward the island, the men noticed something else in the water. It was long, and above it rose some perpendicular objects. Perhaps it was a native fishing boat, they thought, and the objects were the fishermen. They waved, but there was no response, so they decided to avoid the unfriendly thing. Swimming the straight route toward the island, they nevertheless drew closer to it and discovered it was a bamboo tree, its buoyant trunk riding lightly on the surface, its limbs rising toward the afternoon sun. Eager for some rest, they swam to the tree and Jacobson climbed up to have a look at the surrounding area. Howell and Baumgart struggled up beside where he balanced as the ensign scanned the sea. A short way off he saw more swimmers. He began shouting, joined by his mates, their voices carrying across the now-choppy water, their arms waving in excited arcs.

At daylight, when the island was first spotted, Crowley had given the order to anyone within shouting distance: Swim toward land at your own pace. He soon fell behind the rest, alternately swimming and resting when exhaustion overcame him. That he continued to swim is indisputable. What kept him moving is less certain, for unlike young Jacobson and Baumgart, the skipper's faith was a bit complicated. His crucifix still hung from the slender chain that encircled his neck, and there was no question that he had put in his time as a Catholic. He had always attended church faithfully and was generous when he reached toward the offering basket. But he did not, no matter how important such belief was to the Catholic tradition, hold any faith in an afterlife.

What he had to think of as he swam were his wife and children back in Kansas, and his duty.

He had married Louise Paradis, his sweetheart from his Annapolis days, on January 14, 1935. Exactly nine months and ten days later, Louise delivered a daughter, Patricia Louise. Two years later, she gave birth to a son, John Daniel Jr. In their nine years together, the Crowleys had crisscrossed the nation, moving between assignments on the East Coast and the Pacific. Louise was a French Canadian Catholic but had been raised on the prairie by a single mother. She had attended nursing school and then secretarial school, training that led her to a job in Washington. She had met John when her girlfriend brought her along on a blind date. After they married, she tended to his needs and accommodated his tastes: beef, potatoes, and gravy. She was five feet tall. He towered seven inches above her. To her, he was Jack, although he had been called "Gus" at Annapolis. To him, she was the organizer of their social life. She was welcoming to everyone. He was not. To her, he was the leader of the home, the unquestioned ruler. She could appreciate his methodical ways—how he would keep plunging ahead as long as there was some way to plunge.

It was this tenacity, no doubt, that fueled his effort toward the next stroke through the warm Sulu waves—one more breath taken above the water; this, and images of Louise and the children.

Early in the afternoon, Crowley had seen Liddell ahead of him, clinging to another floating tree. The skipper and his executive officer stayed together then until they heard the shouts from Jacobson's group. It took a few minutes for Crowley and Liddell to reach the larger tree and cling to it. For the skipper, the plant had become a lifesaver. Exhausted, he had felt—even with the island in sight—that he could no longer swim. But the shouts from Jacobson and the others gave him new energy.

Breaking branches from the tree for paddles, the five men now straddled its trunk, urging the tree toward the shore. Off to one side, they saw Don Tremaine, swimming alone. He waved back when they shouted and gestured, but he avoided them. Tremaine had seen them but he could not hear them, and had assumed they were natives. If they were too unfriendly to pick him up, he reasoned, he would not chance swimming toward them.

The others were baffled, watching their shipmate struggle toward the island alone. But now they focused on the shoreline ahead and began to see the forms of houses and boats and other indications of civilization. The sea can create some fantastic illusions, and these were among them, for the island called Byan is little more than a shelf of coral, rising five or six feet above the ocean level and covered with a dense jungle. As the men drew closer, they realized that the jungle grew to the edge of small coral cliffs, and that except for one sandy beach about seventy-five yards long, the sea washed directly against those cliffs. They steered for the beach, hoping for a place to lie down.

The water changed from dark blue to a pale aqua a few hundred yards from the shore where the coral reef began, and then it was shallow enough for the men to walk. Their feet were wrinkled and white from seventeen hours in the water, and the entire seabed on which they stepped was coral. It was like walking on crushed glass rather than gravel, and the sharp coral edges sliced into the soft soles of their feet. Abandoning their bamboo tree, they stumbled, trying to keep their balance as the hot afternoon sun dried the salt water from their backs. The pain in their feet was numbed by their eagerness to feel dry land. And up on the beach stood Jim Russo, urging them on.

Staggering ashore, the men could, for the first time since *Flier* sank, see each other from head to toe. The sight was shocking. In the ten hours since daylight, the unrelenting rays of the sun had bombarded their water-softened white flesh. Now, where their skin was exposed, they were scalded red. Baumgart alone had long trousers on, saving his legs from the scorching. But like the others, he waded from the ocean with his face and arms as red as if the seawater had been boiling, and his blood drained into the sand from the coral slashes in his feet.

Liddell was in no better shape. His mouth pleaded for freshwater, his stomach for something to eat, and his muscles cried for rest. But he left the others as soon as he reached the beach and hobbled along the sand; at its far end, he walked back into the water, hoping to find more shipmates.

Byan Island, roughly triangular in shape, is just east of Mantangule Island, the second stop from which the Coastwatchers had evacuated a month earlier. The beach that the swimmers found is on the southern side, facing in the direction of *Flier*'s grave, and its sand is soft and white. In 1944, the island was uninhabited by humans.

As Liddell headed east, most of the men whom he left behind settled onto the sand, overcome by weariness. Someone had found a coconut floating in the surf. When the survivors had gathered some palm leaves and sticks and built a feeble-looking shelter, they tried to open the coconut. They smashed the nut on the coral bank, hoping to crack it.

After an hour, Liddell returned to the beach with Tremaine beside him. Now there were seven survivors—Crowley, Liddell, Jacobson, Howell, Baumgart, Russo, and Tremaine—and they all shared the one coconut. Each man got a couple of tablespoons of coconut milk and a piece of white meat about the size of two postage stamps—their first meal in twenty-four hours.

The meal was quickly finished, and then each man promptly vomited.

A few hours after the men reached Byan Island, the sun settled beyond sprawling Mantangule and the air grew cool. Crowley and Liddell believed they were on Mantangule Island and that the big land to the west was Balabac, which they knew was occupied by the Japanese. To build a fire, if they could manage it, might attract attention, so they faced a night of cold. Even before sunset had cooled the air, they were swept alternately by fever chills and sweats. In the dusk, they huddled together for warmth, lying directly on the sand and, having successfully outlasted death for a day, sought the peace of sleep.

Neither sleep nor peace was to be theirs, however. Roused by their fevers, they would seek a more comfortable position, only to have the grains of the beach rasp across their sunburned flesh like sandpaper. At times, they were awakened by rats nibbling on their feet. Young Jacobson lay awake, his body shaking, the watch on his wrist slowly ticking off the seconds and minutes. He wanted nothing more than for the hours to pass and the day to come, bringing with it warmth.

They had learned, in their first stumbling hours ashore before nightfall, that the area near the beach offered neither food nor water. So when the sun rose on August 15, 1944, the *Flier* survivors knew they had to begin a search. Crowley directed Tremaine, Russo, and Howell, who had injured his knee when he had jumped off the submarine, to stay on the beach and improve the lean-to shelter. Jacobson and Baumgart were to head east and scout out the island, while Crowley and Liddell would head the other way.

Walking any distance was now an excruciating ordeal. Jacobson was struck with the foolishness everyone had displayed when they had discarded their shoes. Of course! They could have simply tied their shoelaces together and slung the shoes around their necks, and now, walking along the shore would not have been such torture!

The Eagle Scout did not think of another measure, taught by the Boy Scouts then, that may well have spared some of the men who, in the dark hours after the sinking, had courageously chosen the time of their own deaths. According to Scout teachings, their trousers could have been their life preservers. The trick was to take a pair of water-soaked trousers, tie the cuffs in knots and button or zip the fly shut. Then, holding the trousers by the waistband, with the legs dangling behind their heads, the swimmers could yank the trousers forward, over their heads, in about the same motion used to swing a sledgehammer. The theory was that the trousers would balloon as air filled the wet legs. If the movement was continued until the hands brought the waistband into the water in front of the swimmer, the inflated legs each would rise like long balloons, the air still trapped inside. Then the swimmer could place the upside-down trousers under his chest, the legs sprouting from under each arm like water wings.

But if Jacobson, the Eagle Scout, was unaware of this lifesaving maneuver, he was not alone, for none of the sailors who got off *Flier* had employed it.

What had kept these seven men afloat had been something no handbook could teach. One swimming stroke following the next had—in the absence of a duty to save their injured friends—delivered them to land. Now they began in the same determined way to take the next small steps toward their survival. Howell, Russo, and Tremaine started gathering scraps of wood and palm leaves in the hope of creating some real shelter for the coming night. At the same time, Ensign Jacobson and the demoted motor machinist mate, Baumgart, hobbled along the shore, Baumgart in trousers and an undershirt, the ensign in his underwear with binoculars dangling from his neck. There were coconuts everywhere along the water's edge. They picked up the ones that looked whole and opened them with their bare hands by smashing them on coral. But each one that broke open left them disappointed, its meat rotten, its milk spoiled.

They trudged for hours without success. And then they rounded a point and ahead they saw a string of islands. Still ankle-deep in the sea and standing on coral beds, they splashed forward until they found a sandy beach where driftwood had gathered. Then they decided it was time to head back. Realizing that if they crossed the island, it should take less time than circling the beach, they tried to climb ashore up the coral cliffs. But the thorns and vines repelled them, and they waded once more into the shallows across the coral, retracing their painful steps toward their shipmates.

That morning, Crowley and Liddell had set off in the opposite direction from Jacobson and Baumgart to explore the western side of the island. They had another reason for leaving together: They wanted to talk about the prospects for the group's ultimate survival. Crowley was familiar with the territory only from having studied nautical charts. Liddell had served on a submarine in the Philippines before the war and had a deeper understanding of the locale. What they had found so far was that they could not stay on this island. It was little more than a coral reef with no food or shelter. The jungle that began at the shore was a tangle of thorns and vines. With no tools to hack their way forward, the men could not penetrate this thicket, even if there were some water and food to be found inland. With their blistered and seeping naked skin, they were no match for the island. Crowley and Liddell agreed that the only hope lay in finding a more hospitable place. They believed they could not afford to delay. What the sinking of *Flier* could not inflict on these men, the loss of food and water, combined with their wounds and the possibility of infection, could.

Rounding the western tip of the island, they saw their two options: To the northeast, beyond two more small islands, lay a large island. Liddell identified it as Bugsuk Island. And behind them, to the southwest beyond the long, flat Mantangule Island, was the mountainous mass they knew had to be Balabac. Intelligence reports that they had reviewed back in Australia said the Japanese were on Balabac. But from what they remembered, there was less chance of finding the enemy on Bugsuk, which was about five or six miles away. The trip could be made manageable by hopping only to the next island, Gabung, and resting before going on. There were tremendous currents that funneled between islands like these, Crowley and Liddell knew, and in their weakened state, the survivors could easily be swept out to sea if they tried to swim across. They needed another plan, and more information. So Liddell decided to leave Crowley behind and explore a bit further on the northern side of the island. The lieutenant had walked some distance when, coming around a curve in the shore, he saw a man ahead on the beach— a white man, clothed only in underwear.

At daybreak the day before, Wesley Miller had lost contact with the other swimmers. But he saw several islands on the horizon, and, since it was in the direction he had been swimming, he kept going for the closest one. As the afternoon wore on, however, he found that the current was sweeping him to his left, past the nearest island. He would never be able to reach it, he knew, so he began to swim for the next island. But when he was perhaps two miles from his target, the current increased, carrying him fast along the beach. Still he swam toward the shore, cutting the distance in half when, to his left, he saw the end of the island approaching. After that, there was nothing, and Miller believed that his long trek from the Oregon ranch to the middle of the Pacific Ocean was at an end.

It was startling when, letting his feet fall below him, Miller felt his toes touch the bottom. He began walking now, and soon the water was only waist-deep, and to his left the coral actually rose above the surface. Then the sun set over Balabac and Mantangule and the water grew deeper. He no longer could wade, but although he must swim again to survive, his arms and legs were unwilling to move. So he willed himself toward the beach, and when he could touch bottom again, he was too tired to stand. Sand and coral rose beneath him, and he leaned forward in the water so that his knees, not his feet, propelled him ashore while his body and arms floated listlessly. Crawling as an infant might, he worked his way out of the sea and partway up the sand, where his thoughts and his will ceased and he fell asleep. Awakened in the middle of the night by rising water, he dragged himself to higher ground, up against the coral cliff, and slept once more.

In the morning, Miller began to walk along the shore, looking for a way to scale the cliffs. As he stumbled on, he searched for clams in the sand. In a mile of hiking, he had found only solid rock cliffs along the bank, with jungle growth snarling out of their cracks.

Then Liddell found Miller and led him back to Crowley. The skipper, perhaps noticing the sailor for the first time, realized that this crewman was little more than a boy, a child who was pathetically grateful to find that he was not a sole survivor.

Later that afternoon, everyone assembled at the beach and reported on their work. Jacobson and Baumgart had found neither food nor water, but they told of locating a pile of driftwood on the northern beach. Howell, Russo, and Tremaine, when they were not working on the lean-to, had set out seashells to collect water should it rain.

And they had found water seeping out of the coral cliffs. They had set some shells below the cliffs and collected some water, one drip at a time—three shells full, in all. Everyone shared it, each person drinking a couple of teaspoons. It was merely seawater that had splashed onto the coral at high tide, but their thirst convinced the men they were getting freshwater.

If they continued to wet their lips with this water for long, they were going to be doomed. The human body, in order to rid itself of excess salt, passes the salt through the kidneys where it is washed away in urine. That means that the body is losing water as well as salt. The more salt in the system, the more water must be expelled. In a short time, the consumption of salt water will actually dehydrate the body, increasing the level of salt in the bloodstream and damaging bodily tissues. Soon, the drinker will die. But first, normal body functions will be damaged. Saliva will dry up, leaving the mouth and tongue without lubrication, exposing them to infection. Drying of the tongue may cause it to swell and split. Death might be preferable.

With the other reports submitted, Crowley told the men of their options. They could head west, eventually reaching Balabac where there was food and shelter—and Japanese soldiers. They would probably be captured and become prisoners of war. (Earlier in the afternoon, another Japanese patrol plane had flown low over the island, the red rising sun insignia on its wings easily seen by the survivors.) Or, they could use the driftwood that Jacobson and Baumgart had found, build a raft, try to reach Bugsuk, and, accepting the uncertainty of finding food and water there, remain free men.

To a man, they chose freedom. They would begin work in the morning.

Settling in for the night, they gazed out over the Sulu Sea, hoping for rain to fill their upturned shells, resigned to ending another day without food. All day, they had seen rain clouds pass on either side of Byan, each with the wet, gray shafts of a downpour slanting toward the sea beneath it. But none had graced Byan or the survivors.

A little after six o'clock, with the sun setting to their right, they saw off on the southern horizon a geyser rise into the air, followed a few seconds later by the sound of an explosion. It could have been the detonation of a drifting mine, or it might have been *Flier's* final convulsion.

In two days, they had had no nutrition. They had each vomited their one small chunk of coconut because it was too dry. And now it had been more than a day since that tiny morsel was momentarily theirs. The lean-to was still little protection against the cold of the coming night. Their individual prayers for the return of daylight would be answered only after long hours of shivering and pain, hunger and thirst. They posted a watch, a couple of men with clubs to fight off potential intruders—and rats. And, like the swimmers they had been, whose stoicism in the face of absurd odds had brought them ashore, they confronted the night.

Sunrise brought all the men back onto their feet. The agony of standing on those festering cuts was not enough to keep them on the beach, and soon the eight were hobbling in the shallow water, where vegetation coated some of the coral, making it less sharp. Splashing up Byan Island's eastern shore, they could see Gabung Island in the distance. When they reached the place where the two islands were closest together—just under a mile separated them—they began building their raft. Liddell and Russo, both strong men, reached into the jungle from the edge of the beach and tore out vines. As some of the men used the vines to lash the bamboo driftwood logs together, Chief Howell sat on the beach, improvising two paddles by splitting slender bamboo poles partway, inserting small pieces in the split crossway, and then tying them in place with thin vines. Occasionally, he would lick moisture that he found on leaves. Not far from Howell, Baumgart and Tremaine, working on the raft, tried summoning humor from their drowsy minds, hoping to lessen their thirst. Their feeble jokes involved inventing celebrity names to commemorate their experience. There was Bing Juiceby and Frank Sinatrajuice. Just offshore, squalls of summer rain blew by, teasing the men who kept searching for shade from the sun blazing over their heads.

Crowley saw how his men slowed in their work as the day wore on, their movements becoming uncoordinated, their attention wan-

dering. Thirst was on everyone's mind. But even though they scoured
the coast looking for edible coconuts, they found none all day.

Crowley and Liddell had observed the currents and determined
that slack tide would come at mid-afternoon, about the same time the
patrol plane had passed on each of the last two days. When the raft
was completed—it was a tiny craft about four feet by seven feet, with
logs four inches in diameter—everyone rested for a while. Then some
began sorting through the coconuts that had floated to shore. Jacobson and Tremaine each found one unopened nut, and everyone had a
small amount of the meat to eat.

It was about two-thirty that afternoon, just before slack tide, when
the eight men surrounded their little raft and pushed it out toward
Gabung. Ahead of them was a crossing of slightly less than one mile.
The water was the pale blue of reef water out for several hundred
yards off the beach, and the reef resumed on the far side of the channel, where dark blue water indicated a depth that no one would be
able to wade. They had brought two long poles with them, and for
the first quarter of the voyage, the younger men took turns poling the
raft, on which Crowley was the only permanent passenger. The rest of
the men leaned on the raft for support as they walked in the shallows
across another long bed of razor-sharp coral. Crowley paddled.

Before they had made it halfway across the channel, they saw the
daily patrol plane coming in low. Crowley and the man poling slipped
into the water, and everyone tried to hide under the raft. The plane
kept going, and the men, clinging to the sides, kicked in the deeper
water, slowly moving the raft across the channel.

Now on the open water, they found themselves directly in the
path of an oncoming squall. Abruptly, they were pelted with large,
pure droplets, delicious on their lips, and everyone tipped his head
back and opened his mouth. But while the raindrops splattered off
their foreheads and cheeks, none of it seemed to find their tongues
before the squall passed on into the ocean, leaving the scorching sun
in its wake.

They had not yet reached the reef on the far side of the channel
when the tide seemed to shift and a new current swept between the

islands. With only a quarter of a mile to go, they suddenly seemed unable to make any progress, and the raft appeared to be drifting away from Gabung Island. The men on the sides kicked with all their feeble power and Crowley, feeling like a very elderly thirty-five, paddled, and the raft circled the end of the island and settled in its lee, the current having deposited the men close enough to shore that they could swim the final leg.

It was seven o'clock, more than four hours since they had left Byan Island a mile to the south, and the sun had already set. They found a sandy beach and were content to collapse where they could find room. The little slivers of coconut they had eaten earlier had done little to curb their appetite, and their thirst was only growing. But no one had the energy to forage. More than food and water, right now they wanted sleep.

Gabung Island was no different than Byan had been, offering only a shallow sandy beach on which to sleep. There was no time—nor any energy among the eight men—for building a shelter, and the night air quickly grew cold. One of the men—perhaps one who had lived near the sea as a child, like Jim Russo, a native of Marblehead, Massachusetts, a town lapped by the cold waters of the North Shore—thought he knew of a solution, one that would insulate his body from the night while keeping any rats at bay. He dug a pit in the sand and then buried himself up to his neck. It was damp, but there were no chilling breezes.

When the others saw this innovation, they all followed suit, and sleep came quickly in eight sandy cocoons. But the fever shakes came quickly, as well, and the sand shook off, leaving the men exposed. They buried themselves again, but before the shakes could get them, they felt sand crabs moving along their tender skin, a tickling that had to be escaped.

Jacobson found that walking helped to settle his fever shakes, so he prowled the little beach until he was calm. Then he buried himself again. He and Liddell thought that perhaps burying themselves together in the same pit would keep them warmer, but the experiment failed when both men shook violently and shed their sand blanket quicker than before.

Sunrise the following morning—August 17—brought with it relief from the tremors of the night and hope that this would be the day the men would eat. Before launching their raft, they gathered to discuss their next steps. It would be another nine or ten hours until the tides allowed them to leave this island for the next one in the chain. Crowley and Liddell took suggestions, and the group decided that their time could be best used by traveling around the island the long way. There would be more chance of finding food if they were covering a longer shoreline. It meant more walking, but now empty stomachs and parched mouths were overpowering the screaming pains from their feet and the swollen and blistered burns on their backs and arms. They pushed the raft into the shallow water and began circling the island to the west. Once more, the coral in the shallow water was softened by plants that grew on it, so wading was less painful than it might have been. But there was a trade-off, because when they were not swimming, their burns were always exposed to the sun as it rose high above the island.

On the eastern side of Byan the day before, the men had walked along the beach with open ocean to their right. Now, walking along Gabung's western coast, they felt surrounded by islands. Mantangule's long, low bulk stretched out to the southwest, and Bugsuk's broad sweep consumed the view to the northeast, only three or so miles across the reef-strewn water. To the north, another large island—Pandanan—was indistinguishable from Bugsuk. And to the northwest, more, smaller islands rose above the reefs to hide the horizon. With their goal of Bugsuk in sight, the men could think of food and water and let those images draw them ahead. But there were distractions. Swarms of stinging insects flew around them, and their thoughts drifted uncontrollably, clouded by the lack of food and water.

There were no good coconuts along that shore. The bank of the island was a coral cliff, just as it had been on Byan, and the jungle hung over the cliff in an impenetrable tangle, home to birds and monkeys. There were occasional sand beaches, but the island was longer than Byan—not quite two miles, compared with just over a mile—and the coral was everywhere along the coast. It took the men until after one o'clock that afternoon to arrive at a place that seemed like a good launching point for their trip to the next island in this chain.

Apo Island was on the far side of a strait nearly two miles across, with the dark blue of deep water again in the middle, between the two shores. The men had about two hours to wait for slack tide and the passing of the next enemy patrol plane, and they gathered more coconuts from the beach, but as so often before, none was edible. Surrounded by a sea full of fish and water, they were dying of thirst and starvation.

The airplane arrived on schedule and continued south over the island. Certain the danger had passed, the men pushed their raft back to sea. The water was shallow enough for them to wade and to keep the weight off their feet as they leaned on the raft. Pushing and splashing, they moved their craft into the dark blue of the deeper water.

They were midway between the two islands, with no retreat possible, when someone noticed the fins. Two sharks cruised just beneath the surface, looking for food. The men kept paddling, splashing and kicking, and the sharks, perhaps sensing the hunger that drove these eight beings, stayed clear. If they had been able to read the minds of the swimmers, the message would have been: *Que sera, sera.*

Aided by the shallow water, the raft crossed between Gabung and Apo islands in only three hours, and the men found a sandy beach just before dark. By now, they knew what to expect. They posted their rat guards and waited in troubled dreams and fitful sleep for the morning.

Sunrise was again their alarm clock, but they lingered until about eight o'clock before gathering around their sole possession, the raft, and heading to the west. Apo is a small, round island, but in all other ways it seemed no different from Byan and Gabung. Again, the men had chosen to take the long way, and each grudging step along the curved shoreline revealed some new aspect of the land ahead. Before noon, they had found the first indication of humans—a dugout canoe abandoned on the beach. The boat was riddled with holes and useless, so they left it and went on. Then they saw a trail leading up over the coral cliff, and Jacobson and Baumgart decided to explore. A trail like this meant human activity. But after a few hundred yards of walking on the coral pavement of the path, the men turned back, leaving the place to the monkeys that chattered and scampered in the trees around them. Joining the other men, they continued north along the shore.

Ancient trees, their trunks varicose and black, their roots writhing like serpents, the weave of their arched branches creating darkened tunnels, grew out from the coral cliffs along the northwestern shore of Apo Island. The men walked under the trees, hidden from observation, until, in the distance, they saw the green shoreline of their destination, Bugsuk Island.

They stood transfixed, for there, under coconut trees that swayed like tall, slender dancers lining the edge of a broad, sandy beach, were houses. There were no Japanese launches on the shore and no sign of activity around the buildings. That did not mean there were no risks. So they would wait and watch.

But not for long.

CHAPTER 15

SPIRITS OF THE LAND

There were eyes behind the towering coconut trees that swayed in the sea breeze along Bugsuk Island's sparkling beach in a gentle hula. The eyes were watching the *Flier* survivors.

All that Crowley and his men saw when they looked toward the island were the apparently tranquil settlement of houses and, in their imaginations, food and water. But they were cautious. With their raft in tow, they worked their way around the northern edge of Apo Island to a point on the beach where they could no longer see the houses. Their plan was to arrive on Bugsuk just before sunset and to use the half-light of dusk to sneak toward the settlement. By now, their starvation and thirst had robbed the men of whatever athletic ability they had once possessed, so when they swam across the narrow channel between the islands, they would lack the strength to swim against the flow. But if they judged the current correctly, they would land about a mile and a half from the houses. Then they would have enough cover to sneak closer, undetected. There was no more than a half-mile between Apo and the far shore, and all of it was the pale blue of reef water. They expected no problems.

Late that afternoon, they pushed the raft off the sandy beach. Most of the men waded at its side, and when they reached the far shore, they climbed out of the water, not on coral but with another long stretch of white-sand beach under their tender feet. Stowing the raft, they walked west toward the setting sun. They were on a narrow peninsula, on the far side of which was the tidal mouth of a saltwater stream. Crossing the peninsula with a wary eye toward the far shore, they waded into the stream. When they climbed the far bank, they were on the same beach that, to the west, passed in front of the Bugsuk houses. Here a grove of baring trees, a species that, like mangroves, sinks its roots in salt water, blocked their view of the settlement. The men worked their way through the shallow water under the trees, with the low rays of the sun slanting between the tree trunks, and then moved ashore, peering through the grove at what appeared to be a once-thriving but now-abandoned village. The houses that they had seen from Apo Island were surrounded by a coconut grove, and between the survivors and those houses were the remnants of bamboo and palm-leaf native huts.

As the others inched ahead, Baumgart and Jacobson, still thinking like a commissary officer, stooped to gather a dozen ripe, green coconuts that had fallen, like welcoming gifts, from the treetops. Meanwhile, the men in the lead moved closer to the buildings. Nothing stirred. And when they peered inside the largest house, there was no one home. This place, it seemed, was safe.

Jacobson and Baumgart were the last to arrive, their arms filled with coconuts. For the first time in five days, the *Flier* survivors would have unspoiled food to eat, and apparently a place to sleep. The main building in this settlement—well built of bamboo and lumber, with a thatched roof—looked like the home of a person of wealth. But the home had been ransacked, the furniture carted out of its now-barren rooms, and any remnant of the former owners' presence stripped from the now-naked walls. There were paper business records of all sorts scattered about the floor, documents recording, among other things, the purchase of cattle and the sale of lumber.

The house had a good, wooden floor for sleeping, probably free from rats and certainly protected from sand crabs. But weary as they were, the men were also excited by their discoveries and were not yet ready for rest. They wanted to explore. Standing in front of the main house and looking south, they could imagine that they were in an exotic resort. A lawn fifty yards deep or more and shaded by the high canopy of coconut trees led to the beach of pure, white, soft sand, framed in this view by drooping coconut palm fronds. Beyond the beach was an island paradise. Stretching out to the left was the chain of islands the men had spent the last four days hopping, and between the last—Byan—and Mantangule, on the right, rose the distant blue mountains of Balabac. A good-size wooden boat—Al Jacobson guessed it was thirty-eight feet long—was beached in front of the house and looked like it had been intentionally destroyed. Nearby was another launch of about the same size that appeared to have been under construction. On either side of the house and inland from it were several clearings, which suggested that the owners had raised vegetables. And farther inland, some of the men reported, there was a stream. In its clear water swam schools of fish, meals for days to come.

Exploring by himself, Earl Baumgart found a curious concrete structure just behind the main house. It stood about five feet high and was another six feet long, and when he climbed atop it he was elated. Someone had built a cistern to collect rainwater, probably from the roof of the house. There was all the water the men would ever need, and more! He called out his discovery to the others, who came running.

Once more, the skipper lived up to his reputation for cautiousness outside of the realm of battle. He told his gathered crew that they should drink sparingly from the cistern. They wanted to guzzle to their thirst's content, he knew. But having gone without water for five days, and with almost no food in the same period, their bodies could not handle much. When he had explained this, each man took a small sip from Baumgart's pool and then went away. Only Chief Howell ignored Crowley's caution. He drank until his belly was full, and then he drank some more.

Now Jacobson and some others set about opening the good coconuts. They found a sharp rock in the ground and smashed each nut against it until they had removed the soft green outer shell. Then they punched out the eye of the inner, hard brown shell, drained the milk, and crushed the nut into pieces that could be chewed.

With these small pleasures, the men began to settle in for the night. Jacobson found a bamboo door that he laid on the floor as his mattress, and he stretched out on it, content. Images filled his head as the palm leaves rustled above him. There were fish and coconuts to eat, a roof over his head, water to drink, and, it appeared, no enemies within miles. There was no more need to walk, so his feet could heal. There was shade from the sun, so his blisters would dry and disappear. This was a place where a man could wait out the war, if he had to.

The last family to sleep in this house had been that of Nazario Mayor. These were his gardens that lay fallow, his motor launch that was wrecked on the beach, and his cistern that held the water. In the forest that bordered the homestead, Mayor had worked as a timber cruiser, selecting the trees that would be harvested by his father-in-law, Thomas Loudon. He knew which stand of Philippine mahogany was ready to be made into lumber, which grove of ipil trees would make good railroad ties. The guerrilla leader's children had spent an often-idyllic childhood at the family home before the war. But there were also family stories that let them know this place, while beautiful beyond description, was dangerous. Their earliest memories harbored images of their grandfather Loudon using his crosscut saw as a weapon. There he was, retreating into the sea, holding off the men who had slaughtered his wife and two of his daughters, and surviving by swimming across a channel to another island.

But when Nazario Mayor's wife and children fled this home, one day ahead of the Japanese raiders, they also carried with them memories of exotic mushrooms and orchids of all hues that grew wild near their home.

The balance between the beautiful and the deadly touched every aspect of life on these islands. The very pool that wetted an orchid's roots also may have nurtured the larvae of malaria-carrying mosquitoes. The same insects may have carried one or more of the four types of dengue fever, a disease that can be as mild as common influenza but that can also cause internal hemorrhaging and death.

By the time the *Flier* crewmen found themselves on Bugsuk, they knew the diseases that surrounded them. Malaria and dengue fever had sent soldiers to field hospitals across the Pacific. There was nothing these eight men could do to protect themselves.

Not long after Chief Howell drank his fill from the cistern, he began to feel ill. His condition worsened during the night, but there was no help for him. If some of the others showed little sympathy, it may have been because they knew his sickness, self-inflicted as it was, was not lethal. In time, his body would acclimate. The little bit of coconut in their stomachs had satisfied their appetites, and they knew there would be more meals to come. With a home around them to keep away the chilling breezes, they succumbed to their exhaustion, dreaming untroubled dreams.

Once more, they arose with the sun and began planning their day. There was work to be done, and Crowley and Liddell started organizing teams. One group would catch some fish, while another would build a fire for cooking. They had no matches, but Jacobson still had his binoculars, and their lenses would make perfect magnifying glasses for focusing the sun's rays in an incendiary beam on dry tinder. Someone needed to scout the area, and the group would need more coconuts.

Jacobson was the first one up, and he was standing looking out a window toward the rear of the house and the jungle beyond when he saw two small boys—they might have been thirteen or fourteen— emerge from the trees. Jacobson told his shipmates what he saw, and they all were quickly on their feet. It was obvious to them that the boys knew the sailors were there, so they filed out of the house and approached the visitors. The boys were wearing ragged shorts and tattered shirts, and their feet were bare, like the sailors'. Crowley stepped forward.

"Americans or Japanese?" he asked.

"Americanos!" one of the boys, Oros Bogata, said, smiling. "Japanese!" he said, drawing a finger across his throat as if slitting it.

The men felt a collective wave of relief. Then the boy pointed to the cistern by the house.

"Don't drink water," he said.

Perhaps they misunderstood his puzzling words, they thought. But with their *Que sera, sera* attitude, they disregarded that comment and asked whether the boys had any food. Oros patted his small stomach.

"Rice," he said, and he motioned for the men to follow him and his silent friend back into the jungle. Stepping in line behind the boys, they found themselves on a narrow path. The boys, seeing that they were being followed, scampered ahead to a spot where they had left poles with small packs tied at the ends. Each balanced his pole on his shoulder, and then Oros led the file of hobbling, nearly naked men while his friend followed, sweeping the trail behind them to camouflage evidence of the group's passing.

In a short distance, they reached an abandoned sugarcane field. Oros motioned for the men to sit down, and he and his companion cut sections of cane a yard long and offered each man his own piece. The heart of the cane was a sweet and juicy bundle of fibers, and for the next half-hour, Crowley and his men chewed in bliss, until they simply had no more strength left in their jaws.

Back on the path, the boys led the men a short way to a clearing about the size of a football field. In one corner of the field was a raised wooden platform with a thatched roof supported on bamboo poles, but with no walls. Again the boys motioned for the men to sit and rest. Then they dropped their poles and opened their packs. One took a stick, sharpened at one end, and placed the tip in a notched piece of wood that he drew from his pack. He spun the stick between his palms, and in less time than it would have taken to remove a match from a box and strike it, he had some tinder smoldering. Jacobson, the Eagle Scout who had been taught to start fires with a bow and a stick, was impressed.

Then the boys produced a small pot, and one left and got water from a nearby stream. They poured rice from their pack into the pot, and while the fire brought the water to a boil, they cut leaves from a banana tree and made plates for their guests. Now the same boy who had cautioned them against drinking from the cistern gave them a cup of muddy water and, by sign language, told them they should drink it. The men hesitated, so the boy drank some himself. *Que sera, sera!* The men drank, as well.

When the rice was cooked, the boys spread it on the banana leaves. Then they produced three dried fish from the bounty of their packs and divided them among the men. There was enough for everyone.

Four days earlier, Crowley and his men had chosen survival with freedom over survival with food when they had elected to head away from Balabac. Theirs was a decision that prolonged the pain of hunger and thirst, which might easily have been cut short had they allowed themselves instead to come under Japanese control. Now, without hesitation, they had turned themselves over to the authority of two small boys whose friendship they accepted as a stray dog does that of a man with a scrap of food. Led by their stomachs, the sailors had followed the boys into the jungle with only the promise of rice, and now, with the smell of steaming hot rice and fish rising to their nostrils, they attacked their meal.

Their focus changed abruptly when, looking up from his food, one of them saw nine men, bristling with weapons—rifles, blowguns, and bolos—stepping into the clearing from every point of the compass.

They were surrounded!

The *Flier* survivors had traded their safety for scraps of sustenance. The price of their meal now stared across the clearing at them.

Wesley Miller was ready to bolt like a startled fawn, but these fierce-looking warriors were everywhere. No one budged. The shredded soles of their feet precluded it.

"Hello!" one of the armed men called. His voice was cheerful and a smile lit his face. He dashed across the grass to the platform where the sailors still sat. Crowley struggled to his feet, as did his men at the approach of this stranger. When the man reached them, he grasped the hands of the *Flier* crew, shaking them vigorously.

"Welcome to Bugsuk Island," the man said. "I am Pedro Sarmiento."

Sarmiento said he was the leader of the local bolo battalion, indicating the men who were with him. He said he had been a teacher before the war, and made a point of telling the survivors that he was a Christian. By the clarity of his English, it was obvious to the survivors that he had received a formal education. The other men were natives of the island, two of them armed with rifles like Sarmiento's, and the other six armed with bolos and blowguns. All of them were dressed in ragged shirts and trousers. Sarmiento said the natives kept lookouts posted around Bugsuk Island, observing the movements of the Japanese, which they reported to him. One of the lookouts had seen the *Flier* men swimming toward Bugsuk and had relayed the information to Sarmiento. But the lookout had been unable to determine whether the swimmers were American or Japanese. (Even now, their swollen faces masked their features, and they were dressed only in underwear, not uniforms.)

So Sarmiento had decided to assemble the bolo battalion. He sent word that night to several nearby islands for the men to come to Bugsuk. During the night, they had surrounded the house by the beach, and when the survivors arose in the morning, Sarmiento sent the two boys to get a closer look. If they found Japanese, they were to act as if they were simply going to the coconut grove. Then the bolo battalion would attack and slaughter the intruders. If they were Allies, the boys were to bring them back to this platform, which Sarmiento explained was a schoolhouse.

Sarmiento had instructions from the guerrilla headquarters that if he found any Allied survivors, he was to ship them to a guerrilla outpost on Palawan's southern tip.

Crowley and Liddell were becoming comfortable with Sarmiento, and they were prepared to follow his instructions. At this point someone recalled the earlier direction from the two boys, to not drink the water in the cistern, and asked Sarmiento to explain.

Oh, he replied, earlier in the war, when the Japanese had driven the owner of the home from his property, Sarmiento had poisoned the water with arsenic in hopes that Japanese soldiers would drink it!

Everyone looked at Chief Howell. The man had a cast-iron gut!

Elton Brubaker and seventy other men had now been gone for six days, the dying screams of those trapped inside *Flier* swallowed by the dark sea, but they lived on in the hearts of those who loved them and knew nothing of their passing.

Nellie May Brubaker yearned for her son more with each day, and although she did not burden him with a nightly letter, she gathered news between letters that she would include in the next one. She tried to paint a picture of the new home that he had not yet known, and the life that awaited him there when he returned from war.

'Tis Tuesday here. Just two o'clock. I have just finished my weekly ironing. I would have been through hours ago if I hadn't worked out in the garden till eleven o'clock. I am preparing for the fall planting which will begin early next month. I still find I prefer working outside to indoors duties.

My flowers are beautiful. The window boxes are gorgeous with petunias. My pot plants are thriving too. My geraniums are the talk of the neighborhood. The lawn here is lovely, spacious, cool, well kept grass. There are four Australian pines in and near the front. There is a large lovely palm near the side-end of the big screened-in front porch. There are four large pecan trees just simply loaded with nuts. We like it better here every day. Yes, it is a dream come true.

[Cousin] Jimmy goes [into the military] Thursday, just two more days. I plan to have [his mother] Lyle over to spend the day with me. How well I remember how I felt the day you left.

This was a momentary lapse away from the news into the deeper thoughts of the mother's heart. She quickly returned to gossip.

Jim was here last night. He, his girl Cathern [sic] Tetter (red headed but attractive), Myron, and most of the gang were here last night.

Charlotte is expected Friday. I'm busy trying to have everything done up when she does get in. I've been painting and varnishing so you would hardly know the old furniture.

Duties are calling again—I'm planning to send you a package for your birthday, which, by the way will be only next month. I'll get it right off—I hear by the radio that we are supposed to get your Christmas packages off next month too.

Then the mother's heart broke through her brave front.

Oh, my boy, how much I love you, and how glad we all will be when you can be home again. Daddy hasn't made the drawing for you yet but I'm sure he will soon. Remember how slow he is. But when he does it, it will be well done.

Love from all of us,
Mom

P.S. Just read your letter written Aug. 4. Romance seems the theme of that particular letter. Yes, I liked Ruth too. Ever so much more than Pauline. There is more personality and character there, so it seems to me.

The Japanese patrol would reach Bugsuk later in the morning, Sarmiento told the sailors, so they could not remain at the schoolhouse. The Japanese soldiers would inspect the area and then would spend the night in the house where Crowley and his men had slept so peacefully the night before. So the sailors would have to hike at least a mile inland to be safe. The Japanese were afraid to penetrate the center of the island, Sarmiento said.

Sarmiento reported that his instructions from the guerrilla leader, Captain Mayor, were to take any survivors all the way north across the center of Bugsuk and then to bring them by boat to the guerrilla outpost at Cape Buliluyan, the southernmost tip of Palawan. He told Crowley and Liddell that it was important to begin the hike soon. When they said they were ready, he told them to finish their breakfast. Then he sent the two boys back to the beach to make sure the Americans had not left any evidence behind.

A few minutes later, the boys returned with the lens that the sailors had removed from Jacobson's binoculars, with which they had planned to start their fires. Someone offered the lens to Sarmiento, who produced a pipe and tobacco that he lit with the lens. He smiled with gratitude. Then, seeing that they had finished their rice and fish, he invited the men from *Flier* to begin their cross-island trek.

CHAPTER 16

BY LAND AND BY SEA

They looked to Earl Baumgart like a line of ballet dancers, these sun-burned white men wearing little more than their skivvies who were trying to balance on their toes as they headed from the clearing into the jungle. Their feet were too painful for them to walk normally. Pus was oozing from the cuts on their soles, and even here, several hundred yards from the beach, the path was mostly sharp coral that only sliced them more. So they rose on their toes, but that did little good. Their toes were as bare as the rest of their feet.

Sarmiento stayed close to Crowley and Liddell, talking with them and encouraging them and their shipmates. Several of Sarmiento's men walked ahead of the column of survivors, hacking the jungle where it grew into the path, while the rest followed the group, guarding against surprises. Ahead, the narrow path rose and fell over gentle slopes and wound beneath trees that soared 200 feet above the jungle floor. All of Bugsuk Island was less than 100 feet above sea level, and although this trail ran the length of the island, it was only about eight miles long. Hikers in good condition could cover that distance in three hours or less, and this group had all day. But they were overwhelmed with fatigue. What they had managed to accomplish in the five prior days, moving from island to island without food or water, they now seemed almost unable to do after their first good night of sleep and their first real meal. Their steps were as labored as those of a Himalayan climber, their pace just as slow. Sarmiento saw that he could not hope to nudge the men all the way to the island's northern shore before dark. He told them they would stop for the night when they had gone halfway.

It was five o'clock that afternoon when the men stumbled into a clearing with three huts built of bamboo, rising on stilts above the vermin and serpents of the jungle floor. Jacobson admired the construction design and the workmanship. To his engineer's eye, these were no shacks. They were decent homes, if rustic. The owners had cleared away enough of the thick underbrush for vegetable gardens. There were chickens in the yards around the houses, pecking here and there, tame as house pets. Jacobson, the budding industrialist, had to admit that nothing in this tiny village could be called progressive, but it seemed to function in a way that appealed to him.

Sarmiento explained that they were at the home of the leading man. They saw that rattan mats had been spread out on the ground. These were beds for them, Sarmiento said. All eight survivors lowered themselves to the mats and, within minutes, were asleep.

Crowley's sleep was broken by Sarmiento, however. The bolo battalion commander had his orders for dealing with these men. The *Flier* survivors may have spent five days in the ocean and its islands, getting slashed, burned, and dehydrated while they nearly starved. But here in the jungle of this remote island, where capture by the enemy was a serious threat, there were military records to keep. Holding a sheet of paper—a precious commodity on any wartime island—the head of the bolo battalion needed to perform a roll call of the *Flier* men. His boss, the guerrilla leader Captain Mayor, would expect a report, Sarmiento said. He told Crowley he needed the names of all of the men and their duty stations.

At just about dusk, all of the men were awakened to the aroma of a wood fire, whose gray smoke curled up and up toward the arch of the green jungle canopy. The village leader had killed one of his few chickens, a puny thing, and was cooking it into a broth in a pot on the open fire. The survivors were impressed with their host's sacrifice.

A pipe made from a hollowed bamboo log carried water for cooking and for drinking from a jungle stream. The stream was muddy and about four inches deep and ten inches wide. The village residents drank from it, however, so the submariners did, too. No tastier beverage and no finer fowl were ever served in a Parisian restaurant than the meal that was spread before the guests. They savored the soup and the wild honey they were given as dessert. Then they fell back on their mats, caught in the webs of deep sleep, having been assured by Sarmiento that he had posted a picket of guards around them as a precaution against the unlikely event that the Japanese chose to penetrate the jungle and raid this village.

Jacobson fell asleep as if drugged, his mind at peace. He awoke abruptly to the news that the morning had come and it was time to continue the hike. Again, the ensign noted, a bamboo water tank was filled from the muddy stream for the next leg of the journey. The natives drank the same water, so he assumed it was fit for Americans.

Sarmiento told the group that they would hike to another village, rest, and have lunch before completing their trip to the northern end of the island. Again, one group of bolo battalion soldiers led the procession, slashing away any impeding vegetation, while the other group followed and covered their tracks. By mid-morning, the sailors began to wonder how far their target could possibly be. They had been hiking for three hours, and their feet felt as if they were walking on broken glass. Their energy was already drained despite the good sleep of the night before, and they wanted to stop. Someone asked Sarmiento how much farther they had to go.

"Just another kilometer," their guide replied cheerily.

Perhaps another twenty minutes had passed when he was asked again: "Are we almost there?"

"Just another kilometer," he said.

Another twenty minutes passed and the reply remained the same. Now the men had something to joke about. Someone would raise the question, and the rest of the men, as a chorus, would respond: "Just another kilometer!"

It was about noon when they entered a clearing with a solitary bamboo hut, the village that Sarmiento had promised. Again the owners of the hut cooked rice for the travelers, but rice with a difference:

It was blue. There was no explanation for its hue, but no one balked. After starving for six days, the men dug into the meal and the subsequent dessert, which was rice with honey. As the sailors rose and prepared to move on, the owner of the hut produced a large basket of rice from his limited supply. Handing it to Sarmiento's men, he explained that it was his donation for the guerrillas on Palawan.

For nearly three hours, the survivors hobbled on, the searing pain in their naked feet a reminder that, despite the hardships they had already endured, they were at least alive. By mid-afternoon, they had reached another hut. The owner greeted the travelers and, through Sarmiento, invited them to join him in a meal. Their shriveled stomachs were still full of blue rice, but the man who, like all of Sarmiento's men, spoke no English, made it clear that his was not an offhand invitation. So once again, the survivors settled to the ground, not entirely unhappy to postpone the trudging, and again, they ate rice.

The hike resumed at about four o'clock that afternoon, only a couple of hours before dark, and with the walking came the recurring question: How much farther?

"Just another kilometer" was met with renewed mirth.

Bugsuk River is a long, narrow lake that bisects the island, almost severing its northwestern corner. The route the men of *Flier* had taken followed not far from the eastern edge of the river for more than half of their hike, and led to a spot near the mouth of the river in a bay on the northern side of the island. Sarmiento had arranged the day before for a boat to be waiting at the river's edge, and when the sailors and their entourage—twenty individuals in all—emerged from the jungle, they were met by the boat's skipper, a Muslim man, taller and thinner than Sarmiento and his soldiers. His name was Su La Hud. The sun had fallen low to the west, leaving everyone in the long shadows of the island's towering mahogany trees. In a short time, it would be night, and while it was desirable to travel by boat at night to avoid being spotted by the Japanese, La Hud had to navigate out of the river before dark.

The boat, which Sarmiento told the sailors was a kumpit, was about sixteen feet long, shorter than the boats Al Jacobson had sailed on Spring Lake in his youth with a crew of two other boys. It was about six feet wide, had one mast with a large, gaff-rigged sail, a deck that began at the mast and went all the way to the stern, and a round bottom. Jacobson recognized it as a "clinker," a type of construction used in Viking longboats. There was a detachable rudder with a tiller for steering, and there was no deck in front of the mast, leaving an opening all the way to the pointed bow where someone could squat with a set of long oars if the wind died. Frames had been built out on either side of the deck, cantilevered over the water and running about nine feet along the sides, for carrying cargo.

Introductions were made all around. La Hud had agreed to take Crowley's crew on a looping ten-mile sail that night across reef-strewn water to Buliluyan Point on Palawan. But neither La Hud nor his two native crewmen, Tom Pong and Kim Jon, spoke English, and Crowley wanted some way to communicate with them, so he asked Sarmiento to remain with the sailors for the next leg. Perhaps Crowley was, according to his nature, being cautious. The navy warned its men that, should they become shipwrecked, they should avoid "Moro tribesmen." Moro was another name for Muslims—a name given them by the Spanish friars in earlier centuries because their dark skin reminded them of the African Moors who lived south of Gibraltar. In this primitive and often lawless corner of the world, the Muslims were traders who sailed great distances in their small boats. But they also had a reputation, a stereotype not always deserved, of being pirates. Crowley probably wanted Sarmiento on board the kumpit not just as a translator.

Sarmiento agreed, and the eight *Flier* survivors, their guide, the boat's skipper, and his two native crewmen prepared to board the tiny sailboat. The river was narrow, the trees on the bank an impermeable barrier to sea breezes. One of the two crewmen got in the open bow of the boat with two oars, prepared to propel the craft downstream, toward the sea. All the other men—a total of eleven—were to crowd onto the deck behind the mast, a space perhaps the size of a small bathroom. What cargo they needed—the basket of rice for the guer-rillas, a rolled rattan mat that could be used during daylight as a sunshade for the passengers, and La Hud's provisions and rifle—had been stowed below the deck. Looking at this wooden boat, Jacobson and the others had difficulty believing it would float. But at six o'clock, with their what-will-be attitude, they found their places on the deck and shoved it into the river.

The crewman in the bow rowed effectively, and the little boat with its heavy cargo made good speed along the river until, just before dark, it reached the mouth of Bugsuk River. Tom Pong stood near the mast as a lookout, scanning the water ahead and the shore behind as they raised the sail, a rag of cotton, patched all over, which began to billow with a light breeze.

Suddenly, Tom Pong erupted in a barrage of words, his voice loud, his finger jabbing toward the shore. The *Flier* crewmen began thinking about the warnings the navy had issued. The instructions had left little doubt that Moros could not be trusted. And now La Hud was turning the boat around and heading back to shore. La Hud's rifle was under the deck, and even in their enfeebled state, the sailors had enough manpower to overcome him and his mates. But Sarmiento was there, and he began translating.

Tom Pong had seen some seaweed on the beach. A doctor had told the natives that the plant could be used as medicine, and so every time they spotted some, they harvested it and ate it.

At the beach, Tom Pong gathered the seaweed and brought it back to the kumpit, where he offered it to his passengers. When they chewed it, it tasted like a bittersweet pickle. Once the crew had gathered some of the seaweed, they again shoved the boat to sea. The wind drew on the sail, pulling the little vessel and its burden north. Su La Hud moved the tiller and the boat weaved in the dusk between the coral heads that were barely washed by the sea. To the northwest, Palawan stretched long and low under the darkening sky, and as the wind drew them farther from land, the passengers began to see the outlines of other islands to the west. To the northeast, there was nothing but sea.

After the last gray vapors of day drained from the sky, there was no moon and the boat was in total darkness. But still, La Hud and Kim Jon somehow steered around the reefs, occasionally poling where the water was too shallow, yet navigating with a competence that assured the navy men they were in the hands of real mariners.

Then the wind, never more than light, ceased, and in the warm night, Kim Jon, whose teeth were black from chewing beetlenut, stood and began whistling, a shrill noise that shattered the darkness like an alarm, and flapped his arms like a bird, apparently hoping to rouse the breeze. When it did not work, he and Tom Pong resumed their paddling. La Hud, with stars to guide him, steered in a long arc, the boat's course turning west and then south. At three o'clock the next morning, the rowers slipped over the side of the kumpit and pulled the boat ashore at Cape Buliluyan. There were muffled voices everywhere and the sounds of men splashing out into the water. The entire contingent of guerrillas assigned to this outpost, having heard who was coming, were there to greet the *Flier* survivors.

Before the war, the beach at Cape Buliluyan was a village of bamboo huts built out over the water by the fishermen who lived there. Stilts—sunk in the soft, white sand that stretched out a hundred yards from shore—supported those structures and made docking and unloading boats more convenient. But these houses were out in plain view to the Japanese airplanes and boats that patrolled these waters. So the guerrillas had set their camp back in the coconut trees, hidden from the beach. They led Crowley's men to their headquarters and began producing documents to identify themselves. They were all Filipinos—Christians with roots in Manila—and they were all, like Sarmiento, educated. Before the war, they had been teachers, engineers, and other professionals, but since 1941 they had devoted their lives to soldiering. This outpost was where they had made their stand against the invaders.

Cape Buliluyan was a spectacular setting. Palawan, with rough mountains rising like a backbone for most of its slender length, flattens a few miles north of the cape and narrows to less than three miles across. Palm trees lined the long, sandy beach, and from the shade and shelter of those trees and the jungle behind them, the guerrillas had a clear view of the South China Sea to the west. Between here and Ramos Island, where the Coastwatchers had first landed, was the

North Balabac Strait shipping lane. Its approaches from the north were visible from the cape, as well. There were islands between the cape and Ramos, and with care the guerrillas could slip across to Balabac to talk with the locals and gather intelligence on the Japanese. Information seeped from the garrison on Balabac and became gossip among the residents. Any details that the guerrillas could learn from their visits there were reported to guerrilla headquarters in Brooke's Point, where Nazario Mayor could use them in planning his deadly harassment of the occupiers.

At the camp headquarters, Sergeant Pasqual de la Cruz, the commanding officer, introduced himself and took responsibility from Sarmiento for the *Flier* survivors. He was pleased to be their host, but he told them they could not stay long. They would have to keep traveling north, to Brooke's Point, another fifty miles. It was too dangerous for them to remain at Cape Buliluyan. In Brooke's Point, they would be protected by Captain Mayor.

All the men at the cape spoke English. (The language was brought to the Philippines by the Americans following their turn-of-the-century defeat of the Filipino patriots, led by Aguinaldo.) Not only was the sound of spoken English reassuring; more important, the survivors were overjoyed to meet people who understood their military needs, could explain the hazards of this unfamiliar land, and were able to provide for their survival. First, Crowley wanted to know whether the guerrillas had any medicine to treat their cuts and burns. De la Cruz went to a shelf and took down a jar of white salve, handing it to the submarine commander. Crowley looked inside. Bugs and dirt were embedded in the medicine, and the skipper handed it back to de la Cruz with thanks. So far, none of his men's wounds appeared to be seriously infected. He was unsure whether coating their cuts with this rancid-looking salve might change that. The sergeant apologized, saying the salve was all that they had.

De la Cruz's men then took the sailors to their bamboo barracks and showed them to bunks—actually, platforms that were little more than tables. Again, there was a meal of rice, followed by sugarcane snacks. And for a while, no one slept. They wanted to talk, and the conversations went on until nearly dawn. With the decision finally reached that they would sail the following night, everyone settled on their beds for some rest. While the sailors slept, the guerrillas went foraging for spare clothing, and by the time their guests rose in mid-morning, they had trousers for everyone and shirts for a few, most of them too small for the tall Americans, who nevertheless tugged them on to protect their burned backs and arms from the sun.

Now the sergeant had a question to ask. His men had learned from their trips to Balabac that two weeks earlier, the Japanese had moved four Allied prisoners from Balabac to Puerto Princesa. He explained that there was a prison camp there, filled with American soldiers and sailors. De la Cruz told Crowley that the prisoners had survived the sinking of an American submarine with two other men, who had been killed on Comiran Island. He wondered if Crowley and his men were from the same submarine. Crowley knew it could not be. *Flier* had sunk only eight days earlier. The skipper realized another boat must have been lost before his own had hit the mine.

Since they could not set sail until later in the day, Crowley and his men were given a tour of the guerrillas' compound. The primary structure was a bamboo building about forty by fifty feet and raised on bamboo stilts, six feet above the ground. Trenches had been dug around and under the building, and there were trapdoors in the floor. If the enemy attacked, the guerrillas could drop into the trenches to defend themselves. Outside, there was a huge iron pot used to refine salt from seawater, and sugarcane had been planted in a clearing nearby. As at Captain Mayor's home in Bugsuk, there was a cistern where rainwater was collected from the roof of the building, and, as in the native settlements on that island, chickens roamed freely about the compound, pecking at the ground, waiting to become a meal.

On this particular day, the chickens were safe. A dinner was prepared in the early afternoon, and the sailors sat down to a main course that included carabao, or water buffalo, meat, sliced paper thin. Accustomed as they were to a submarine's burgeoning food locker, where ground meat was given away to make room for filets, the men of the *Flier* had all tasted better cuts of meat. The carabao was as tough as leather, but no one complained as they chewed, happy to have any food. For a treat, they were given a coconut and honey spread for dessert.

Out on the beach, a steady breeze was blowing from the west that afternoon, and when the Japanese patrol boat went by at three o'clock, Sergeant de la Cruz decided it was safe for the sailors to begin their voyage to Brooke's Point. They would have about three hours of daylight, although most of the trip could be made in the dark; by morning, they would arrive on Ipolote Bay.

Sarmiento said good-bye to the men, wishing them well. He had sent the members of his bolo battalion to visit the islands around Bugsuk in hopes of finding other *Flier* survivors. They had fanned out to Mantangule and Bancalan, the largest islands in the Bugsuk group, as well as Canabungan, Malinsono, and Patawan, smaller islands arrayed in the reefs between Bugsuk and Balabac. All of these islands could be reached easily by kumpit or banca, the local outrigger boats, without crossing the open sea, and the search was already under way. But Sarmiento felt he needed to oversee the search himself and should leave immediately. Knowing that fifteen men had escaped *Flier*, he could not dismiss the possibility of finding more submariners.

From Cape Buliluyan to Brooke's Point was a straight sail up the coast, with the wind pushing from behind. But fifty miles is a long way for any sailboat to cover in a day. If, loaded with a dozen passengers, the little craft could make an average speed of four knots, the trip would take more than twelve hours. By leaving in mid-afternoon, the boat might well reach its destination before sunrise. They shoved the kumpit into deeper water and everyone—Crowley and his men, La Hud, Sergeant de la Cruz, Kim Jon, and a new crewman, Kong— climbed aboard. When La Hud raised the big sail, it stretched tight and the boat moved quickly in front of the wind.

Among themselves, the survivors, who by now had dubbed La Hud "The Sailor," were confident that they would soon be in Brooke's Point. They got comfortable for the coming long night at sea.

It was still daylight—they had been under way for about two hours—when La Hud steered without warning toward the beach, speaking to de la Cruz in Tagalog. Never completely comfortable with a Muslim guiding their fate, the sailors asked the sergeant what was happening. He pointed out to sea, where they saw a Japanese patrol boat.

La Hud dropped his sail to make the boat less conspicuous. The patrol boat passed without incident, but by the time it was gone, the wind had died and it was dusk. One after another, La Hud, Kim Jon, Kong, and de la Cruz took turns in the bow of the boat, handling the long oars and rowing the boat sluggishly. After a while, the wind returned and the speed improved. Now it was dinnertime, and La Hud, still steering with the tiller, became not only skipper but cook as well. He had a sheet of steel on the deck, and from his supplies beneath the deck he produced some wood and a tripod. Lighting the wood on fire, he hung a pot from the tripod to boil water for rice. All the time, he was trimming his sail and steering the boat with his bare feet, which were as nimble as the fingers and thumbs of his hands.

By three o'clock in the morning, the little vessel had brought its dozen passengers roughly twenty miles from Cape Buliluyan. It was clear that they would not reach Brooke's Point by daylight. La Hud steered toward shore once again, bringing his boat into the mouth of the Tuba River, a broad tidal stream that historically was the first port on Palawan where Muslim traders from Borneo would stop. The water was deep, but the wind faltered close to shore and the rowing resumed. The moon had risen by now, and from the boat, the survivors could see only the low shoreline jungle. La Hud told them that they were going to spend the night at the home of a local man about two miles upriver, so they scanned the bank in anticipation, unconcerned that navigating this same river were crocodiles nearly twice as long as their boat.

Still under the moon, La Hud turned the boat up to the northern shore of the river, where the passengers unloaded and climbed up the bank 100 yards to a large, rambling house built not of thatch and bamboo but of lumber. The owner and his wife, a Muslim couple, welcomed La Hud and his new friends to their home, showing them where they could sleep. In the morning, the *Flier* men awoke to a bustling house and the aroma of a chicken being cooked. The daughter of the couple, it seemed, had just been married, and she and her groom were there. The mood was festive.

In the long wait for the afternoon Japanese patrol boat to pass by the mouth of the Tuba River, there was time for the host to ask a favor. His daughter and her husband wanted to go to Brooke's Point. Could they hitch a ride on the kumpit?

And so, at three o'clock, Crowley and his men welcomed the bride and groom aboard the crowded deck of the sailboat. The couple brought luggage—a live chicken and rice and household items—and when everyone was aboard, there was room only to sit with knees up under chins.

With the addition of the newlyweds, the passenger list had grown by only one because Su La Hud wasn't there. Sergeant de la Cruz explained that the skipper had business to attend to on shore and would rejoin the boat later, so they cast off with Kim Jon and Kong, the new skipper and mate. As he steered the boat, Kim Jon began singing. He did not speak English, but he knew the words of a song made popular by Sammy Kaye—"Blueberry Hill," Glenn Miller's number-one hit in 1940—and his serenade was unending as the little boat moved back down the Tuba River.

The sail filled with wind and the boat left the mouth of the Tuba and headed out across the Sulu Sea, turning northeast to follow the coast of Palawan. The crew had sailed a couple of miles off the coast when a man was spotted in the water, swimming from shore toward the boat. It was La Hud, who had stayed ashore to visit his family. He climbed aboard and soon was cooking an evening meal of rice pancakes. His foot was on the tiller, steering, and the line that controlled the sail was between his teeth. While he cooked, he also made good on an offer to sew a rip in Earl Baumgart's trousers.

And Kim Jon sang on.

When he was not needed rowing, Kong indulged himself with cigarettes he rolled out of native tobacco, using a nipa leaf for paper. The smell of the smoke wafted across the boat and, deprived of nicotine for ten days, Russo and Baumgart motioned that they would each like a cigarette. Kong was happy to share and rolled one for each sailor, who, expecting perhaps a Lucky Strike, got the sensation of hot tar being poured down their throats. The butts went sizzling into the sea after just a few puffs.

Just before dark, several boats appeared in the distance in front of the kumpit. From a closer range, they proved to be bancas. Natives were diving from the drifting boats and spearing fish. La Hud recognized the fishermen as friends and pulled closer. The natives handed him two types of fish and some eel that the skipper cooked for dinner later on, when he lit another fire on deck.

The boat sailed on with no moon, although they did have a map of stars overhead. By staying close to shore, encounters with the enemy were avoided; but until they were about ten miles from Brooke's Point, their closeness to land meant they were sailing through a maze of coral reefs. Once they cleared the reefs, they were in water that a Japanese boat could patrol, and then the dangers would increase. Even on a night dark as a closed vault, La Hud seemed to know where the reefs were and was able to avoid them, but when the last of the reefs was off their stern, de la Cruz began to worry.

The wind was light but steady, and La Hud was able to sail rather than row. His passengers relaxed in the quiet until out of the dark there came shouting. The skipper dropped the sail and his passengers braced themselves for trouble, when suddenly another boat appeared beside the kumpit. La Hud and Sergeant de la Cruz recognized friendly voices, however. De la Cruz turned to Crowley and explained that the boat had come from the north and might have intelligence on Japanese along the coast. De la Cruz turned back to the other boat and asked what the men had seen. Nothing, they said, and the boats parted, continuing in the night toward their separate destinations and destinies.

CHAPTER 17

INTO THE JUNGLE

The moon, halfway into its first quarter, had risen by five-thirty on the morning of August 23, and daybreak was only a short time away when the kumpit rounded the point at the southern tip of Ipolote Bay. On board, Sergeant de la Cruz waited for the call from the sentry, whom he knew was posted there to hail the boat, but there was no sound. Alone in the dark, many is the soldier whose mind has drifted from the burden of staring into the blackness and listening to the silence. The sergeant called out, but there was no reply. He called again and again until the voice of the sleeping guard came from shore like an echo. De la Cruz told the man to report the arrival of the boat to guerrilla headquarters.

Scores of guerrillas were on the sun-washed gray sand at eight o'clock when the kumpit nosed ashore at Buligay. Stepping out in front of his men to greet the submariners was Captain Nazario B. Mayor, who identified himself as acting commander of Section D of the Sixth Military District. The guerrilla leader was a muscular man about five feet, nine inches tall with a square face, deep creases dividing his cheeks from his mouth. He spoke English perfectly and invited the sailors to his home, a few hundred yards deep in the coconut trees behind the beach. The *Flier* men were barely able to walk up the slope of the beach, their muscles cramped from sitting all night on the crowded deck of the kumpit, their feet still slashed with raw wounds unprotected by shoes. Slowly they hobbled off the sand and up under the coconuts toward the Mayor home.

A crowd of guerrillas and townspeople who had gathered at the beach surrounded the men as they struggled ashore. Stepping from this group, Harry Edwards introduced himself and welcomed them to Brooke's Point. He was tall, middle-aged, and athletically built. The warm greetings continued when the sailors finally approached the Mayor home, a large structure with a thatched roof and open walls. Mary Mayor, her children around her, ushered the sailors into her home. Showing them where they could wash away the grime of their ordeal and bathe their wounds, she then began preparing a meal.

The fact that the Mayors spoke fluent English and that both had been educated in the United States did not completely allay the fears among Crowley and his men that they could be misplacing their trust. For ten days, the eight men had been the beneficiaries of a string of incredible fortune. First, they had escaped *Flier*. What brought Al Jacobson the stroke of luck to trade places with Herbert Behr shortly before the explosion that sank the submarine in less than twenty seconds? Or caused Earl Baumgart to be disciplined and sent topside when he would rather have spent his watch in the engine room? Or allowed Liddell and Russo to survive being rocketed from the conning tower in that shaft of air with no major injuries, while other men had been so wracked by the experience that they were unable to swim?

Once in the water, what had kept a man like Miller, who had failed his navy swimming test, afloat for all those hours? And how would all of them, including Howell and Tremaine, have survived had there been a monsoon churning the Sulu Sea, or had the currents swept them not northeast, away from the Japanese, but—like the men of the *Robalo*—flushed them like so much debris onto the beaches of Balabac?

And when they all finally reached land, how likely had it been that, physically shredded and starving, they would be found by apparently friendly forces? Indeed, from what they had been taught, were not the chances great that any "Moros" they met, rather than being Good Samaritans, would have slaughtered them as the history books said they had Magellan?

All those hours at sea, they had not been attacked by sharks. Their little boat had slipped through the mangroves without a serpent attack and had sailed through crocodile-infested waters unharmed. Through-out the journey, they had turned their fate over to the elements and to total strangers, their only decisions being to follow obediently and unquestioningly. Those choices had brought them here, to a place where they were surrounded by natives, many of them fiercely armed. And not all among the eight were convinced that these dark-skinned people were their friends. Even the loyalties of Harry Edwards—an American who had chosen to leave his country—could be questioned. The Mayors sounded educated and could talk of life in the States, but where was their patriotism if they had abandoned America to live here?

Certainly the sailors could have been killed by any of the people whom they had met along the way, from Oros Bogata, the teenage boy on Bugsuk who gave them their first food and drink, to the men of the bolo battalion with their bolos and blowguns, to La Hud and his crew on the kumpit. But at each turn, Crowley had recommended accep-tance, showing no desire to avoid what appeared to be help.

And now they were surrounded by natives in a corner of the Phil-ippines that had had no contact with the rest of the world since the war began. Then Sergeant Amando Corpus arrived at the Mayors' home, and for the first time, the sailors felt relieved. He was a GI, as much as they were. Everyone relaxed.

Mary Mayor brought food to her guests, who had many questions. They learned from Corpus that the Coastwatchers had radios, and that contact with the submarine headquarters in Australia, 2,000 miles to the southeast, was possible if not predictable. From Captain Mayor, they learned that they should not stay close to the beach. The guer-rilla recommended that they move inland, to the Edwards property in Macagua. If they stayed in Buligay, they would be unable because of their injuries to evacuate quickly should the Japanese decide to invade. While there had been no invasions since the one repelled early in the war by the guerrillas, there had been occasional attacks by air. Brooke's Point had been bombed eleven months before, and four months ago, a Japanese bomber had strafed the area with machine-gun fire. As recently as four weeks ago, a Japanese gunboat had anchored offshore and randomly opened fire on the beach with heavy and light machine guns. The guerrillas had returned rifle fire from shore, and the enemy had failed to attempt a landing. No one could predict if the planes and gunboats would return.

Up in the mountains, the submariners would be somewhat protected, even if the threat of malaria was greater. Already, they had been exposed to the disease in their time hopping from island to island. Crowley and Liddell decided to take the risk and follow Mayor's advice.

While the men consumed their midday meal, the guerrillas located two carabao carts. Once the food was finished, the eight men were loaded into the two carts, each drawn by one carabao, and the trip up to the mountains began. Al Jacobson was in the same cart as Crowley and three other men. A big, old bull carabao was hitched to the cart, which was about five feet wide, six feet long, and made from boards, with an open back and rough wooden wheels. With a slap to the bull's rump, a native man got him moving away from the Mayor home.

Although for most of their trip, the *Flier* men had been spared the seasonal rains, they had traveled only a short way inland on a dirt road under a hot sun when they saw evidence of the monsoon season. The road was rutted, with puddles from rain the day before in every low spot. The pools came about every 100 yards, and the bull took every opportunity to lie down and wallow in the mud. His driver would kick and slap him, but the massive animal ignored this pest until he was sufficiently refreshed to move on. Then the cart would lurch from side to side, moving at a pace no more rapid than a leisurely stroll.

For the first couple of miles, the beast's hooves fell on a path that, while uneven, crossed a flat landscape where the tall trees of the coconut plantation stood in ranks on each side, spreading a parasol of frothy green fronds. Then the trail entered a gradually rising landscape, with small hills to the north and south. The jungle underbrush began to press in from either side. Occasionally the cart passed a native hut with chickens pecking the ground outside and perhaps pigs and dogs resting where there was shade. Always in the distance, over the carabao's head and shoulders, were the mountains.

As the two carts approached a small stream, the passengers could see a large house ahead, higher on the mountainside. Harry Edwards was at the stream, attempting to repair a rice mill—a cast-iron contraption for processing rice, with a funnel on the top and a wheel on the side, attached by a belt to an aging diesel engine. Edwards dropped his work and greeted the sailors once again. Then he sent one of the natives who had been helping him up to the house on the hill to make it ready for the guests.

Snorting and straining, the carabaos pulled the two carts the last quarter-mile from the stream, up the steep path to the house, where a new group was gathered to welcome the survivors. Rosario Edwards, Harry's wife, was flanked by the rest of the Coastwatchers unit and by three Americans—William Wigfield, George Marquez, and Charles Watkins. If any of the survivors had felt lingering doubts about their hosts, those qualms now evaporated in the clear mountain air.

The Edwards home was built like almost all the other structures the submariners had seen—with bamboo stilts and a thatched roof—except that it was larger than any of the others. When they had climbed the steps and were inside, the sailors were offered seats in real chairs. They felt civilized for the first time in ten days.

Next door to the Edwards home was another house, built by Nazario Mayor—a retreat for his family should the enemy invade. The house was not occupied because the guerrilla wanted to keep his children away from the swarms of mosquitoes harbored by the mountains. The Coastwatchers were living in the Mayor home, and they invited the enlisted men from *Flier* to join them, while Crowley, Liddell, and Jacobson were invited to stay with the Edwardses.

When the greetings and chatter had subsided, the men had time to admire the view from this mountainside. Below, they could see the route they had followed from the beach, which began beyond the plantation about five miles away. The blue of the Sulu Sea spread to the east, to the horizon beyond the coast, and the green of the jungle's bamboo, mango, and star apple trees, etched by late-afternoon shadows, stretched north and south from Macagua for many miles.

No warrior ever defended from a more strategic position. Their backs to the mountain and all approaches within view, surrounded by friends, the survivors could hold out here indefinitely. Al Jacobson, for one, was ready to kick back for a while.

Jacobson's father, at this hour some 7,000 miles away, was distraught. He sat down to write to his sons, and once again the news from the foundry was uncharacteristically low on his agenda.

As far as peace goes, this last week has been one minus— when Uncle Asthor [sic] passed away, it was like cutting off a leg or an arm; but time will help heal many things, and some day it will pass.

One thing I would like for your boys to do is to stick together through thick and thin—one of you may have a fault; but, if the others chip in and try to help out, the faulty one will soon get rid of his faults, and you will have a team that cannot be beaten.

The Fisher boys are a good example—they built up the Fisher Body and then sold out to the General Motors—the General Motors crowd tried to get too strong, and the Fisher boys just resigned, and are now going to start up something for themselves so their sons can carry on.

One of you boys will be good in, say, sales and management; one in production; and, perhaps, another in accounting. You have some sisters to take into consideration, which will make brothers-in-law some day; and if you can surround yourselves with keen men, you can build up an organization that is tops.

To see the way some of these men carry on is disgusting— all they think of is a good time; and when they get old they belly-ache and moan that they have a raw deal, when it is in reality their own fault.

Build your foundation so strong that no storm or depression can knock you down.

I had every expectation that Uncle Asthor some day would have been one of the top executives of Chevrolet Motors. He started in from a utility book-keeper to work up to Comptroller, and the good things I heard about him made me proud of the fact that he was my brother. And that is the way I want you boys to be held in esteem by your fellowmen [sic].

To everyone at Macagua, the *Flier* survivors were not only esteemed but genuine heroes. Their wounds were like badges, signifying, to a man, their determination. But they were badges well left behind, so the Coastwatchers brought their medical supplies and, even before another meal could be prepared, they swabbed sulfa ointment onto the raw cuts and blisters. Then the Coastwatchers dipped into their other supplies, bringing cigarettes, soap, and some clothes from their emergency rations. Finally, they laid out cheese and crackers and poured some army coffee for the sailors.

All the while, there were urgent discussions between Crowley, Liddell, and the Coastwatchers. Having heard that these men had radios, the sailors wanted to know when they could contact Australia. Crowley wrote a note and handed it to one of the Coastwatchers. The simplest message was his first: "*Flier* lost. Don't use Balabac Strait."

The Edwards place was a beehive, with men coming and going, children hanging around, wood smoke wafting from the open cooking fire, and the smells of a meal being prepared. In the midst of their discussions with the Coastwatchers, the submariners were joined by a short fellow with a thick Scots brogue, Reverend Alexander "Sandy" Sutherland. He had come from the family's hut near the coast in the barrio of Paratungan. The minister was buoyant to find more Americans on Palawan. The arrival in July of the Coastwatchers had given the Sutherlands a sense that their time on the island was coming to a close. Theirs was only a feeling, but one perhaps fueled by the youngest Sutherland, Alistair. The germ of this feeling had been planted two years before.

It was in 1942 and the war was only a year old. Every evening, the family knelt in prayer, and on this night the father noticed that his son remained kneeling when everyone else had finished. The boy's whispered words were inaudible, so Sutherland waited a few days before mentioning anything to the four-year-old. Each night he heard the same muffled plea. When he finally asked Alistair if he had a special worry that he would like to discuss, the boy looked concerned. "Father, I heard you mention in one of your sermons that God wants to help those in need, and you used a scripture to explain that God is everywhere and can come to us from even the sea that surrounds this island."

Sutherland urged his son on.

"So I have been praying that God would send a ship to take us off this island before the Japanese can find us."

From that day on, the entire family prayed Alistair's prayer. Now there were navy men in Macagua, along with the radiomen from the army. Alexander Sutherland could be excused if he read more into these events than the rest of the community.

Visiting the sailors at Macagua, Sandy Sutherland was effusive. When Crowley asked the minister if he could lead a church service for the *Flier* survivors the next day, Sutherland promised to return.

Later, vapors from the cooking pots mixed with the smell of wood smoke, and soon a feast—the second of their day—was laid before the submariners. There were coconut sprouts, rice, *kalamay hati*—a dish of cooked ground sugarcane and coconut milk—and a fruit similar to a grapefruit. When the meal was completed, Harry produced news reports transcribed by the Coastwatchers from recent radio broadcasts and normally typed and distributed in the community. There was nothing to suggest that the Philippines would be liberated soon. The Allied war effort continued to make progress against the Japanese, however. In the time since the August 13 evening report received aboard *Flier*, Allied troops had gone ashore in southern France following shelling from ships offshore and bombings by the Army Air Corps. And on this same day, the navy had shelled Aguijan Island in the Mariana Islands, east of the Philippines and south of Japan.

Below Macagua, the Sulu Sea had turned from blue to gray to black, and the sun had long since fallen behind Addison Peak when, in the dark of night, the men of *Flier* slipped into a deep, embracing sleep.

Alexander Sutherland returned the next day to conduct a church service outside the Edwards home for the men of *Flier* and all the nearby residents. With his guests' souls restored, Harry Edwards had a way to restore their bodies. He had sent one of the natives to bring a native doctor to the village. The man arrived that morning with his few medical supplies, and he offered to inspect the sailors' wounds. They were polite, letting him change their dressings, but they trusted the American medicine of the Coastwatchers more. Already, they had begun taking daily doses of Atabrine, the Coastwatchers' anti-malaria medicine. Atabrine, developed by a German scientist before the war as a synthetic substitute for quinine, which came from tree bark, was not pleasant. The yellow pills were bitter and turned the skin pallid, at times causing headaches, nausea, and vomiting. The medicine was so distasteful that officers—like the parents of toddlers—often had to oversee soldiers to assure that they took their doses. But Crowley's men had already experienced enough bodily discomfort that swallowing a bitter pill seemed inconsequential. They prepared to take their medicine religiously. And when, later in the day, the Coastwatchers brought a native woman who they had trained as a barber, everyone got a haircut.

Life for the Coastwatchers in Brooke's Point had been without military reward. No longer consumed as they had been on Ramos and Mantangule islands with their own survival and the need to evade the nearby Japanese, they focused on making reports to Australia. But that work had not gone well, a fact that Teodoro "Butch" Rallojay recorded daily in his diary.

In the latter days of July, when it seemed to rain every day, the issue had been building a shack near the shore in Buligay, where the radios could be kept dry. Most of the spare equipment had been hauled to Macagua to keep it safe in case of invasion. By July 20 the shack was finished, and the crew expected to begin broadcasting to Australia the next day. But at the hour chosen to make the first contact, there was no reply. The next day proved just as fruitless. The following day was Sunday, and accepting an invitation, the six men hiked about five miles to Tubtub, where the Rodriguez family from Brooke's Point had their evacuation home.

"It was raining," Rallojay began his diary report that night. "We went to visit Judge Rodriguez. Met his wife and lovely daughter, Connie, who is a very interesting little girl, and very charming too." Distracted as he was by Conchita Rodriguez, who was actually a young woman, Rallojay's mind remained on his job. "This afternoon at 3:00 p.m. local time, we again sent two messages. We hope they are getting through as we have not yet received anything from them."

Radios on Palawan and Australia finally sparked the next day, and Rallojay, who was at the key sending the Morse code message, was elated when the keyman on the other end, a friend of his, replied: "Hi Butch."

The Coastwatchers, so accustomed to radio failure, couldn't believe the reply, and so sent a message to repeat. Again came the dots and dashes, the "dits" and "dahs" of radio Morse code with Rallojay's initials and the message: "Hello Butch." An excited Rallojay responded: "Okay Buck." Finally the men could communicate with General MacArthur's headquarters. Their work could begin.

But two days later the Japanese gunboat unleashed its machine guns on the beach and the Coastwatchers decided their hut in Buligay was unsafe. This time, they moved everything to Macagua—everything except their antenna. So once again they could not communicate with Headquarters.

Even had they been able to respond, they had little to report. They had failed to spot any enemy convoys, the type of information that Headquarters needed. Then one of their receivers stopped working, leaving them with no good short-distance radios since the spare had been ruined when it was soaked on Mantangule Island.

Frustrations were mounting as July ended. On the last day of the month, a Monday, Carlos Placido, whose natural leadership had always eclipsed that of Sergeant Corpus, the group's assigned commander, decided to take action to improve their performance. Setting out by banca that morning for Cape Buliluyan, he explained that from this location, he could watch shipping in the North Balabac Strait and in the South China Sea. He would take a radio with him and make reports to Brooke's Point that could be relayed to Australia. No one objected to his initiative, and twice during the day the men at Macagua reached Placido by radio. But over the next two days, his signal weakened and finally disappeared. All of the radios were now performing fitfully.

During their whole first month in Brooke's Point, the Coastwatchers had been planting and cultivating victory gardens. It was one of their assignments, that they should grow their own food when they could. By early August, their first crops were ready to harvest. They toiled in the rain, trying to keep their plants from rotting. Bugs were beginning to eat the stems of the plants. The radios were failing at every level. Placido had disappeared completely. There was nothing to report to Headquarters even if they had been able to get through. And it rained—every single day.

Not everyone was failing so miserably. The world news that came in over one radio receiver on Friday, August 11, reported that American planes had bombed Davao on the island of Mindanao. The day before, the Japanese had ended their resistance on Guam. But it rained all day on the mountains of southern Palawan, and there was nothing to report to Headquarters that day or the next.

After nearly two weeks away, Carlos Placido returned to Brooke's Point on the night of August 12, bringing with him a horse, two cows, and a huge quantity of rice that the natives in Buliluyan had gathered and sent as a donation for the Coastwatchers, whom they called the Australians.

The next day, *Flier* sank after hitting a mine.

The guerrillas in Buliluyan already knew that a submarine—it turned out to be *Robalo*—had been lost. Perhaps a more effective Coastwatcher unit would have known about the mines in Balabac Strait and could have warned Headquarters. They failed in this assignment, although their radio problems would have precluded them from warning anyone; whether they had had information or not, they could not have saved *Flier.* Now, even though they had occasional radio contact, the reports were few and the intelligence-gathering almost nonexistent. In the ten days after *Flier* went down, things improved slightly for the Coastwatchers. On Saturday, August 19, they reported to Headquarters that they had sighted a Japanese convoy, and two days later, they saw a ship far out in the Sulu Sea, although they could not identify it.

Crowley's arrival with his seven subordinates was the first real news the Coastwatchers had to report. Baumgart, Tremaine, and Howell wrote their own names and addresses in Rallojay's small notebook. The Coastwatcher entered the names of the other men. The following day, Rallojay's radio key clicked out a message to Headquarters, giving the names of the survivors.

Headquarters was furious. Why had the Coastwatchers not informed them of the mines in Balabac Strait before *Flier* had been sunk, one officer's message demanded? This response came like a sucker punch, knocking the wind out of Sergeant Corpus and his five men.

Life for the individual Coastwatchers had been conflicted. Rallojay, for example, lamented the disgusting weather and the depressing performance of his unit. But at the same time, he had been seeing Conchita Rodriguez for three weeks, his young heart swept away. His joy was his own. The rest of the Coastwatchers were dealing with the failings of their war effort, each in his own way, and their leader, Amando Corpus, was sinking deeper into the depression that had paralyzed him earlier in the summer, back on Ramos Island.

Now, for Ensign Jacobson, life in Macagua was almost like R&R leave. He began amusing himself by reading six-year-old copies of *Reader's Digest* and whittling cribbage boards and other items out of bamboo. Sitting in front of the Edwards home under a large shade tree, he had a view of the nearby rice paddies and the distant sea, beyond which, somewhere, there was a war being waged. Al remained barefoot. He tried to make sandals, but none were comfortable. They all rasped against the sores on his feet, and finally he abandoned the effort. His feet were on the mend, anyway.

One day, Jacobson agreed to join George Marquez, with whom he had become friendly, and tag along with some natives who were going boar hunting. The party headed down the hill toward Tubtub, into a mountain jungle valley. Al and George were armed with a carbine they had borrowed from the Coastwatchers. The natives had blowguns, six-foot-long slender bamboo poles hollowed to fire a poison dart. Al had hunted in Michigan—pheasant and ducks—but he had never seen anything like a boar running through the forest, big enough and sufficiently fast to knock a man down. The Americans never fired a shot, and the natives missed with their blowguns, although they did bag some birds.

One day, bored with his diversions, Jacobson walked down the hill to the stream where the submariners had first encountered Harry Edwards and his rice mill. The mill had been hauled up the mountain from the family's Brooke's Point home, and it had served to process the raw rice ever since. At first, the machine's engine ran on oil salvaged from barrels that washed up on the beach of Ipolote Bay from sunken warships. Now it was running on coconut oil. But it needed work. The belt between the mill and the diesel engine was tattered, and Jacobson, familiar with all sorts of foundry machinery, took on the job of repairing it. Finally, he felt he was earning his keep.

For the survivors, life on Palawan became a series of single events, no two seemingly connected but each a part of the cockeyed life of people stranded by war.

The tranquility of Macagua was shattered one afternoon when the shock wave of an explosion somewhere near the beach thundered up the mountainside. It sounded like gunfire, bringing everyone to their feet to stare down across the coconut plantation, looking for landing craft. But the Sulu Sea was quiet and free of ships, and the source of the noise remained a mystery.

Crowley and his men had been in Brooke's Point for four days when the time came for a party that the locals had planned sometime earlier, to entertain the Coastwatchers. Perhaps someone had recognized their boredom and malaise. The party was to be a dance, and the local girls had been enlisted to entertain the young men. There would be tuba—a drink milder than beer and made from the sap from coconut blossoms. Perhaps there would be romance for more men than just young Rallojay.

All of Corpus's men dressed in their best coveralls and, corralling the *Flier* men, three of them began to head down the hill that morning after breakfast. Corpus was still in the camp, and Placido and Dacquel were also waiting there for Captain Mayor and his wife. Everyone seemed to be in high spirits. Suddenly, there was a muffled shot and young Robert Mayor, the guerrilla's son, cried out. Placido raced toward the boy's voice and found Corpus lying on the ground. He felt for a pulse and tried to make his commander talk, but the sergeant was already dead. Butch Rallojay, Ray Cortez, and Slug Reynoso, the three who had already left, were about a half-mile away when they heard the shot. Racing back up the hill, they found Placido with Corpus's body lying where he had dropped. Corpus had put a gun to his heart and fired. His suicide was the culmination of his guilt at failing to discover and report on the mines that sank *Robalo* and *Flier*. Already prone to despondency, Corpus took the reprimand from MacArthur's headquarters personally and chose to administer his own censure.

Stunned by the suicide, the community canceled the party and planned a funeral instead. They needed a coffin, but there were few boards in all of Brooke's Point because the sawmill at the beach had been idle since the war began. The coffin they made for Corpus was a bit small. That night, after the sergeant had been buried, a somber Butch Rallojay returned to his diary. "At 7:45 this morning est. Sergeant Amando Corpus took the easiest way out," the soldier wrote. "Shot himself to death. He got discourage [sic]. His moral [sic] was very low. May God have pity on his soul."

CHAPTER 18

ESCAPE

Radios were the problem. While the shortwave set with which the Coastwatchers contacted Australia now worked regularly, the sets for communicating at closer range functioned only fitfully. And if the crew from *Flier* were to be evacuated, these radios would be critical.

No one ever suggested there should not be an evacuation; not Crowley or Liddell or any of their shipmates. Life on Palawan, while it presented problems of disease and occasional food shortages, could be endured in relative safety. But the submariners saw it as their duty to return to battle until the war was won. Every day, sailors, marines, and soldiers were dying at sea, on the beaches and in the jungles of the Pacific, as well as the fields, villages, and cities of Europe. They knew this instinctively, even if they did not get detailed daily reports from Headquarters.

Most recently, the invasion in July of the Marianas—Guam, Tinian, and Saipan—had taken the lives of 4,000 American marines and 500 American sailors. Another 400 would die later due to complications from their wounds.

Every able sailor and soldier was needed, so Crowley set to work designing a plan for the evacuation. To deal with the radio problem, Crowley turned to Arthur Gibson Howell, at thirty-five, Crowley's contemporary in age if not rank.

Howell had joined the navy in 1942, already fascinated by electronics. In the late 1920s, after high school, he had sold Singer sewing machines. In 1930, when he was twenty-one, he joined the East Moriches, New York, fire department, and four years later he met Irene Swanson and opened his own store, selling and servicing radios. A year later, he married Irene.

One day in June 1942, Howell, the father of two boys, came home to the house he and Irene had built a few years before with some unexpected news. He had joined the navy! Irene may have been startled by his announcement, but she remained his wife, and during the next four years she got letters that traced his career across the globe and up to the rank of chief. The letters often began: "Darling Irene" and were signed "Your loving man," or just "Gibson," the name by which his shipmates had known him."

The navy chose to build on what Howell had already started in his life. Three months after he enlisted, he completed training at the navy's elementary electricity and radio material school in Grove City, Pennsylvania, as one of the top students. Almost a year later, after finishing submarine school in New London, across Long Island Sound from his home, he graduated from radar and sound operator school with a 3.81 grade point average. And two months later, on October 18, 1943, he was among the submarine's first crew members, standing in formation to watch Mrs. Anna Smith Pierce break a champagne bottle across *Flier*'s bow.

His most recent mail to Irene, cleared for the censors by Lieutenant Liddell on August 1, just before *Flier* left Australia, was a package. The chief had filled a box for shipment back to their home in East Moriches, New York, including in it some new navy uniforms, as well as one felt woman's belt for Irene, three twine necklaces, one crystal necklace, three children's books for the boys, three felt children's neckties, and one miniature submarine pin.

He did not send the Bronze Star that he had received after the successful first patrol—not in this package. He had earned the medal as the submarine's top radar operator, a man on whom Crowley relied when it came to electronics.

As soon as Howell heard the Coastwatchers were having trouble with their radio equipment, he volunteered to help. Hiking back from

Macagua to their hut near the coast, he began working with the cranky sets.

With Howell tending to the radio problem, Crowley moved on to the other elements of the evacuation plan that Headquarters had directed him to develop, once they had received the radio message about the *Flier* survivors. He knew that help would come in the form of a submarine and that the rendezvous would have to be after dark. The location would, of course, be in water deep enough for a submarine and free of reefs. And since there were no docks on all of Palawan that were not in Japanese hands, the people being evacuated would have to meet the submarine offshore.

The skipper needed charts. Captain Mayor's fighters had salvaged a set of Japanese charts from a supply boat that had run aground on Palawan. Some pages from the set had been cut up by Harry Edwards for use as currency in the Brooke's Point economy. Crowley and Liddell huddled over the surviving charts and concluded that the best place to rendezvous with a submarine was right in Ipolote Bay. A line of reefs shadowed the coast not far from the beach, but beyond the coral the bay was thirty or more feet deep, enough water in calm seas for a submarine.

Next, there was the issue of transportation to the submarine. Crowley had been told that Datu Jolkipli, the Muslim leader, had boats at his disposal. A runner was sent and returned with a message that the datu would provide two boats, one with a motor, whenever Crowley needed them.

Finally, there had to be a method of letting the evacuation submarine know that the survivors were ready to rendezvous. At the northern corner of Ipolote Bay, near the beach in Brooke's Point, was an old lighthouse—a concrete structure that stood perhaps sixty feet tall, taller than the trees and any of the buildings in the community. It was only a couple of blocks from the schoolhouse where the guerrillas had slaughtered the Japanese landing party. Crowley arranged with Mayor to hang three lanterns, one above the other, from the lighthouse on the night of the submarine's arrival. This would be the signal that the coast was clear of Japanese soldiers for twenty miles on either side of Brooke's Point.

With this detail settled, Crowley went to the Coastwatchers with his plan. Butch Rallojay began tapping his radio key. A confirmation came back: The message had reached Australia. It would be held in complete secrecy for future transmission to the evacuation submarine.

Already, *Redfin*—the same boat that had deposited the Coastwatchers on Ramos Island nearly three months earlier—had been given cryptic orders by Headquarters. On August 23, while the submarine was on patrol in the South China Sea off the western shore of Balabac, the message had arrived: "Proceed immediately to Latitude 8 degrees, 40 minutes north, Longitude 118 degrees, 15 minutes east, and await further instructions."

Redfin's skipper, Commander Marshall H. Austin, turned his boat toward the Sulu Sea and spent the next three days sneaking through the Japanese-controlled water until he reached the designated spot, thirty miles southeast of Ipolote Bay. It was noon on August 27. That evening, *Redfin*'s radioman received a transmission that he relayed to his skipper: instructions for Austin to patrol the central Sulu Sea until he received further orders.

As Howell's work on the Coastwatchers' radios continued, he got some help from his enlisted shipmates. The electricity for the radios came from a generator attached to a stationary bicycle. Baumgart, Miller, Russo, and Tremaine took turns pedaling the bike, and in time Howell managed to get the radio sets working. The final piece of Crowley's escape plan—kept secret from all but the survivors and the Coastwatchers—had fallen into place. All that was left was the wait.

When not pedaling to give Howell electricity, all the men spent time talking with the oddball collection of Brooke's Point expatriates and the American soldiers and sailors who had settled there. They bonded almost instantly with American servicemen Watkins, Marquez, and Wigfield. There was less contact with the others—just the one church service performed by Alexander Sutherland. The most intriguing stories were about Vans Taivo Kerson, the Finnish adventurer who, some days before the *Flier* crewmen had arrived, had left alone on a banca, sailing for the far side of Palawan.

Kerson, a man twice as old as Ensign Jacobson, clearly had an extensive résumé as a soldier of fortune. He had traveled the world, working as a seaman, diver, and engineer. For five years, he had worked for China's national government. In 1932, he had fought beside the Chinese against the Japanese in Shanghai.

Kerson had arrived in the Philippines in 1936 and worked in the mining industry with Henry Garretson, who later became the war-time houseguest of the Sutherlands. Kerson and Garretson had helped salvage the ship *Panay* after the Japanese invaded the islands, and together they later made their way to Brooke's Point, where Garretson, an older man, had become infected with malaria.

Jacobson was enthralled by the stories of how Kerson had organized the Brooke's Point residents into a resistance force before the guerrillas got organized. The engineer in Jacobson was further impressed by tales of how Kerson had retrieved gunpowder from Japanese mines that floated up onshore. Kerson had packed the gunpowder into old shotgun shells and then added pebbles from the beach, replenishing the depleted supply of ammunition for the guerrillas' few weapons.

During the days when the *Flier* survivors had been swimming and island-hopping, Kerson had sailed around Cape Buliluyan and up the western coast of Palawan, searching for food and other supplies for the Americans and guerrillas in Brooke's Point. On the day when Jacobson and his shipmates were swimming from Apo Island to Bugsuk, Kerson had been due west of the Tuba River, on the coast far beyond the surreal, smokestack-shaped mountains that divided the Tuba on the east from Bonbon Point, on the west. He had seen a large ship offshore burn and sink. In the days since, he had loaded his banca with supplies and trimmed his sails once again to round Cape Buliluyan.

It was with mixed feelings that the people in Macagua awaited Kerson's return, they told the survivors. He was an important part of their community whose presence made life around Brooke's Point easier, but they would like him to be able to leave if the evacuation occurred, and so they wished he would get back soon.

On the night of August 29, Kerson's banca nosed onto the sand of the beach at Buligay, loaded with rice. Soon the soldier of fortune made his way inland to Macagua, where he began telling his own stories to Jacobson and the others. On his outward journey, he had loaded the banca with the beer and whiskey he had salvaged from the Japanese supply ship that grounded earlier on Palawan. He knew that the natives—particularly those on the rugged western shore of Palawan—had scarcely enough rice to feed themselves. To encourage them to donate from their supplies for the guerrillas, Kerson—like American pioneers preying on naive Native Americans—traded his alcohol with the native leaders. On this trip, in addition to the bags of rice that swelled above the sides of his banca, he also brought the promise of enough rice from the far side of the island to keep the guerrillas fed for the next six months.

The shortwave radio in the Coastwatchers' quarters in Macagua had come to life earlier this same day. Headquarters in Australia was calling, and the news was good. *Redfin* had been assigned to handle the evacuation, and it would arrive off Ipolote Bay at eight o'clock the next evening. Commander Austin had already been informed. Waiting in *Redfin* offshore just after midnight on this day, he had received orders from Australia telling him to be five miles off Brooke's Point by sunset the following day. *Redfin* was about fifty miles southeast of Tubbataha Reefs, some distance north of Ipolote Bay. Austin, who still had no details of the rescue operation, waited until nighttime and then headed south on the surface, aiming for an island thirty miles north of Brooke's Point where he could loiter until the hour of the rendezvous.

At seven o'clock that night, about the time that Vans Taivo Kerson was steering the kumpit ashore at Buligay, *Redfin*'s radio received the message from Australia with all the particulars of Crowley's plan: The submarine would be meeting two small boats off Brooke's Point carrying eight survivors of *Flier*, including John D. Crowley.

Until now, neither Austin nor anyone else in the submarine fleet had known that *Flier* was lost. Austin was four years younger than Crowley, who had graduated the spring before Austin arrived in Annapolis. They were aware of each other, however. In the close-knit submarine officer fraternity, their paths had crossed on numerous occasions. Most recently, in July, they had spent several days together in Fremantle, on break between patrols. Austin was no doubt relieved to learn that his colleague was alive, and, given the nature of *Redfin*'s prior exploits, rescuing Crowley and his crew must have seemed like a relatively problem-free assignment.

Austin had been *Redfin*'s commander since March. On the boat's hectic second patrol, which began March 19, the crew had first sunk a 1,900-ton Japanese destroyer off Mindanao. A week later, *Redfin* sank two Japanese passenger-cargo ships in a nighttime attack. The following week, responding to a distress call from six Australian agents in Borneo, Austin sent a landing party ashore in a rubber boat to evacuate the agents. The proper security signal had been displayed on shore and, in the darkness, voices on land had responded with the correct password. So the landing party headed for shore. As the rubber boat reached the beach, a Japanese soldier with a fixed bayonet lunged out of the night. A gun battle followed, blinding muzzle flashes punctuating the darkness, and the landing party escaped in the rubber boat to *Redfin*. The mission was aborted. At least two Japanese soldiers were dead, while all of Austin's men were back on board, uninjured.

Redfin's third patrol started on May 26, with six army soldiers aboard. The submarine had deposited these men—the Coastwatchers—on Ramos Island, and then began scouting the Japanese naval base at Tawi Tawi, where on June 11 the crew had sunk a Japanese tanker. Austin was able to report to Australia that the Japanese naval task force was departing Tawi Tawi, thus preparing Allied forces in the Marianas for what would become the decisive Battle of the Philippine Sea. In late June, *Redfin* sank another Japanese passenger-cargo ship before returning to Australia.

Redfin left Fremantle in August two days after *Flier* and laid a minefield off the west coast of Borneo before getting the call to sail to the Sulu Sea. In the few days the submarine had been cruising off

Palawan, Austin had seen nothing of the enemy—good news for the rescue effort. And the plan that Crowley had created, with its signal lights and radio code names, seemed almost foolproof. Compared with some of *Redfin*'s earlier assignments, the evacuation of Crowley and his men, along with a Scottish missionary family whom his orders had included, would no doubt be almost effortless.

Earlier that same day, James Liddell had found a typewriter and composed a short note.

29 August 1944
CONFIDENTIAL

Dear Mr. Sutherland:

It is a pleasure to offer transportation for yourself and family to Australia at the discretion of the commanding officer of a submarine passing near here. While this is not a definite promise, I personally feel that it will be approved unless there are unforeseen reasons on board the boat.

Should you desire to take this opportunity, please be at the house of Captain Mayor with your family and possessions at 3 p.m. August 30th. I wish to call your attention to the confined space aboard a submarine, making it impossible to carry any large or bulky item, and would suggest that your personal effects be limited to about one suitcase per person.

In any event, please keep the knowledge of this ship passing here confined to your immediate family. This is necessary for the proper safety of this enterprise.

A runner took the typed note from Macagua to the Sutherlands' home in Paratungan, near the coast. Alistair Sutherland's prayer, first uttered more than two years before, was finally being answered. The Sutherlands would be in Buligay the following afternoon.

People were moving well before sunrise in the hillside jungle in Macagua on the morning of August 30, 1944. Some livestock was gathered and then the trek back to the beach began. Crowley's feet were infected and he was unable to walk. With help, he climbed on the back of a carabao for the slow descent through the coconut plantation. Others like Jacobson were in better shape, and began walking down the hillside from the Edwards homestead. They covered the miles slowly and arrived at the Mayors' beach home by mid-afternoon. Looking out to sea, where they were to meet *Redfin* after dark, they were stunned.

For the first time since the war began, a Japanese freighter was anchored just off Brooke's Point, between the beach and the reef, just inshore from the spot where the rendezvous was planned.

Earlier, in the unsettled gray light just before daybreak, *Redfin* had begun heading south along the coast of Palawan, submerged but close to the reefs. Austin was using his soundman to navigate, and he was recording where the peaks in the reef were located. He found that he could keep track of his position with no other means but the sonar equipment. There was neither a periscope wake nor a radar signal to alert the enemy, and the submarine was deep enough to avoid being spotted by airplanes. Austin could move freely. By noon, he had mapped the peaks sufficiently to allow him to move inshore to the rendezvous point after dark without a problem.

The Japanese ship arrived at about one o'clock that afternoon. It came from the north—a small Sea Truck cargo vessel, heading toward Brooke's Point. At two o'clock, the ship dropped its anchor only one mile from the spot where *Redfin* had been told to meet Crowley and his crew. Austin, still submerged, moved to within 3,000 yards of the ship, stopped, and raised his periscope. The ship appeared to be unarmed, and there was nothing to indicate that its arrival was anything other than an unfortunate coincidence. But there was radio equipment on the ship. Concerned that if *Redfin* was spotted, military vessels and aircraft would be contacted, Austin decided to remain cautious.

Crowley's heart sank when he saw the ship. He didn't know whether word of the evacuation plan had been leaked. Perhaps one of the Coastwatchers told a friendly local, or maybe the datu had broken his confidence. Of course, it could all be just chance. But the ship's arrival was not good luck. Already, it had eliminated one part of the skipper's plan. No lanterns could be hung from the lighthouse to signal *Redfin* without also making the men on the freighter suspicious.

Crowley and Liddell walked east along the curve of the beach from the Mayors' home toward Brooke's Point to inspect the ship more closely. Seeing that it appeared to be a harmless freighter, they decided to go ahead with the rest of the plan. Datu Jolkipli, true to his word, had delivered two kumpits, one with an outboard motor. Chief Howell arrived from the Coastwatchers' shack and told Crowley that the two portable radios were both working; one could be taken aboard the kumpits, and the other could be left on the beach in case help was needed.

Now, as the sun sank and cast a long, sharp shadow east from the tip of Addison Peak, the rest of the evacuees began arriving at the Mayors' home: Alexander and Maisie Sutherland with their children, Alistair and Heather; Vans Taivo Kerson and his friend, Henry Garretson; and the three GIs, Charlie Watkins, William Wigfield, and George Marquez—a total of seventeen men, women, and children, including the men of the *Flier*.

The sun fell behind Mount Mantalingajan, and shadows spread across the barrios, where residents all seemed to be in on Crowley's secret plan. In the dusk, a small crowd gathered near the beach to wish the travelers farewell. At eight o'clock, once darkness had consumed Buligay, Crowley took the Coastwatchers' radio, pushed the key, and spoke the code words into the mouthpiece: "Violet, this is Rose. Violet, this is Rose."

The skipper tried several times, but no sound came from the other radio, being manned in the kumpit nearby. When Howell checked, he found that the problem was with Crowley's set. Switching radios, Crowley again called *Redfin*. Still there was no answer. For the next two hours, with the clergyman's family, the expatriates, the stranded GIs, and the *Flier* survivors poised around them, the Coastwatchers cranked the radio's generator and Crowley spoke the code words into the microphone. Hope among the evacuees drained lower with the silence of each passing minute. There were two possible explanations. The most logical was the same problem that had dogged the Coastwatchers since June 6—the radios. Unuttered was an even worse concern: that *Redfin*, like so many other submarines, was at the bottom of the Pacific.

It was about ten o'clock that night when Crowley decided there was no alternative but to put to sea. Everyone was gathered on the beach, and the two kumpits, each about twenty feet long and four feet wide, were loaded with passengers and crew. A couple of the Coastwatchers were on board to work the radios, and some of the guerrillas and townspeople were there to operate the boats. Someone started the outboard motor, and a line was passed between that boat and the other.

Jose Santos, the son-in-law of Harry Edwards, had brought along two steel barrels, hoping to get some diesel fuel from the submarine for his father-in-law. The barrels were on board the boats, along with the evacuees' and the guerrillas' weapons. The gunwales of the small boats rose only slightly above the ripples of the sea on which they floated. Nearly thirty individuals shared the tiny cockpits of the boats as they were shoved out to sea.

From the Mayors' beachfront, Brooke's Point was due east, about two miles away at the north end of the curving sand of Ipolote Bay. The Japanese freighter was just beyond the point. The spot where the kumpits were supposed to meet *Redfin* was about a mile south of the ship, and so, with the outboard motor running, Crowley directed that the two boats head in that direction. The whirring sound of the radio generator being cranked came back through the darkness to the passengers in the rear boat, who could hear Crowley's hushed voice repeating the same call.

"Violet, this is Rose. Violet, this is Rose."

Russo was handling a flashlight, the signal *Redfin* had been told to watch for. He shielded the beam to keep the crew on the Japanese ship from seeing it, but swung it in a broad arc. The kumpits moved farther offshore, beyond the town point, keeping a mile or more away from the ship but drawing close to the rendezvous point.

"Violet, this is Rose."

Aboard *Redfin,* Austin was frustrated. His radio operator had first heard Crowley around eight o'clock, but when he responded there was no reply. And when he looked for the three lamps hung from the lighthouse, Austin saw nothing. At ten o'clock, he received a message from Australia to return to Darwin when the mission was completed, but he was beginning to wonder if that would happen. At just before eleven o'clock, Austin noted in his log that the radio of the evacuees could still be heard, but no contact had been made, and there were still no signal lights onshore. The Japanese ship remained at anchor, apparently oblivious to the commotion brewing on the darkened sea. Austin waited ten minutes and then moved within 4,000 yards of the Japanese ship and flashed a semaphore signal four or five times. Austin thought there was a very slim chance that the ship was being manned by the evacuees. But there was no response, so he turned *Redfin* out to sea to charge its batteries. Austin was discouraged and confused.

It was closing in on midnight when Crowley thought he heard a faint reply. The voice coming over the radio directed him to switch to Morse code keying on the radio because the voice transmission was too weak. The radioman moved a switch and began sending code.

Offshore, Austin, hearing the reply, swung *Redfin* around in a tight circle and headed back toward shore. His radioman was now keying the submarine's radio, and messages were getting through. At half past midnight, the radioman reported that the two kumpits were five miles southeast of Brooke's Point. Six minutes later, Austin spotted the boats three miles away. Everyone on *Redfin* was at battle stations, with one sailor manning the deck gun and lookouts perched above the bridge, straining to see the kumpits. On everyone's mind was the aborted attempt to rescue the Australians, who turned out to be Japanese soldiers with blazing machine guns. Each man aboard *Redfin* prepared himself to react to treachery from the kumpits.

Ten minutes after Austin had seen them, the evacuees heard the *Redfin*'s engines and then spotted the submarine, less than two miles away. The radios were silenced as the submarine, using its sonar, and the kumpits, now being paddled by guerrillas who were feeling their way through the waves and the breeze, approached each other under a moon that was three days short of full.

It was precisely one o'clock in the morning when *Redfin* drew abeam of the kumpits. The guerrillas raised their paddles. The deck gunner, confused, abruptly swung his .50 caliber weapon toward the boats.

"They have guns, Captain!" the gunner shouted. "Shall I let them have it?"

Everyone froze.

"No, hold your fire," replied Austin who, standing on the bridge, began singing the chorus of a quartet favorite. "Sweet Adeline," he sang.

> *My Adeline,*
> *At night, dear heart,*
> *For you I pine . . .*

Now Austin heard in reply the high-pitched voice he knew to be John Crowley's, scratching through the warm air over the silvery ripples of the Sulu Sea.

> *In all my dreams,*
> *Your fair face beams.*
> *You're the flower of my heart . . .*

You could imagine the harmony when both skippers joined together for the final line.

> *Sweeeeeet Aaaaa-de-liiiine!*

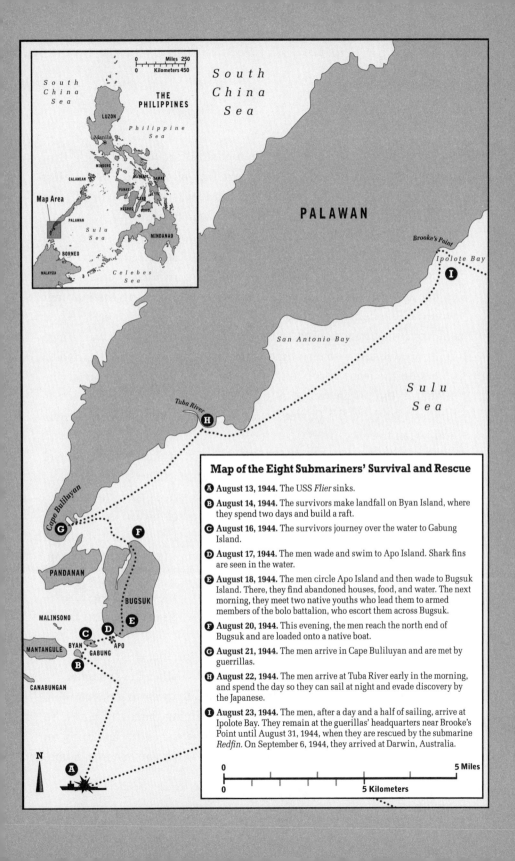

*South
China
Sea*

PALAWAN

Brooke's Point

Ipolote Bay

I

San Antonio Bay

*Sulu
Sea*

Tuba River

H

Cape Buliluyan

G

F

PANDANAN

BUGSUK

MALINSONO

C **D** **E**

MANTANGULE

BYAN

B

APO

GABUNG

CANABUNGAN

N

A

Map of the Eight Submariners' Survival and Rescue

A **August 13, 1944.** The USS *Flier* sinks.

B **August 14, 1944.** The survivors make landfall on Byan Island, where they spend two days and build a raft.

C **August 16, 1944.** The survivors journey over the water to Gabung Island.

D **August 17, 1944.** The men wade and swim to Apo Island. Shark fins are seen in the water.

E **August 18, 1944.** The men circle Apo Island and then wade to Bugsuk Island. There, they find abandoned houses, food, and water. The next morning, they meet two native youths who lead them to armed members of the bolo battalion, who escort them across Bugsuk.

F **August 20, 1944.** This evening, the men reach the north end of Bugsuk and are loaded onto a native boat.

G **August 21, 1944.** The men arrive in Cape Buliluyan and are met by guerrillas.

H **August 22, 1944.** The men arrive at Tuba River early in the morning, and spend the day so they can sail at night and evade discovery by the Japanese.

I **August 23, 1944.** The men, after a day and a half of sailing, arrive at Ipolote Bay. They remain at the guerillas' headquarters near Brooke's Point until August 31, 1944, when they are rescued by the submarine *Redfin*. On September 6, 1944, they arrived at Darwin, Australia.

0   5 Miles

0   5 Kilometers

EPILOGUE

In the North Florida heat of a September afternoon, Charlotte Brubaker took what would, for the next fifty-eight years, be her last steps as a free woman. Her father, Emil, was back at work in the railroad yard. Her mother, Nellie May, was teaching in St. Augustine's public schools, which had opened for the year a couple of weeks before. Charlotte had finished summer school at Florida State College for Women in Tallahassee and now awaited the beginning of her senior year in college. Going to college during the summer would allow her to graduate the following spring, a year early. Then she could contribute both to the family's needs and the war effort. With no demands on her time right now, however, she decided to go out on the front porch, on the cooler north side of the house. She settled in the porch swing, hung by chains from the porch roof rafters, not far from the flower boxes her mother had painted orange, and began to relax.

A taxi broke the stillness, stirring a swirl of dust from the gravel of Vedder Street as it approached number 11, where, with its tires crunching quietly on the sand, it came to a stop. Charlotte was surprised to see the driver get out and come directly toward the porch. In his hand, she saw, was a telegram. Almost instantly, her mind shifted into neutral, like a motorist coasting up to an unfamiliar intersection. She reached and took the telegram.

She knew, without opening it—knew with an instinctive dread—that inside the telegram the message began: THE NAVY DEPARTMENT DEEPLY REGRETS TO INFORM YOU . . .

The cab driver left and Charlotte, with the unopened telegram in her hand, sank back onto the swing, trying to collect her thoughts.

The message remained sealed. It seemed to the young woman that by the act of opening it, she would be verifying the awful news. So she refused to act. She didn't know how long she had been sitting on the swing when finally she got up and went to her aunt's home. Something told her to go there. She was just reacting, not thinking, because thinking might lead her to confirm her fears.

She left her aunt's home and went to the railroad shop and told her father. It was he whose permission had allowed Elton to join the navy, against Nellie May's wishes. Charlotte knew Emil bore the burden of having sent his son to his death.

Emil and Charlotte returned to Vedder Street and waited for Nellie May to get home from school. When Mother arrived, the family called for one of Emil's relatives, the Reverend Lauren Brubaker, a Presbyterian minister.

Stunned, the whole family read the telegram, dated September 14, Elton's birthday.

THE NAVY DEPARTMENT DEEPLY REGRETS TO INFORM YOU THAT YOUR SON ELTON STANLEY BRUBAKER FIREMAN FIRST CLASS USN IS MISSING FOLLOWING ACTION IN THE PERFORMANCE OF HIS DUTY AND IN THE SERVICE OF HIS COUNTRY. THE DEPARTMENT APPRECIATES YOUR GREAT ANXIETY ABOUT DETAILS NOT NOW AVAILABLE AND DELAY IN RECEIPT THEREOF MUST NECESSARILY BE EXPECTED. TO PREVENT POSSIBLE AID TO OUR ENEMIES AND TO SAFEGUARD THE LIVES OF OTHER PERSONNEL, PLEASE DO NOT DIVULGE THE NAME OF THE SHIP OR STATION OR DISCUSS PUBLICLY THE FACT THAT HE IS MISSING. VICE ADMIRAL RANDALL JACOBS, THE CHIEF OF NAVAL PERSONNEL.

Never had Charlotte thought she would lose Elton. The three of them—Elton, Lewis, and she—had been a unit. At times they were divided, two against one. Each of them had taken turns being on the outs. But there was a bond of love between them that they believed would always be there. And now Charlotte had to either admit that the bond had been forever dissolved, or, against all the evidence, believe her brother would return. She chose the latter, and her emotional collapse began. Within two weeks, as if steered by an automatic pilot, she returned to Tallahassee. One weekend night, she felt something come over her and she went first to the home of the dean of women for her department. Finding no one there, she tried to reach her Presbyterian student leader,and then some of her friends. No one was around, and so she went to the infirmary, where she was admitted. The weeks that followed were a blank and would remain that way in her memory for decades to come. She recovered enough to graduate from college, having been given credit for work she could not complete. But she was never again the same innocent, happy young woman she had once been. And when she returned to Vedder Street, she discovered that her brother's death had driven a wedge between her parents, causing a fissure that, even with the help of many years, forgiveness never seemed able to patch.

Another seventy-seven families across the country got messages like the one delivered to the Brubakers on that day in St. Augustine. One reached the home in Castle Rock, Washington, of Jessie Daggy, the mother of Waite Hoyt Daggy, the sailor who had been injured on Midway when he was slammed by the huge wave against the steel conning tower. Another message went to Slayton, Minnesota, where Cora Gerber waited for word of her son, Clyde Arthur Gerber, nervous no doubt after his miraculous survival on Midway, where towering surf had washed him ashore. A third message went to the home of Lena Rodoni in San Jose, California, the sister of that heroic sailor, George Joseph Banchero, who had saved Gerber's life more than a year before. And, yes, Janie M. Pope got a message in Greensboro, North Carolina, reporting the probable death of her son, the rascally Chief Charles DeWitt Pope, who one day was being dragged back to his ship by the Shore Patrol and on another, was saving his shipmates in the middle of a Pacific storm.

But eight families got a different, and more welcome, message.

Edna Jacobson was on her way to a Thursday meeting of the Missionary Society at church when she got a letter that began:

Dear Daddy, Mother, and All:

You won't receive any letters between this one and the last letter I wrote before going on patrol. It's not that I wasn't think-

ing of home and all of you, and it's not that I didn't write any. Some time in the future, I will be able to tell you why.

Edna was overcome. She read on.

There isn't a heck of a lot I can say until I get in and receive your letters. However, there is one thing that is extremely important—remember, regardless what you read in the near future, I am not aboard the U.S.S. Flier. *I am in good health and safe. Do not mention the fact that I have made that point strong to any one but those in the family. More about this later.*

By the time she left for the Missionary Society, Edna was bursting with thankfulness and more than a little frustrated that there was no one she could tell! Nor was her excitement relieved that evening when Alvin Sr. arrived home. There apparently was company, so Edna couldn't even tell her husband. Finally, when he went to bed, she told him, and neither of them got a good night's sleep.

The next morning, a man who was doing some work for the Jacobsons approached Edna. "I signed for a registered letter for you. Here it is," he said, handing her the mail.

"Your son, Ensign Alvin Emmanuel Jacobson, Jr., United States Naval Reserve, who was aboard a ship the loss of which will be announced in the near future, is safe and well," the letter began. "The circumstances of his rescue are such that information concerning it should not reach the enemy, and it is requested that you do not divulge any reports that may come to you concerning his experiences, or disclose the name of the ship in which he served."

These letters began arriving two weeks after the moonlit Philippine night when the submarine *Redfin* flooded its tanks off Brooke's Point to lower its deck and receive seventeen evacuees aboard. Young Jacobson, schooled in the naval tradition of requesting permission to board a vessel, said nothing that night when a hand reached down for his and hauled him up from the small, crowded native boat. Hushed greetings were exchanged. John Crowley received a warm hello from Marshall Austin, *Redfin*'s captain, who also recognized some of the Coastwatchers whom he had last seen when they had paddled their rubber raft ashore at Ramos Island.

When the native boats were emptied, *Redfin*'s crew began handing supplies down to the guerrillas on board. Jose Santos presented the two barrels he had brought in hopes of getting some diesel fuel for his father-in-law, Harry Edwards. The barrels were filled and loaded on the boats, along with six machine guns, four rifles, ten pistols, and three carbines. The little boats, riding light after disgorging their seventeen passengers, settled once again under the weight of 25,800 rounds of ammunition for the weapons, 200 cartons of cigarettes, three bags of medical supplies, containers of flour, yeast, coffee, and other food, packs of playing cards, radio parts, and soap.

Austin told the Coastwatchers that as a parting gift, he would shell the Japanese ship anchored off Brooke's Point. He instructed them to capture the ship's crew if they came ashore and to salvage what they could from the wreckage. Then the Coastwatchers and guerrillas shoved off from the submarine and disappeared in the dark. As they motored back toward shore, they heard the shelling of the Japanese ship begin.

The moon was setting at just after two o'clock that morning, and the gunners on *Redfin* had trouble seeing the ship. They fired twenty-seven rounds from their four-inch deck gun and another sixty rounds from a 20-millimeter gun. There was no return fire, but Austin saw only a couple of hits on the ship before it raised its anchor and began steaming away, protected by a reef from pursuit by *Redfin*.

Between the bursts of gunfire, Austin could hear the sweet, childish voice of Alistair Sutherland, the preacher's son who had prayed for God to send a rescue submarine.

"Kill the Japs!" the boy kept shouting.

It took six days for *Redfin* to reach Darwin, Australia. Maisie Sutherland—who, like the others in her family, and all of the *Flier* survivors had arrived barefoot—was given her first shoes in two years. Her husband and children, who had not eaten bread or butter in nearly three years, feasted on the submarine's stock of these and other foods. In return, Maisie mended *Redfin*'s flag.

Each of the refugees and survivors was treated for malaria. Donald Tremaine had contracted the disease in the eighteen days since his boat had sunk, and two days into the trip he began showing the symptoms. Crowley's feet were infected, but a treatment was found in the ship's medicine chest.

With little to do, Ensign Jacobson found a typewriter aboard and composed his first letter home two days before the submarine arrived at Darwin. Once in port, the eight survivors, who had clung together to overcome all obstacles, were escorted aboard Admiral Christie's private plane and, after a twelve-hour flight, arrived in Perth, where their paths began to separate. Christie invited Crowley to stay at his home. Jacobson and Liddell were given a suite at the bachelor officers' quarters. The enlisted men were shipped to barracks in another part of Perth. Two days later, Christie decided to send all the survivors except Crowley 300 miles inland to Kalgoorlie. The admiral thought it would not help morale if the survivors, who had terrifying stories to tell, were allowed to settle onto Perth barstools beside submariners about to embark on patrol.

Ten days later, with a new set of uniforms and revised pay records, Ensign Jacobson had orders for his next assignment. He boarded a "China Clipper" cargo airplane, headed for two weeks of leave before joining the USS *Ling,* a submarine under construction in Boston. If his life aboard *Flier* was not forgotten, his time with the boat's survivors was over. *Ling* was launched a few months later, and Jacobson was aboard when the boat passed through the Panama Canal on its way back to the war. *Ling* had just left the canal the day word arrived that the war was over. *Ling*'s new orders required the boat to fire off all its torpedoes and fill the torpedo tubes with Scotch and whiskey before returning to New London for a celebration.

By now, the *Flier* survivors were all traveling on their individual courses.

John Crowley, a career man and Naval Academy graduate, remained in the navy. His next assignment was as commander of the submarine *Irex,* which was under construction in New Hampshire. He retired with the rank of captain after thirty years of service. Then he began another career, working for the Maryland civil defense department, before finally retiring to a home near Annapolis, Maryland.

Over the years, Crowley kept in touch with James Liddell. His children thought of Liddell as a sort of Jolly Green Giant, a man with a warm personality who physically towered over their rather short father. Liddell had left the navy after the war and became an executive in a Lancaster, Pennsylvania, flooring company before starting a prosperous business of his own.

Earl Baumgart returned to Milwaukee where, in 1949, he joined the police department. He settled back into his community, serving his city for the next twenty-eight years before retiring.

Arthur Gibson Howell remained in the navy until the war ended, assigned to duty in the States. On August 13, 1945, he wrote to his "Darling Irene" and thanked her for a pillow she had "fixed up" for him to make his train rides between his assignment at the Submarine School in Groton, Connecticut, and his home in East Moriches, Long Island, more comfortable. He said he hoped he would be returning to civilian life soon. "Will be extra special when trains can come and go and I don't have to leave our nice home and go for a long tiresome, uninteresting ride on them. It has been such a long, long time since June of 1942. So many things have happened and so much water has gone over the dam."

Just a week before, the first atomic bomb had been dropped on Hiroshima, emphasizing the Allies' recent demand that Japan surrender unconditionally. The end of the war could now be anticipated, although Howell feared some "treachery" by the Japanese if the Allies lowered their guard. He told Irene about the weather in Connecticut and about a hot plate that he had rigged into an oven. He talked about fellow sailors and about friends and family at home.

But on this date, the anniversary of the sinking of *Flier,* he made no mention of the ordeal he had survived in the Pacific.

Japan's representatives finally surrendered on September 2 on board the battleship USS *Missouri*, signing documents that were then signed by General Douglas MacArthur. By October, Arthur Gibson Howell was back home with Irene, hanging up his uniform with two bronze stars and a Purple Heart. He returned to his radio repair business in East Moriches, where he was already a member of the fire department. He went on to become a successful businessman and fire department official in his hometown, and over the years, he kept in touch with his skipper and contemporary, John Crowley. Their friendship, and the one between Crowley and Liddell, were the only ones among the *Flier* survivors to outlast the war. The rest of the crew had little contact with each other.

But if young Al Jacobson was representative of the rest, they never forgot each other, or their swim in the shadow of their shipmates' deaths.

When he arrived home in Grand Haven, Michigan, after leaving Australia in September 1944, Jacobson had sat down with his mother, a skilled stenographer, and dictated in remarkable detail the events that began on August 13, 1944. Because his country was still at war, and the ensign was concerned that his memoir might fall into enemy hands, he did not name any of the individuals involved. But he did make a separate list of those names, and after his parents had read his report, he secured it for the duration of the war.

The war ended, and Alvin Emmanuel Jacobson Jr. returned to the University of Michigan, where he earned his engineering degree. He got a job in Chicago, but it was not long before he was back working in the family business, the Grand Haven Foundry, just as his father had wished. He spent a few bachelor years of skiing, sailing, and developing his business skills. Then young Al met Mary Eileen Chace, a Nebraska girl who was a friend of one of his sisters, and he married her, starting another branch of the Jacobson family and propagating the proud family name.

The Brubakers in St. Augustine had lost Elton, and although his younger brother, Lewis, was there to continue a lineage that had begun centuries before in Switzerland, Elton's death had created a huge void, an ironically frigid crevasse in the hot Florida landscape, a chasm into which plummeted Charlotte Brubaker's soul. But in many ways she got on with her life. She married and bore two daughters and two sons. In 1959, when Frank, the second oldest, was in the second grade, Charlotte met his teacher, Elaine Morrison Foster, a transplanted West Virginian. The two women soon were commuting together to night school as they pursued degrees in education. A convenient acquaintance grew into a friendship, and Elaine observed in Charlotte Brubaker an underlying struggle. If she thought she understood the source of her friend's trouble, Elaine never broached the subject with Charlotte. And then, in 1978, Elaine moved north, to Washington, D.C.

The two women allowed their friendship to fall victim to the distance that now separated them. It was nine years later when, for no reason that she could defend, Elaine picked up the phone in her apartment on C Street Northeast and dialed Charlotte's number. It was two days before New Year's Eve, 1987. Unbeknownst to Elaine, Charlotte's mother, Nellie May, had just died of leukemia the day before. Charlotte was distraught, and Elaine, concerned for her friend, made a point of calling again the next day. The conversation flowed across their years together in Florida and their individual families. For the first time, the two women discovered they shared an interest in genealogy, and that Charlotte's ancestors had lived in the West Virginia county next to Elaine's home county. Their friendship blossomed brighter than it ever had before.

In 1991, Elaine invited Charlotte to visit her in Washington. Now they began making trips together and visiting each other's homes, as if they were not separated by 800 miles. On one of these visits, when Elaine had traveled to Florida to spend time with a daughter there, they were sitting in Charlotte's home on a barrier island a short distance from downtown St. Augustine when Charlotte produced a trove of her brother Elton's letters home from the war. She simply set them in front of Elaine, almost without comment, except to say that her brother had died in the war.

Perhaps it was the sterility with which Charlotte presented the shocking story of her brother's drowning that signaled to Elaine that something was wrong—that her friend was being eaten up by the grief that by now was nearly fifty years old. It is sufficient to say that Elaine saw something in Charlotte that needed to be set free, so she set to work to make that happen.

Elaine had, many years before, acquired the skills it would take to liberate Charlotte. When she was an unmarried student at the Shenandoah Conservatory of Music in Virginia, a piano teacher had taught Elaine's class how to conduct academic research, and Elaine was an able student. Later, when she was working on a doctoral dissertation at Florida State University, she had employed the same talent, and now she was working in Washington as a freelance researcher at the Library of Congress and the National Archives. She took Elton Brubaker's letters home to Washington and began typing them so that they could be entered into a computer, thinking that Charlotte would benefit from an organized telling of Elton's story.

As she pored over the letters, Elaine became intrigued with the saga of the *Flier* and wanted to learn more. To her amazement, she found that eight men had survived the submarine sinking that had taken Elton. These were the only World War II submarine disaster survivors to evade capture by the Japanese. Their story gripped Elaine, who contacted members of the Submarine Veterans of America for help in her research. They gave her the names of the survivors and some of the addresses, and she began writing to them. All eight, she learned, were still living, and one by one, they responded to her letters. Encouraging each of them to tell her more, she shared the survivors' letters with all of their old shipmates. Elaine Foster's effort to help a friend was beginning to have a much broader impact than the rescue of Charlotte Brubaker Johns from her years of denied grief.

As the fiftieth anniversary of *Flier*'s sinking approached, a lot of memories had been stirred among the survivors. Al Jacobson had taken out his memoir to share with Elaine Foster, and now he rewrote it, adding new information that he had discovered. With the squall of correspondence among the survivors after all these years, he had more with which to shape his tale. And it occurred to him that a gathering of his shipmates would be a good idea. He contacted Crowley, who suggested a reunion in Annapolis, near the old skipper's home. Jacobson sent out the invitations.

They gathered in Maryland on August 4, 1994, those who could make it. Jacobson and Crowley were joined by James Liddell, the executive officer and navigator who had guided the survivors ashore, and Wesley Miller, the sailor who had once flunked his swimming test, and James Russo, who, swimming alone, had been the first among the survivors to reach the beach. Baumgart had a scheduling conflict, Howell was at home with his ailing Irene, and Tremaine, too, was missing.

Four years later, Jacobson, who had never shared the story of his ordeal in the Philippines with his children, took his adult son Steve on a journey back to the islands. They toured all of the places where the survivors had been, and paused for an emotional moment over the spot in the Sulu Sea where, according to the crew's recollection, *Flier* had disappeared with seventy-one men. Again, upon his return to Michigan, he reported his findings to his shipmates.

Three years later, as he contemplated attempting with this author to tell the complete story of the submarine *Flier*, Jacobson reached out to his old shipmates once again. By that time, Crowley, Tremaine, Miller, and Russo had died. Liddell's son reported that his father had Alzheimer's disease, and Howell's son said his father had lost his memory.

Then, in 2003, only Jacobson and Baumgart, among the survivors, were still alive. Earl Baumgart was confined to his Milwaukee home, suffering from Parkinson's disease. Jacobson, at age eighty-two, still sailed on Spring Lake in the summer and went to his office at the family business most days. He was embarrassed by the hero's welcome that had greeted him in 1944 when he returned to Grand Haven. "I wasn't a hero," he said sixty years later. "I just survived." But he, like his father, became a pillar of the community, an influential local captain of industry. His optimism—the same quality that never allowed him to doubt his own survival—was intact, and to him each day was "great." And yet, there remained a place in his heart that ached for those who rode *Flier* to their grave while above them, he and seven other souls swam for their lives.

In preparation for this book, Al Jacobson visited Earl Baumgart in 2003 at his home in Milwaukee, where he was confined to a life-support machine. Baumgart succumbed to complications of Parkinson's disease in 2005.

Jacobson lived on. Despite numerous illnesses associated with aging, he never failed, when asked how he was, to respond with a genuinely enthusiastic "Great!" In 2008, he joined all the other eighty-five *Flier* crewmen on eternal patrol.

ACKNOWLEDGMENTS

This book would not exist were it not for the efforts of three individuals: Mike Hamilburg of the Mitchell J. Hamilburg Literary Agency brought the *Flier* story to my attention. Alvin Jacobson shared his "Survivor's Story: Submarine *Flier* Lost August 13, 1944" and his sources selflessly. And Elaine Foster eagerly gave me the entire product of her exhaustive professional research on *Flier*.

Elaine Foster introduced me to Charlotte Brubaker Johns, who, with her brother, Lewis Brubaker, provided honest details of their family history and of their brother, Elton. Charlotte guided me on a tour of northern Florida and shared family correspondence and photos from more than sixty years earlier. I thank them both.

Elaine Foster also provided me with copies of her correspondence with all of the *Flier* survivors, all but two of whom had died by the time I heard their story.

Al Jacobson took me to Milwaukee to visit Earl Baumgart, who at the time was battling Parkinson's disease.

At every step in my research, I was aided enthusiastically by those whose assistance I sought.

Submarine newsletter editor Larry Legge led me to Heather Sutherland Danielson, whose family had been trapped in Brooke's Point. Mrs. Danielson and her husband, Paul, welcomed me to their eastern Ohio home and helped me reproduce the collected letters of Alexander and Maisie Sutherland. Later, when I planned a visit to the Philippines, Mrs. Sutherland helped me make contacts and arranged for accommodations in Brooke's Point.

Mary Ellen Crowley and her sister, Pat Hrubiak, graciously provided me with details of Commander Crowley's family history and his family life.

Equilla Hackett shared her memories of her older brother, John Clyde Turner.

Conchita Rallojay provided great details of the experiences of her husband, Teodoro "Butch" Rallojay, as a Coastwatcher. She also gave me copies of his wartime diary, the most detailed observations of the activities of that Coastwatcher unit.

Nazario Mayor's oldest son, Robert Mayor, and his youngest daughter, Mary Ann Ancheta, told me the story of the Palawan guerrillas, providing details I would not have otherwise had.

In Brooke's Point, I was told the wartime history of that community by Josephine Rosario, Jose and Beth Santos, Imelda Garcia, Eduardo Villapa Jr., and Emerita Verano. Their help was invaluable.

While in Brooke's Point, I stayed with Dana and Kelly Danielson. They loaned me a motorcycle so that I could follow Dana up into the mountainside in Macagua, where we visited with members of a native community who had lived there during the war.

I was taken to Brooke's Point from Puerto Princesa by Colonel Elpidio Loleng. The long trip in his van—and the trip farther south to Rio Tuba, and the return trip to Puerto Princesa when my visit was completed—was a generous contribution to the project by Colonel Loleng and his family.

I was met in Rio Tuba for the boat excursion to the islands of southern Palawan, including Bugsuk, by Domingluito de la Torre, the Mayor family caretaker at Bugsuk. Mr. de la Torre was an invaluable guide and remains in my thoughts.

I am grateful for the help provided by Terry Howell, son of Arthur Gibson Howell, in sending me his father's wartime correspondence, documents, and artifacts.

Keith Wallman, editor at Lyons Press, has my undying gratitude for taking a chance on telling the *Flier* story.

And, finally, my thanks to Robert Fowler, for his critical eye and his encouragement.

BIBLIOGRAPHY

NAVAL DOCUMENTS

History of the Medical Department of the United States Navy in
World War II, The Statistics of Diseases and Injuries

Narrative Report of Rescue of Eight Survivors from USS *Flier* and
Nine Other Persons Marooned at Sir John Brooks [sic] Point,
Palawan Islands

Palawan Military Police Report No. 56, 28 August 1944 (Japanese)

Puerto Princesa during the Second World War: A Narrative History
(1941–1945)

Record of Proceedings of an Investigation (*Robalo* and *Flier*) 14 September 1944

Report of a Board of Investigation Looking into the Grounding of the
USS *Flier*

Report of a Board of Investigation Looking into the Loss of the USS
Macaw

Report of First War Patrol: *Flier*

U.S. Submarine Losses, World War II

NATIONAL ARCHIVES

International Military Tribunal for the Far East, pages 15,196 to
15,278

BOOKS

American Caesar, by William Manchester

Guerrilla Submarines: A Bantam War Book, by Edward Dissette and
Hans Christian Adamson

Palawan's Fighting One Thousand, by Diokno Manlavi

Silent Victory, by Clay Blair Jr.

Submarine! by Edward L. Beach

Take Her Deep! A Submarine Against Japan in World War II, by
Admiral I. J. Galantin

INTERNET SOURCES

http://battlebelow.com—Submarine war against Japan

http://realmagick.com—Phases of the moon, 1944

http://ussvi.us/mem/spritz.htm —The "Volunteers" of Spritz's Navy

www.cdc.gov/dengue/

www.cyberhymnal.org—Lyrics for "Eternal Father, Strong to Save"

www.fleetsubmarine.com/personalities.html#c —John Crowley
    service

www.geocities.com/egjustimbaste/guerrillas/guerrillas8.html—
    Leyte's Guerrillas

www.history.navy.mil—Naval casualty statistics

www.infoplease.com—Sulu Archipelago

www.madsci.org/posts/archives/jan2002/1011652570.Gb.r.html—
    Why does drinking salt water make your tongue swell?

www.Navsource.org/Naval/1944.htm—Chronology of World War II,
    1944

www.pbs.org/wgbh/amex/dday/timeline—World War II timeline

www.sagehistory.net/worldwar2/topics/WWIIChron.htm—World
    War II Chronology

www.worldatlas.com—Australia map

www.worldwar-2.net/timelines/asia-and-the-pacific/asia-and-the-
    pacific-index.htm

PERSONAL AND TELEPHONE INTERVIEWS

Ainley, Stan—telephone interview concerning Spritz's Navy

Ancheta, Mary Ann—personal interview (October 9, 2002) and tele-
    phone interviews

Baumgart, Earl—personal interview (October 9, 2002)

Brubaker, Lewis—personal interviews (2002)

Brubaker Johns, Charlotte—personal interviews (2002); telephone
    and e-mail interviews

Crowley, Mary Ellen—personal interview in Baltimore

Danielson, Heather and Paul—personal interview (2002) in Ohio

Garcia, Imelda—personal interview in Brooke's Point, February 2003

Hackett, Equilla—telephone interviews concerning John Clyde
    Turner

Jacobson, Alvin Emmanuel Jr.—numerous personal and telephone interviews May 2001 through February 2004.

Mayor, Robert—telephone interviews 2002 through 2004

Rallojay, Conchita—telephone interview October 2003; e-mail correspondence October through December 2003.

Rosario, Josephine—personal interview in Brooke's Point, February 2003

Santos, Jose and Beth—personal interviews in Brooke's Point, February 2003

Verano, Emerita—personal interview in Brooke's Point, February 2003

Villapa, Eduardo Jr.—personal interview in Brooke's Point, February 2003

LETTERS/DIARIES

Baumgart, Earl, letters to Alvin Jacobson and Elaine Foster, 1994 to 1998

Collected letters, Jacobson family—wartime

Collected letters and diaries, Sutherland family—1932 to 1945

Collected letters and documents, Brubaker family—wartime

Collected letters and documents, Howell family—wartime

Crowley, John D., letters to Elaine Foster 1994

Jacobson, Alvin E., "Survivor's Story: Submarine *Flier* Lost August 13, 1944," 1997–2002

Miller, Wesley, letters to Elaine Foster 1994

Rallojay, Teodoro, diary—wartime

Russo, James, letter to Elaine Foster 1994

Tremaine, Donald, letters to Elaine Foster 1994

NEWS CLIPS

Chicago Daily Times—James Liddell May 5, 1943

Evanston Review—James Liddell May 6, 1943

Looking Aft, September 2001, Larry Legge—Alistair's prayer

Northwestern University Alumni News—James Liddell January 1945

SOURCES

CHAPTER 1: TREACHEROUS PASSAGE

Unless otherwise noted, descriptions of action on board *Flier* are drawn from three Navy documents: *Flier*'s deck log from its first patrol, "Report of a Board of Investigation Looking into the Grounding of the USS *Flier*," and "Report of a Board of Investigation Looking into the Loss of the USS *Macaw*." Reports of investigation include transcripts of testimony by all decision-makers involved, as well as from others with eyewitness observations. These three documents include specific onboard communications that are quoted directly in the text.

The view of the men on board during the ground is based on a May 12, 1994, letter from Earl Baumgart to Elaine Foster. Generic descriptions of life aboard *Flier* are based on interviews with Alvin Jacobson and on my own visits aboard the submarines *Becuna* and *Silversides.*

The actual experience of traveling on the breeches buoy was related by Baumgart in the same 1994 letter.

CHAPTER 2: PACIFIC PERIL

The deck logs of *Flier* and *Florikan,* as well as the Board of Investigation transcripts for *Flier* and *Macaw,* provide the details for entries involving *Flier* after Midway and the loss of *Macaw.*

Elton Brubaker's life has been re-created through the Brubaker family's collection of letters and from interviews with his siblings, Charlotte Brubaker Johns and Lewis Brubaker.

A description of Chief Petty Officer Charles Spritz and his "Navy" of submarine trainees is based on an interview with Stan Ainley of Greenville, Rhode Island, who was Spritz's assistant. I supplemented Ainley's recollections with information from the Web site http://ussvi. us/mem/spritz.htm.

Alvin Jacobson's recollections, captured in several interviews between 2001 and 2004, provide the basis for much of his story. In one of these interviews, he related his experience facing the board of navy officers who approved him for service, including direct quotes he recalled from that experience.

Correspondence between Jacobson and his parents is included in a family collection of letters from the period.

CHAPTER 3: MISSING FROM ACTION

Disciplinary action against *Flier*'s crewmen at Mare Island is taken from the submarine's deck log.

The history of problems with torpedoes is based on information in *Silent Victory* by Clay Blair Jr., 1975.

Mare Island improvements on *Flier* are found in the submarine's deck log.

CHAPTER 4: A GATHERING OF MEN

Alvin Jacobson's recollections during interviews are the basis for much of the narrative in this chapter, as are his comments in letters written to his family. Jacobson detailed his family's history in these interviews.

Those details of James Liddell's background not provided by Jacobson were found in publications of his alma mater, Northwestern University, and his employer, Armstrong Cork Co.

The nickname "Cautious Crowley" was explained in a June 18, 1994, letter from Earl Baumgart to Elaine Foster.

The description of Commander Crowley and details of his family life are based on interviews with his daughter, Mary Ellen Crowley.

Biographical information on Earl Baumgart was drawn from his letters to Foster and Crowley, and from my personal interview with him in Milwaukee in 2003.

Details of the life of John Clyde Turner were provided by his sister, Equilla, in a 2003 telephone interview.

CHAPTER 5: A SECOND CHANCE

Flier's deck log and Jacobson's recollections are the basis for the description of the boat's departure from Mare Island.

The story of Elton Brubaker's travels to Australia and of his family life in Florida are based on his letters home and on interviews with his sister and brother.

The description of the flow of the war effort is based on William Manchester's book, *American Caesar.*

The casualties resulting from guerrilla action in the Philippines was taken in 2003 from the then-available Web site www.geocities .com/ebjustimbaste/guerrillas/guerrillas8.html.

The explanation of Coastwatchers was provided by Conchita Rallojay, widow of Coastwatcher Teodoro J. Rallojay.

An explanation of the Ultra system of decoding and communications is found in Clay Blair Jr.'s *Silent Victory.*

Statistics on lost submarines is found in the U.S. Navy's publication, *U.S. Submarine Losses, 1949 issue, World War II.* The exchange between Commander Morton and Admiral Lockwood is reported in Edward L. Beach's book, *Submarine!*

CHAPTER 6: WELCOME TO THE WAR

The scenes from *Flier's* first patrol have been re-created from the boat's deck log and from interviews with Alvin Jacobson. The attack on John Clyde Turner was recalled by Jacobson in detail.

To describe the construction and interior of a fleet-type submarine, I used diagrams published by the U.S. Navy, combined with observations I made and photographs I took on visits to two such vessels.

Admiral Galantin's reflections on submarine warfare are taken from his book, *Take Her Deep! A Submarine Against Japan in World War II.*

CHAPTER 7: STRANGERS IN THEIR NATIVE LAND

The Coastwatchers' experiences are drawn from Teodoro Rallojay's diary, provided by his widow. The diary includes such details as the number of pesos left in the Coastwatchers' tin and the amount of sleep they were getting.

Nazario Mayor's story and that of his family was told to me by one of his daughters, Mary Anne Ancheta, in an interview with her in her Wisconsin home, and in telephone interviews. Her brother, Robert Mayor, added details to the story.

Some of the details of Mayor's movements are found in *Palawan's Fighting One Thousand* by Diokno Manlavi.

I was introduced to Thomas Edwards's story by Alvin Jacobson. During my visit to Brooke's Point, I interviewed several of his relatives and neighbors who were alive during World War II. The description of the role Edwards and his family played in the town is based on those interviews with Josephine Rosario, Jose and Beth Santos, Imelda Garcia, Eduardo Villapa Jr., and Emerita Verano.

CHAPTER 8: THE WAGES OF WINNERS

Flier's deck log and Alvin Jacobson's recollections are the sources for the submarine's movements.

Letters from Elton Brubaker provide the details of his life in Australia.

The events in the war that do not involve *Flier* are drawn from the Web site, U.S. Naval Chronology of World War II, 1944 (www.nav source.org/Naval/1944.htm).

Teodoro Rallojay's diary is the source for information on the Coast-watchers' activities.

CHAPTER 9: MINES AND MARINERS

Information on *Darter* and *Tsugaru* is provided in a September 3, 1985, letter from Vernon J. Miller to John Crowley, and on the Web site, IJN Minelayer *Tsugaru*: Tabular Record of Movement (www.combined fleet.com/tsugaru_t.htm).

Robalo's story is based in part on testimony found in the "Record of Proceedings of an Investigation into the Loss of the USS *Robalo* and the loss of the USS *Flier*." The story of the survivors of the *Robalo* is drawn from the Japanese Palawan Military Police Report No. 56, August 28, 1944. This report summarizes the interrogation of the four *Robalo* survivors in the Puerto Princesa prison camp.

The story of the massacre at the Puerto Princesa prisoner of war camp is drawn from the official transcript of a war crimes tribunal, officially designated Case Number 337, held at Yokohama from August to November 1948.

CHAPTER 10: BACK TOWARD GLORY

Flier's departure from Australia for its second war patrol is based on the "Record of Proceedings of an Investigation into the Loss of the USS *Robalo* and the loss of the USS *Flier*."

In interviews, Alvin Jacobson elaborated on the story of the trip north from Australia, including the tale of the commandoes who devised the radar reflector and Ensign Behr's work rebuilding the damaged engine. He originally wrote down his recollections of the experience in 1945 when he returned home from the war. He compiled those memories then in a tract he called "Survivor's Story: Submarine *Flier* Lost August 13, 1944."

Speculation on how Elton Brubaker spent his time aboard *Flier* is taken from the comments and letters of his surviving shipmates, including Jacobson. It attempts to reflect the minimum that Brubaker would have had to experience aboard a submarine. The family history reported in this chapter is based on interviews with Charlotte Brubaker Johns and Lewis Brubaker.

CHAPTER 11: TRAPPED IN THE PATH OF WAR

The Coastwatchers' material comes from the diary of Teodoro Rallojay.

The description of Macagua is based on notes I took when I visited the site in 2003.

Thomas Edwards's life on Palawan is pieced together from interviews with his relatives and neighbors, as are the description of survival tactics adopted by the residents of Brooke's Point and the guerrilla ambush of the Japanese soldiers there.

The story of the Sutherlands' desperate lives during the war is based on interviews with Heather Sutherland Danielson, the daughter; Mrs. Maisie Sutherland; and letters written during the period by Alexander and Maisie, and provided by Mrs. Danielson.

CHAPTER 12: CHANGED ORDERS

Details of life aboard *Flier* on the night of the sinking are based primarily on the recollections of Alvin Jacobson, with details added from the correspondence in the 1990s between Elaine Foster and the other survivors.

Excerpts from Brubaker family letters to Elton are provided from their collected letters of the period. The collected Jacobson family letters are the source of those quotes.

Admiral Christie's orders are discussed in the "Records of Proceedings" (investigating the loss of *Robalo* and *Flier*).

Crowley's deliberations on his route are reported in the "Records of Proceedings."

The accounts of *Flier*'s sinking given by the eight survivors are found either in their letters to Elaine Foster, or in their testimony, found in the "Records of Proceedings," or both. In numerous interviews, Jacobson described his own observations in detail. The stories of those who escaped *Flier* but did not survive are pieced together from the recollections of Jacobson and other survivors.

CHAPTER 13: IN THE SHADOW OF DEATH

The account of events once the survivors found themselves in the water is based primarily on Jacobson's tract, "Survivor's Story," and on interviews with him. Letters from the other survivors to Elaine Foster provide more details of each man's experiences and thoughts.

Wesley Miller's comments to Chief Hudson were taken from a June 20, 1994, letter from Miller to Foster. Earl Baumgart, in a letter to Foster, told the story of Chief Pope's decision to quit swimming. Jacobson told me the story of Ed Casey's disappearance in the dark. Jacobson tells a similar story in his tract, where he also reported reciting the Twenty-Third Psalm.

In a June 24, 1994, letter to Elaine Foster, Donald Tremaine wrote that he knew Elton Brubaker, and that he had encountered him in the water following *Flier*'s sinking.

Chapter 14: Choosing Freedom

Commander Crowley's religious sentiments and the details of his personal life were provided by his daughter, Mary Ellen Crowley, in an interview.

The activities of the survivors on Byan Island are based on Jacobson's tract and on interviews with him.

Wesley Miller's survival story is told in letters that he wrote to Morrison.

Information about the dangers of drinking salt water is found on the Web site, MadSci Network (www.madsci.org/posts/archives/jan2002/1011652570.Gb.r.html).

The decision by Crowley and Liddell to attempt a crossing to Gabung Island in the afternoon is reported in Jacobson's tract, as are the other details for the island-hopping, and was expanded upon by Jacobson in personal interviews.

Chapter 15: Spirits of the Land

The encounter by the survivors with the native boys is related by Jacobson in his tract. I heard the same story from Oros Bogata, whom I met when I visited Bugsuk in 2003.

Chapter 16: By Land and by Sea

Jacobson's tract provides the rough outline for the trek across Bugsuk Island and their voyage beyond. His recollections during personal interviews provide more detail, as do letters from other survivors to Jacobson, Crowley, and Elaine Foster. Baumgart in a letter to Foster told of Kim Jon's chewing of beetlenut and other fine details.

Chapter 17: Into the Jungle

Details concerning the *Flier* survivors' treatment by the Coastwatchers and their use of the Coastwatchers' radios to contact Australia is found in Jacobson's tract and is amplified by comments he made during personal interviews.

The story of Alistair Sutherland's prayer comes from Larry Legge's submarine newsletter, *Looking Aft.*

Jacobson's tract is the source of information on the medicine and haircuts the survivors received.

Teodoro Rallojay's diary is the source of information on the final success of the radio transmissions, and the Coastwatchers' victory gardens.

Jacobson's daily activities are presented in his tract.

The events surrounding Amando Corpus's suicide are found in both Jacobson's tract and Rallojay's diary.

CHAPTER 18: ESCAPE

Allied losses are documented in *U.S. Navy and Marine Corps Personnel Casualties in World War II* by the Naval Historical Center.

Howell's story is re-created through a collection of wartime letters and documents provided by his family.

Jacobson's tract details the arrangements made for kumpits and signal lanterns.

Details of *Redfin*'s preparations for evacuating the *Flier* survivors come from Commander Austin's subsequent report, entitled, "Narrative Report of Rescue of Eight Survivors from USS *Flier* and Nine Other Persons Marooned at Sir John Brooke's Point, Palawan Islands."

The description of the rendezvous between the survivors and *Redfin* is taken from the recollections of Jacobson and several of the others, recounted in letters written later.

EPILOGUE

In interviews, Charlotte Brubaker Johns described the setting when her family received the navy telegram advising them of Elton's loss.

Jacobson, in personal interviews, told how he sent word home of his survival and how his parents reacted.

Marshall Austin's report on the rescue detailed provisions that were sent ashore for the guerrillas and locals.

Jacobson, in personal interviews, related the experience aboard *Ling* when the war ended.

INDEX

ABOUT THE AUTHOR

Douglas A. Campbell is the author of *The Sea's Bitter Harvest: Thirteen Deadly Days on the North Atlantic*. He worked as a reporter for the *Philadelphia Inquirer* for twenty-five years. He also writes for *Soundings* magazine. He has covered topics ranging from the American economy to Atlantic eels, and has had a lifelong interest in the sea. For this book, he interviewed survivors of the sinking of the *Flier* and visited the Philippines location where the sailors washed ashore. Campbell lives near Philadelphia in Beverly, New Jersey.